Tears for Food

My tears have been my meat day and night,
while they continually say unto me,
'Where is thy God?'

(Psalm 42, verse 3)

Tears for Food

by

Charles Parker

Grosvenor House
Publishing Limited

The right of Charles Parker to be identified as the author of this
work has been asserted in accordance with Section 78
of the Copyright, Designs and Patents Act 1988

The book cover is copyright to Charles Parker

This book is published by
Grosvenor House Publishing Ltd
Link House
140 The Broadway, Tolworth, Surrey, KT6 7HT.
www.grosvenorhousepublishing.co.uk

A CIP record for this book
is available from the British Library

This book is a work of fiction. Any resemblance to
people or events, past or present, is purely coincidental.

Paperback ISBN 978-1-80381-027-0
Hardback ISBN 978-1-80381-028-7
eBook ISBN 978-1-80381-029-4

ACKNOWLEDGEMENTS

I should like to thank the following people who helped in the production of this book:-

Jill Hogben for her support and encouragement. Mrs Williams who worked at the Home Office with me who very kindly typed the original manuscript some forty years ago. Chris Hogben of **CHRIS HOGBEN CREATIVE** for designing the beautiful covers for this book. Sharp Printing, Broadstairs, for their help in printing out all the drafts and last, but not least, Julie Scott at Grosvenor House Publishing for guiding my work through the maze of publication requirements.

Also by Charles Parker

'Red Duster to White Ensign': editor

Cuthbert the Crocodile: a children's story

DEDICATION

For my brothers and sisters

Contents

PART ONE: TRINITY

Chapter 1: **Stink bombs and bangers**

A seagull glided languidly over the chalk speckled fields still warm from the rays of the gentle autumn sun. As the swollen globe began the final stage of its slide to earth, partly obscured by the trees, the dark crimson rays reflected off the orange and gold leaves of the Beech trees surrounding the churchyard. These contrasted sharply with the now fragile golden yellow leaves fluttering on a solitary lime tree, which stood among the other trees of Oak and Horse Chestnut. Some Chestnut trees were almost bare while others, seeming to gain strength from the nearby, more hardy, Oaks still clung tenaciously to their summary greens with only here, and there, a hint of yellow and brown heralding the onset of winter. Other rays glancing off the field turned the pieces of broken white chalk scarlet as if they too, like the sun, oozed blood.

The sun seemed to fall faster the closer it got to the horizon. Thin trails of clouds, gradually obscuring its already failing light. The seagull cried and turned away from the darkening, slightly somnolent fields, which just over a decade ago had reverberated to the roar of engines and staccato rattles of gunfire from airplanes from nearby Manston Airbase, towards the sea where it would roost on the chalk cliffs for the night. In the churchyard a pall of mist floated, seeming malevolent among the shrubs and gravestones then suddenly flew away, when caught by a draft of air, like an errant spirit called back to the grave.

Leading up to the churchyard was a muddy narrow track. On one side lay the field, on the other a smaller field, which gave way to a wood made in penetrable by thick gorse bushes surrounded by a sea of broken rotting ferns while here and there clumps of stinging nettles acting as spindly guardians of a forbidden domain. The wood's isolation was heightened by the 'PRIVATE – KEEP OUT' notices nailed at intervals on the trees nearest the boundary. The autumn had not changed the wood a degree in its forbiddingness. Those trees, which had lost their leaves standing seemingly awkwardly, near those which had not.

All of this was lost on the two boys who were now cycling along the track that led to the church of St. Peter. Their bicycles rattled and jolted from one rut to another which in their hurry to get to their destination they made no attempt to avoid.

"Hurry up or we'll be late" the boy known as Richard cried out as he tried to go faster by standing on his pedals. He brushed his auburn hair angrily out of his green eyes, which reflected his impatience as his friend spoke.

"Let's not bother tonight", cried his best friend Barry, whose blond hair, also obscuring his blue eyes, seemed to torment him whichever way he turned his head. "Let's go scrumping instead: I'm hungry".

Richard sighed and slowed sufficiently to allow Barry to catch up, but in doing so making it difficult to keep his bicycle on an even course.

"No!" he cried in exasperation as Barry drew level. "Don't you remember?"

By his puzzled expression Barry obviously didn't. "There is a wedding tomorrow", continued Richard, "and if we are picked for it", as we will be he thought to himself, just by turning up, "then we'll get half a crown each, and anyway what about the bangers?"

Barry looked aside. "Oh", was all he said. He had completely forgotten about the wedding and the bangers but now mollified by these thoughts he refrained from making any further comment and merely concentrated on trying to keep up with Richard.

They continued to bounce along the muddy track, which had been rutted by other bicycles and horses hooves, trying to avoid the horse 'buns' scattered here and there like, Richard imagined, overcooked doughnuts whilst the nettles, which lined both sides of the track, though only driven by the wind of their passing, seemed to lean menacingly towards them as they rode by. The autumn sun, now on the final leg of its slide to earth, was rapidly disappearing behind the many-hued trees that marked the boundary of the churchyard as the boys turned into it.

Richard sighed with relief as they arrived at the churchyard, the front wheel making one final bump as it lifted itself onto the narrow tarmacadam path, which ran along the churchyard up to the church. Richard turned at the sound of Barry's bicycle also bumping up onto the path and gave him a smile of encouragement. They had almost made it in time; only a few hundred yards more and they would be there. Not being able to see the clock on the church tower Richard strained his ears in order to hear it when it struck the hour.

An old man, weeding at a grave, hesitated and then raised his head, disturbed by the noise of the rattling bicycles. Espying the two boys, through his watery eyes, he cleared his throat noisily and, in a cracked voice, shouted out hoarsely. "Oi, you're not allowed to cycle in the churchyard."

Richard and Barry although momentarily taken aback continued cycling. "What shall we do?" hissed Barry, urgently.

"Ignore him", whispered Richard, cycling even faster, "pretend you haven't heard him."

On they went followed by the indignant cries of the old man who stood there leaning on the gravestone whilst holding a dirt encrusted trowel in one hand and branding a fist with the other. "I know you, I'll tell the vicar!" His final threat hanging in the air like a cloud.

Richard and Barry went on; hurrying passed the tower of the flint church, which leaned slightly on one side owing to a large crack in the turret of the tower, said to have been caused by an earthquake in Elizabethan times nearly four hundred years ago, and the gaping black south door of the church to the main gate.

St. Peter's church still remained as the hub of the village to which it had given its name, standing on the top of a 'T' of a road junction. Facing down from the church to the east was the High Street, with the Red Lion pub on one corner and on the other a chemist. Next to the pub in a yard set back from the road was a small riding school from which Richard could hear the horses whinnying as dusk fell. On the other side of the High Street, next to the chemist, was 'Bantocks', the confectioner's shop where they bought their sweets. Jammed between that and the pork butchers was a small toy shop, now advertising 'Astra' fireworks, with a poster showing a lurid display.

Richard and Barry turned left, passed the war memorial and free-wheeled down to the entry to the vestry next to Vye & Son the grocer. A group of boys there were playing conkers. Richard looked up as the clock on the church tower slowly chimed the hour followed by the deeper notes of the bell striking six, 'Just made it' he thought.

"Ow, that hurt", said the fair haired boy called David, as he rubbed his knuckle which was throbbing from a savage blow from the other boy's conker. "You're supposed to hit the conker, not my hand."

The other boy with dark hair called Jim laughed. "Well it serves you right", he replied. "Don't move your hand when it's my turn to hit." Jim turned, hearing the approaching bicycles, "Oh, hello Ricky, hello Barry."

"Hello Jim, hello Dave" they replied in unison.

Mr Owen not here yet?" asked Richard as he leant his bicycle against the wall, as did Barry with his, before rejoining his friends.

"No!" replied Jim, "and the vestry is locked so we can't get in."

"It's gone six," said David, "perhaps we ought to go and look for him in case he's forgot; he did once."

"Nah", said Barry, "if he's coming, he's never late, like clockwork."

At that moment Mr Owen came into view round the corner of the chemist. He was a wizened little man in his late sixties, with a slight hunch back. Thin white hair lightly covered his head so you could see his skull but underneath his surprisingly bushy eyebrows his dark eyes glinted with vitality; as sharp and bright as a freshly broken flint. Oddly enough for an organist and choirmaster he was slightly deaf. Although there was no sign of any traffic, he looked carefully right and left before crossing the road.

"Good evening, boys", he said.

"Good evening, sir, Mr Owen", the boys chorused their mixed replies.

Mr Owen surveyed the boys smiling benignly whilst he rhythmically chewed a piece of gum. The boys had never seen him without his gum and looked forward, with some hilarity, to the times when it stuck in his false teeth and he had to remove them. Using the chain Mr Owen pulled his watch from his waistcoat pocket, looked at it briefly, nodded to himself and replaced it then walked towards the vestry door. Fumbling with a bunch of keys for a moment Mr Owen found the one he wanted, unlocked and opened the door then led the boys, who had followed him, into the vestry, switching on the lights as he went. A damp mustiness greeted them, which Richard liked since it made him think of all the other choristers who had sung there before him.

The vestry was of panelled oak. In the wall opposite the door was set a large partly stained glass window practically the whole width of the floor, beginning from about four feet from the floor and reaching up to the ceiling, through which you could see the churchyard. Some of the gravestones, all but hidden by the dense undergrowth of weeds, ferns and wild flowers, had a skull and crossbones carved on them so that Richard and his friends were certain that pirates were buried there. High up on the right hand wall of the vestry was a portrait of an 18th Century vicar of St. Peter's, the Rev

John Dean, whose eyes, the boys thought, seemed to look at you eerily no matter where you stood in the vestry. Underneath the portrait were the oak cupboards where the choir kept their cassocks and surplices and for the boys their ruffs. On the opposite side, also set into the wall were cupboards where the anthems and other music was stored. A long oak bench ran along that wall, whilst under the window there was a row of chairs. The only other pieces of furniture being the battered upright piano, an old beech wood table and a leather upholstered chair used by the churchwarden to count the Sunday collections and for the signing of the register at weddings.

Mr Owen took a chair and sat down in front of the piano while the boys talked and shivered in the damp air.

"Alright, boys", said Mr Owen, "settle down and we'll do a few scales."

"It's cold, sir," said Herbert, a chubby freckle-faced boy with a sandy coloured hair and glasses, "can we have the fire on?"

"Alright", said Mr Owen as he played a few chords on the piano and moved his chair to a more comfortable position. "Right then, let's see how far we can get passed top 'C' tonight shall we?" He chuckled to himself as he waited for Herbert to get back to his place in the line of boys, after turning on the fire.

Whilst the boys sang the scales, and Mr Owen nodded his head in time with the music, Jim nudged Barry and took out from his trouser pocket two stink bombs protected by some cotton wool. He moved his eyes in the direction of Mr Owen then back again. Barry smiled and nodded, then elbowed Richard in the stomach, making him look round at his grinning friends. When he saw the stink bombs he raised his eyebrows in alarm, shook his head and whispered, "Not tonight, there's a wedding tomorrow."

His friends took no notice. Egged on by Barry, Jim carefully rolled the stink bombs towards Mr Owen's chair. The stink bombs progress was watched wide-eyed by the other boys as with mounting excitement the stink bombs stopped to the right of Mr Owen's chair.

Mr Owen stopped playing the piano and with a frown on his wrinkled face turned to the boys, saying, "Has someone brought their cat to choir practice tonight?" The boys giggled nervously. "Well someone is singing out of tune – who is it?" The boys stayed silent. "Alright", said Mr Bowen, "let's try again but this time without the probationers."

Mr Owen moved his chair, and in doing so put a chair leg on one of the stink bombs which broke, releasing its contents. Almost immediately the foul odour began to fill the air. Jim grinned with satisfaction as Mr Owen resumed playing, seeming not to notice the smell, which had begun to pervade the room. The boys, trying to suppress their laughter carried on singing while one young probationer; Roger Overton who had joined only last week, started to feel queasy and wished, not for the first time that he hadn't insisted on having two fried egg sandwiches for tea. At length he could stand it no longer and rushed out of the Vestry to the toilet from where the boys could hear him being violently sick.

Mr Owen turned on hearing the noise, raised his eyebrows questioningly and then took a large handkerchief from his pocket and blew his nose thunderously.

"Excuse me, boys", he said, "but I don't seem to be able to get rid of this cold." He snorted loudly several times. "I've had it all week", then snorted again before turning back to the piano.

Richard sighed inwardly 'thank heavens for that'. Roger, meanwhile, looking very white returned to the Vestry and sat down, while Jim, disappointed at having wasted a good stink bomb tried to think of a way to retrieve the other before Mr Owen broke it, to no avail, like the first.

Herbert who was sitting next to Roger looked worriedly at him a couple of times then raised his hand, saying quickly, "Can I open a window please, Sir?"

Mr Owen turned and looked at him quizzically for a moment before commenting, "I thought you said you were cold! If you open the window all the heat will go out."

"It's Overton, sir, he's not well", retorted Herbert somewhat desperately.

Mr Owen looked searchingly at Roger, then enquired, "Not well, hm, have you been sick?"

"Yes, sir", mumbled Roger weakly.

"Well in that case", said Mr Owen, "you had better go home."

Not wanting to, Roger spoke up, "I'll be alright in a minute, sir", he maintained, sitting up straighter and trying to smile.

At that moment the smell from the stink bomb finally infiltrated Mr Owen's nose, causing him to sniff noisily as he surveyed the boys all watching him. "Hm", he finally said, almost to himself, "it is a bit musty in here tonight". He pointed at Herbert. "Open the window wide and let some air in".

Herbert leapt up onto his seat and, with the assistance of one of the other boys, since the windows were very stiff from rust, over-painting and so little usage, finally forced a window open. Fog floated into the room from the churchyard inspiring Jim to do a Dracula impression, but giving it up when he got no response from the others.

"Right", said Mr Owen, "let's get on with it shall we?" and he resumed playing the piano.

The rest of the choir practice progressed without any further incidents. The canticles for Sunday were sung very briefly, just to try out a new chant. This was quickly followed by the psalms and hymns for Sunday; then a new version of the versicles and responses, which had just been received from the Royal School of Church Music. Having done this there was a short respite whilst Mr Owen dug some anthems and Christmas carols out of the various cupboards, muttering to himself as he did so, picking some up hurriedly then just as quickly discarding them in favour of others. These were all practiced diligently until finally the church clock, which had faithfully been recording the passing of the quarters chimed the hour itself.

Richard looked expectantly at Barry, raising his eyebrows as he did so, as Mr Owen stopped playing the piano, bringing a ragged ending to the hymn they had just been practising, 'In the bleak mid winter'. Mr Owen fumbled in his waistcoat pocket for his watch and seeming to have difficulty in finding it finally pulled on the gold chain, thus extracting the reluctant watch from its hiding place. Flicking the watch cover back he looked at it for a moment, snapped the lid shut then gave it a few turns, gazing absently at the music in front of him whilst humming to himself before returning the watch to his pocket. The boys, who had started to chatter, fell silent as Mr Owen, turning in his chair, cleared his throat, and then eyeing the boys in turn said.

"I think I may have mentioned last Sunday that there is a wedding tomorrow at 2 o'clock."

Mr Owen surveyed the expectant boys who sat eagerly, poised on the edge of their seats, while waiting for his next pronouncement. Clearing his throat again he added, "How many of you can make that time?"

With the exception of a few probationers, who knew they would be unlikely to be picked anyway, all the boys raised their hands.

"Right", said Mr Owen, "they only want eight so....." and he proceeded to point to eight boys, including Richard and Barry as well as their friends, Jim, David and Herbert. "You eight stay behind, the rest of you I'll see you Sunday: don't be late".

Mr Owen paused, watching those boys who were going home putting on their coats, scarves and for some their school caps; others picked up their bicycle lamps from the window sill and experimentally switched them on. All of them gradually drifted through the door, saying their goodnights to Mr Owen as they did so. He in turn smiling and nodding in reply, all the time chewing his gum rhythmically until the last boy had left.

Turning to Richard, Mr Owen pointed to a cupboard, "Richard, please get out the music for 'O Praise the Lord' by 'Goss' will you. We'd better practise it as we are singing it tomorrow" then he chuckled to himself.

Richard got to his feet, went to the cupboard and rummaged among the packets of anthems until he found the one he was looking for. Closing the cupboard door he took a copy out of the envelope and gave it to Mr Owen who nodded his thanks. Richard then gave copies to the rest of the boys, keeping one for himself and putting the remainder down on the empty seat beside him. While Mr Owen played the boys followed the music through to the end, some silently, others humming to themselves whilst Herbert spontaneously burst out into song.

"Right", said Mr Owen as he finished playing, ending with a flourish, "not too fast now, one, two, three and off we go".

He resumed playing, this time the boys all singing with the music. Mr Owen played contentedly giving shouted words of encouragement and instruction as the anthem progressed. Richard sang cheerfully with the others; he never felt so happy and at peace as he did when he was singing. Although they had been singing for over an hour, with the reward in sight the next day, this additional practice was no hardship. Once, twice then a third time they sang this particular anthem and then quickly ran through the other hymns and the psalm to be sung at the wedding. All of which as they knew them by heart were sung with the added pleasure that you got as if you were meeting old friends. At last there was nothing left to practise save the Gloria of the psalm which, with the Amen, Mr Owen finished on the piano with a great flourish and suddenly slammed the lid down hard and stood up.

"Good, good", he look quizzical for a moment, "very good in fact; right, off you go, boys, the men will be here in a moment for their practice". He surveyed his charges as the boys put on their coats, school caps and scarves.

Richard helped by Barry collected up the music and put it back in the cupboards.

"Goodnight, goodnight", said Mr Owen as one after another the boys left, some tipping their caps to him. Richard was also about to leave with Barry when Mr Owen called him back. "Ah, Richard, may I have a word with you?"

Richard had stopped at the mention of his name, as had Barry to whom he whispered, "See you outside in a minute".

Barry nodded and was going to continue but his curiosity got the better of him. "What's it about?" he asked quietly, but noting the impatient stare of Mr Owen had to content himself with Richard's quick, barely noticeable shrug of his shoulders. Barry walked the remaining few steps to the wooden door, pulled it open and stepped into the ill-lit short narrow passage. On his right was the toilet, smelling of vomit; while ahead of him was the door to the small courtyard. He continued on his way as Mr Owen, having accepted Barry's departure resumed speaking to Richard. Although tempted to stay and listen Barry carried on walking to join his friends outside.

* * *

"How long do you think he will be?" asked David, drawing his coat belt tighter around his waist in the vain hope that it would somehow stave off the cold.

Barry looked up at the illuminated clock on the tower; it was almost a quarter passed seven. He took a packet of liquorice Imps out of his pocket and handed them round to everyone before replying.

"Not long; the men's choir practice starts in a few minutes so he can't be". As if to lend weight to his words several men loomed out of the darkness into the dim light outside Vye & Son and with a cheery "Good evening boys" disappeared into the vestry.

David sniffed in mock disapproval. "They've been in the Red Lion – again". The others nodded solemnly in agreement as the Vestry door opened again and Richard walked out. He was spotted first by David. "Where are the bangers, Ricky?" he enquired as Richard approached.

Barry however had other things on his mind at that precise moment. "Wait a minute, Dave" he said to David before turning to Richard and continuing, "Well", he hesitated, "what did he want then?"

Richard looked in turn at each of them before replying. "I'm going to be made Head Chorister on Sunday", he announced, barely able to control the quiver of excitement in his voice. "Graham has left the choir as his voice has finally broken." The others at first sighed with relief then crowded round Richard, congratulating him. They had never liked Graham Poole who, a year and a half older than them was, in their eyes, a bit of a big head and a bully. He had been Head Chorister for two years and had been particularly obnoxious to Richard – who he had regarded as a rival for his post – and as a consequence to his friends as well. There was no envy in Barry's or any of the others' voices as they took turns in congratulating him. They all knew that he had the best voice and it was right that he should be chosen.

After the excitement had died down David repeated his earlier question. "Where are the bangers?" he asked excitedly.

Richard went to his bicycle and slowly opened the saddle-bag as Barry, Herbert, David and Jim crowded round impatiently. Taking out the brown paper bag he unrolled the top and showed it to the others, their eyes lighting up at the sight. As the tallest, he had been volunteered to buy the fireworks as they were all under age.

Barry reached forward eagerly and took a banger out of the bag. Making sure that the bottom of the banger was secure and the blue touch paper tightly wound he gave it a squeeze to be reassured by its firmness. "I'll bet these will go off with a loud bang" he declared defying anyone to say otherwise. He need not have worried as everyone nodded their heads solemnly in agreement. Satisfied, he took a last look at the banger and put it back in the bag.

"Have we got everything, torches?" Those with bicycles held up their bicycle lamps to Barry. "Matches?" he continued. Richard rattled a box. "Right, let's go."

As if they were a troop of soldiers they marched out of the vestry courtyard, turned left passed Vye & Son, the grocers, and then sharp left again along the muddy track. On their left side was the wall of the grocers and two small cottages, which backed onto the churchyard while on their right the pigsties and a large barn. It was a very clear night overhead; the stars played hide and seek with the few wispy clouds which seemed to rush along driven by an unfelt wind. They walked along the rutted track, often stumbling over lumps of flint and broken bricks, which had been put down by the farmer to provide a grip for his tractor's tyres. After a few yards they had passed the cottages and the barn. Now on their left was the low flint wall of the churchyard and on the opposite side the old concrete air raid shelter, thought by the boys to be haunted by the ghost of the Luftwaffe pilot whose fighter plane had crashed during the war in the field which lay directly in front of them beyond the shelter. Although the wreckage was no longer there they had all seen the twisted propeller which now had pride of place in the public bar of the Red Lion at the top of the High Street.

Barry marched towards a gap in the wall. The mortar which held the flints together was old and powdery. Years of wind, rain and frost had at last loosened some of the flints which now rested in a small heap on the ground. Others had been added over the years by the choristers who, using this gap as a shortcut to get to the church, had widened it so now it was quite large. Barry crouched down by the wall and rubbed his finger back and forth on the mortar by a loose flint. The dry mortar turned to powder at his touch, sprinkling his knees with gritty white dust. Barry brushed the dust off as he stood up. "Let's try a couple here to see if we can get this flint out."

The other boys came over and examined the spot. Although loose, like a rotting tooth, the flint defied all their attempts to pull it out. Richard the last to try, looked up at Barry who had been watching intently and declared, "We'll never shift that." He gave the flint a kick with his boot. "You'll need a bomb to even move it!"

Barry was not so easily put off. "Let's try a couple of bangers and if it doesn't work we'll try something else."

No-one disagreed, so taking two bangers out of the bag he jammed them tight behind the flint, giving the latter an extra tug and twist to see if he could shift it. To his surprise he felt it move in his hand. He looked up but doubted if the others had noticed the movement in the dark. The feeble light from David's bicycle lamp was waving to and fro instead of concentrating on the point where he was working. "Perhaps another one would make all the difference," he said blandly and held out his hand to Richard who, on receiving no signs of dissent from the others, reached into the bag and took out a banger larger than the rest.

"I bought this tuppenny one as well", he said as he handed it to Barry, who grabbed it eagerly, his eyes lighting up at the sight. "This'll do the job." Jamming it next to the other two he picked up a lump of damp clayey earth and packed it tight round the fireworks like he had seen on war films on the television. He was making sure it was firmly in place and was about to reach for another piece to make certain it was all secure but was deterred by a plaintive cry from Herbert.

"Hurry it up will you, it's cold just standing about. My ears will drop off in a minute." Barry tutted and asked resignedly, knowing he wouldn't be allowed to make this the work of art he had hoped it would be, "Where are the matches?" Richard thrust out his hand holding the matches which Barry took. Taking a match out of the box he crouched closer to his home-made 'bomb' and struck the match, which after lighting was promptly blown out by the wind. He threw it down in disgust and tried another but the same thing happened. "This is ridiculous," he declared, "We'll never get the bleedin' thing lit."

Richard came closer and putting the bag of fireworks on the ground tried to shield the flame as Barry struck another match. "It's no use," he finally declared after several more tries, "we will have to think of something else." He paused deep in thought while the others looked at each other mystified. At last Richard spoke out. "Has anyone got any Bengal matches?"

The others looked at one another, all shaking their heads except David who, half raising his hand said reluctantly, "I have a few, but I was saving them."

Barry stood up. "We only want one, go on," and added, noticing David's reluctance, "It'll be worth it, you see. David took the box of Bengal matches out of his pocket and handed it over to Barry who opened the box and took one out leaving two behind. "Only one, right?" David nodded and all of them watched as Barry crouched down, his hand poised. Looking sideways he asked, "Ready?" They all nodded. Barry struck the match which, despite the valiant attempt of the wind to extinguish it, blazed luridly, his face taking on a hellish hue from the roaring red flame. Barry applied the match to the blue touch papers and having made sure all the bangers were alight he dropped the match and ran the few paces to join the others who unconsciously had backed off a few yards. Nothing happened at first then one banger, quickly followed by the other two, fizzed into life. The fizzing reached a crescendo and one banger exploded loudly followed almost immediately by the other two. Herbert had clapped his hands over his ears so did not hear the second bang properly but both he and the others were spattered with pieces of mud.

"What a fantastic bang," cried Barry as he rushed forward, the smoke from the 'bomb' being quickly dispersed by the wind. He reached forward and pulled away the scorched flint from the rotting mortar and waved it in the air triumphantly. "See, what did I tell you," he said, passing the flint around for everyone to inspect.

David looked at the flint cursorily and gave it to Herbert before inspecting the hole, probing it with his fingers. "It hasn't done all that much damage, has it?" he asked.

Barry looked at him scathingly, his moment of triumph already beginning to fade. "Well, what do you expect, you twit, it's not a bleedin' atom bomb!" and turned away in disgust.

David was not daunted by the sneer in Barry's voice and wanted to blow something up himself like he had seen on television, but what? His eyes probed the dim light given out by his bicycle lamp but he could see nothing suitable. He was about to give up when he saw two snails on the ground near the wall. He cried out to the others, "Hey, how about blowing these snails up?" The others paused from dismissing the merits and effect of 'Barry's Bomb', as it was already being called, and looked at David and then at the snails on the ground. From the expression on the others' faces David felt some further justification was necessary. "Well, why not, I don't like snails; they eat all the vegetables in our garden at home."

Barry looked down at him disbelievingly, annoyed at David's disparaging remarks about his bomb he was not prepared to let this remark pass without comment. "They can't eat all the vegetables in your garden otherwise you'd have snails as big as pigs." The others sniggered at this remark so Barry pursued it, prodding David in the chest as he did so. "Well, have you?" he demanded.

"Have I what?" replied David.

Barry looked away, exasperation clearly written all over his features; looking back he repeated "Have you, or have you not got snails as big as pigs in your garden?"

Even David had to smile at the ridiculousness of the question. "No, they're as big as bleedin' elephants", he replied, mimicking Barry and using his favourite swear word.

The other laughed out loud at this so Barry gave up, shrugging his shoulders in resignation and walked off a few paces, muttering "Who in their right mind would want to blow up a snail?"

Herbert looked at him and felt compelled to say, "I quite like snails." He was going to say that he had a couple as pets at home but the look Barry gave him made him think better of it. Barry dropped a flint on the ground and kicked at it as Richard handed David the bag of bangers, which was taken eagerly from him.

Crouching down, David took a banger out of the bag and handed the bag back to Richard.

"Let's have some light," he demanded.

Jim turned on his bicycles lamp to illuminate the snails. Leaning forward David pushed the banger into the soft earth underneath the snails so that only the blue touch paper remained above ground. Barry, who had now returned from kicking the flint, put the matches in David's outstretched hand. Surrounded by the other boys David crouched over the banger, his face only inches from the firework. He struck the match and in one sweeping motion, while it still burned fiercely, applied it to the touch paper which immediately caught alight.

He jerked back suddenly, banging into the others in his wish to get out of the way, shouting, "Get back, get back!"

The others did so, running back to what they considered to be a safe distance, turning in time to see the banger fizz into life. Herbert, not wishing to witness the imminent destruction of two snails, closed his eyes as the fizzing reached a crescendo. He would have liked to put his hands over his ears and in fact started to do so, but not wanting to be thought a cissy by his friends deterred him from doing so. The loud bang, when it came caused him to squeeze his eyes tight shut for a moment. Then he hurriedly opened them as he heard the others run forward, and followed belatedly

The boys stood around a miniature smoking crater, within which lay the split remains of the banger. Of the two snails there was no sign.

Barry looked at the crater and then at David for moment and then at the others before speaking. "Well", he said, then paused for effect, "that was a bleedin' waste of time, wasn't it?!"

David was mortified. It had not gone as expected. He had hoped to see the snails fly through the air, but it was too dark. He looked around for the remains of the snails as Jim sniggered.

"Probably in orbit by now, I shouldn't wonder". He looked up at the sky as if expecting to see them pass overhead, "Britain's contribution to the space race." The others laughed at his remark, and the look on David's face.

Barry stopped them short. "Let's go down the old air-raid shelter. There might be some rats we could throw bangers at." The others all gave their assent save

Herbert who was not too keen on the idea. The thought of rats gave him the willies.

"I, I think it's time I went home", he said, hoping to avoid having to go down the air raid-shelter.

Richard felt that he ought to be making his way home too: knowing his mother was very strict about how much time he spent out of the house and with whom. But since he was enjoying himself, didn't want to split up the group just yet. "Don't be silly Bert; we've got plenty of time yet." But on seeing the doubt on Herbert's face he added, "Well, just a few more minutes anyway, OK?"

"OK", replied Herbert and with Richard followed after the others to the entrance of the air-raid shelter.

A remnant from the Second World War, the air-raid shelter lay like a partially submerged angular grey whale in a sea of earth and weeds. Although the top was still mostly clear it was bespattered by moss and other fungi. At the sides an accumulation of long grass, weeds, dead leaves and other debris had collected over the years to soften the outline and conceal this unnatural growth, as if its very being was an affront, which nature now tried to cover up. In size it was about fifty feet long and twenty feet wide. At approximately half way along its length a steep concrete slope, on which nature was also beginning to encroach, led down in to the shelter; the bottom of which was twenty feet below ground level. At the bottom, the entrance, about eight feet square, was a gaping black maw.

Barry, David and Jim stood at the top of the slope and waited until Richard and Herbert caught up. All five watched, looking down at the darkness, which their bicycle torches were unable to dispel. Leaves swirled round in circles driven endlessly by the wind, the rustling and scraping making an unnerving sound. Herbert twitched involuntarily as Barry looked down and even he was wondering, looking at the damp moss and lichen covered concrete as well as the lightless entrance, whether this was a good idea after all. It was clear to Herbert that the others were waiting to see what he would do next.

Richard looked at his friend, aware of his dilemma. Clutching the bag of fireworks Richard walked down the slope, occasionally his feet losing their purchase on the concrete made slippery by the rain and rotting leaves. He looked back; no-one was following, not even Barry.

"Come on", he said "we haven't got all night", and resumed his walk until he reached the bottom. The others hesitated then Barry followed by the others, and most reluctantly by Herbert, joined him at the bottom of the slope.

Whilst waiting, Richard had been shining his bicycle lamp into the gloom but its weak light was unable to penetrate the absolute blackness which faced him. "Well, what do you think – shall we go in?"

The others look uncertainly into the solid blackness. Even in the daylight the air-raid shelter was a little bit eerie; at night it was even worse. Getting no response, Richard took a banger from the bag and lit it. Waiting until it started to fizz before throwing it into the darkness and watched as the fizzing missile appeared to be swallowed by the gloom before it exploded with a loud bang, which echoed back and forth.

The five boys stood transfixed; stunned by the ferocity of the explosion, which had hardly begun to die down when suddenly three rats emerged from the gloom and hurtled past the boys, continuing up the slope.

Herbert shrieked and ran up the slope, seeking to run away from the entrance to the shelter and any more rats that might suddenly emerge but in doing so almost caught up with the rats who, having run out of the shelter, had now paused, at the top of the slope, and turned around to see what was happening.

Giving another shriek, Herbert skidded to a halt and then ran back to where the others were still standing watching him, whilst the rats, having seen enough, scuttled off into the undergrowth. "Help!" he cried, "we're surrounded by rats".

The others burst out laughing at this and the look of panic on Herbert's face as his eyes darted here and there, looking for rats.

"Don't be silly, Bert", said Jim, grabbing him by the shoulder. "There aren't any rats – they've all gone."

Herbert stopped his frantic motions and looked slowly around. Seeing no rats, or any other form of wild-life, he let out a great sigh, his head falling forward and shoulders drooping, "I've had enough", he said and when no-one immediately responded continued, "I'm going home now".

With that Herbert turned and walked slowly up the slope. Watched by the others he reached the top where his determination to brave the dark journey back to Church Street, past probably packs of rats lurking in the mist now beginning to form, deserted him. He turned around. "Is anyone else coming?" he asked.

Richard nodded his head. He was late as it was and although he had two excuses for being later than usual, the additional practice caused by tomorrow's wedding and his being made head chorister, he knew he had better not be too late. Reluctantly he handed the bag of bangers to Barry, who having taken it, shook his head. "No, we might as well all go home now."

David and Jim agreed and together they climbed up the slope to join Herbert who tried to make his relief not too apparent. Returning to the vestry courtyard they collected their bicycles, listening for a moment to the men singing at their choir practice. "How about going to get some conkers tomorrow?" said Jim.

David looked at him as if he were deranged. "Are you mad – you've got hundreds!"

Jim merely shrugged. "Not hundreds, anyway they don't last long and I'm keeping a few for next year." Noting everyone's reluctance he added a final inducement. "I know where there's a hazelnut tree that hasn't been touched yet." He noted with satisfaction that Richard and Barry's eyes lit up.

After some humming and hawing they all agreed to go looking for conkers and hazelnuts after the wedding, if it wasn't raining too hard, when Jim would show them where the hazelnut tree was in the dense wood that led from the graveyard down to Dane Court Road. Saying their various 'goodnights', Jim, David and Herbert cycled off on their separate ways home, leaving Richard and Barry behind.

"How many bangers have we got left?" asked Richard just as Barry was about to stuff the brown paper bag into his saddlebag.

Barry looked inside the bag, then up at Richard. "Five", he said, putting them away, making sure the leather straps on the saddlebag were tight.

Richard nodded, seemingly content with this number but not divulging why. "Will you bring them with you tomorrow; we could let them off after the wedding?"

Barry nodded. "Might as well". He thought for a moment before adding, "Do you have to go home yet; we could go down the seafront". Barry didn't want to go home to an empty house. His father was out down the pub and his mother usually visited his Gran on Fridays so he was in no hurry to get home.

Richard grimaced, aware of his friend's reluctance to say goodnight. "Sorry, I'm late enough as it is and I don't want to get further into trouble, you know what my mum is like".

Barry nodded; he knew only too well. "You can come home with me if you like", Richard added in a flash of inspiration.

Barry shook his head. "Err. No thanks, but I'll cycle with you for a bit". Richard nodded, welcoming the companionship.

The mist was now getting thicker and the pale yellow light from the lamps on their bicycles made little difference to the gloom which preceded them. The mist, making them cold and damp, spurred them on to cycle fast along Church Street and turn left at the ambulance station into Northdown Road, past Tuckers, the newsagents, which was on their right. For a night, which had started off bright and clear, then with only traces of mist, it had now turned into a very thick fog. Richard and Barry cycled slowly along the remainder of Northdown Road until they arrived at the junction of Northdown Hill and Westover Road. Both stopped; Barry was the first to speak.

"Well, see you tomorrow then?"

Richard nodded, "Yes, I've got some messages to do in the morning."

Barry did not need to be told that 'messages' meant shopping. He was used to these Scottish sayings, which

Richard got from his mother. "OK, then, see you tomorrow." With a brief wave he cycled off disappearing quickly into the fog.

Checking that his lamp was working, Richard cycled up Northdown Hill on the pavement because he thought the fog made the road unsafe, passed the Crown and Thistle pub to his house next to the small green on the corner of Northdown Hill and Pearson's Way. Reaching the house, he opened the front gate, wondering how to explain away his lateness, reciting the reasons to himself as he wheeled his bicycle up the path. First was the extra practise for the wedding tomorrow afternoon, then when the others had left he had to stay behind to be told he was to be made head chorister, and finally the fog. He wasn't late very often and the news about his being made head chorister would please his mother and might in itself be enough to explain away his lateness so that not too many questions would be asked. Feeling that, should he need it he had, like a mediaeval knight, girded sufficient armour about himself in the form of excuses for protection against the darkness he might have to face indoors; Richard put his bicycle in the porch and leaned it against his brother Robin's bicycle, opened the back door and stepped into the kitchen.

Richard unbuttoned his coat and then went to drape it over a hook in the hall. He was about to go into the back room when he noticed that his jersey still hung on him oddly. He stopped and considered whether he should take it off but its absence was bound to be noticed since it was too cold just to be in shirtsleeves. Very quickly he pushed his jersey back into shape as much as he could. The boy at school who had pulled it for a joke that day hadn't realised how flimsy and threadbare it was since it had been bought at a jumble sale. He had been immediately apologetic but it hadn't made much difference. The jersey just wouldn't go back the way it had been. Taking a last look at his jersey he left the protection of the hall, turned the handle of the door and stepped inside the back room.

Everyone was there. Saying a brief hallo, he walked over to sit on the pouffe and watch television. Nothing happened immediately and he was beginning to think he would get away with it when his mother's voice suddenly cut through the air like a butcher's cleaver. "Richard!" He turned his head as his mother added "What's the matter with your jersey?"

Richard sighed silently to himself. It was best just to own up and get it over with. "It got pulled at school," he volunteered.

"Stand up!" commanded his mother from her seat in the corner. Richard did so and then as directed walked over to his mother when she beckoned. Standing still, in order to prevent provoking his mother by being accused of fidgeting, he waited whilst she inspected the jersey, the front of which had been so badly stretched it hung like a dark blue fold of skin. His mother looked up at him.

"You let someone do this to you – do you think we can buy jerseys for you every week?" She paused before punctuating the question. "Well?"

Richard shrugged helplessly. "He was bigger than me," he started to explain. The words were hardly out of his mouth when his mother grabbed hold of his hair and pulled him down so that his face was only a few inches away from hers.

"I don't care if he's six feet tall. The next time someone pulls your jersey you had better hit him good and hard because it'll be nothing to the beating you'll get from me when you get home, get it?" she said; releasing Richard who now began to slowly straighten up.

"Yes, mum," he replied. "Good," said his mother and fetched him such a clout across his face that it caused lights to flicker in front of his eyes.

Feeling backwards with his hand he groped for the pouffe and sat down, the lights in his head continuing to flicker on and off for a few minutes. That wasn't too bad, thought Richard; it could have been a lot worse. He felt Robin's eyes on him so moved his head slightly until their eyes met. Richard winked slowly, reassuring his brother, who half smiled in return before resuming watching the television. Richard too turned back to the set but his eyes did not follow what was on the screen. One thing's for certain, he thought, the next time someone pulls my jersey I had better do something about it.

Chapter 2: **A wedding and visit to the church tower**

Richard and Barry stood on the pavement outside the entrance to the vestry, dressed in their ruffs and cassocks, watching the wedding guests arrive. Old cars and new cars, taxis and even a jeep with two American airmen from nearby Manston airport, drew up and disgorged the guests before driving off down the High Street to park or try to find a vacant spot in the already crowded Church Street and Vicarage Street. An usher dressed in his morning suit hurried from one car to the next, making sure that no-one parked outside the main gates, a space reserved for the arrival of the bride. In contrast to yesterday's chill wind and rain the air was clear and bright. The blue sky scattered with white fluffy clouds the gentle sun offsetting the cool wind, which blew up from Broadstairs and the sea, just over a mile away. Richard was distracted from the goings on by a gull hovering in the wind overhead, occasionally diving downwards as if to get a closer look at what was happening on the ground below, then finally coming to rest on the tower. He was startled from watching the gull by a well-placed elbow from Barry. "Look," he hissed, "over there."

Richard looked in time to see some men dressed in morning suits stagger and lurch out of the Red Lion pub.

The usher, who a moment ago was shepherding cars out of the way, saw them and rushed across the road shouting, gesticulating and pointing at his watch. As if on cue the church clock chimed the quarter to the hour, whilst the usher started to push the men towards the church, muttering all the while, whilst the men moved slowly off with large grins on their faces. Barry stuck his finger between his neck and the ruff which, because of the starch, was beginning to chafe his skin. He pulled at it for a moment to ease it then grinned to himself.

"Come on," he turned, "we'd better get ready." Richard sighed and followed Barry into the vestry as Barry continued, "I wonder if anything will happen today?" He smiled wistfully for a moment then spoke, thinking his thoughts out loud. "Perhaps the bride will faint, or perhaps the bridegroom will be sick like the one we had last year."

Richard had stopped with his friend and listened to his musings for a while then reached up and pulled roughly on his arm. "Come on, stop daydreaming. Things like that happen only once in a blue moon. Let's go and get the books ready."

Reluctantly Barry followed Richard into the dark coolness of the vestry still dwelling on the many possibilities. "Perhaps the bride won't turn up after all. That hasn't happened for a while." Richard held the inner door open for Barry then turned, as Barry caught it, and opening a cupboard took out some sheet music. Closing the door to the cupboard he turned to Barry and gave him some copies of the anthem just as the curate burst into the vestry from the corridor that led to the church.

"Ah," he exclaimed, "just who I wanted to see."

Barry groaned audibly, "Oh no!" raising his eyes up to the ceiling.

The curate, unheeding, gathered Richard and Barry together. "Good afternoon, sir," they both said as he looked down on them, nodding his head in acknowledgement of their greeting. "Now I wonder if you would both do me a favour."

Richard automatically nodded his head in affirmation as the curate looked at him whilst Barry shook his head from side to side, changing to a nod as the curate looked at him, so rapidly that it sent a jolt of pain down his neck, making him wince involuntarily. The curate looked oddly at Barry for a moment, his brow furrowed, then his face cleared.

"Thank you. Now," he continued breathlessly, "after the wedding service would you go up to the tower and bring down the flag?" He looked fondly at Barry. "I know you've been up there before, for me." Barry nodded his head and smiled grimly to himself. He remembered all too well and often remarked he could still smell the dust and cobwebs on his clothes from when he had tripped up in the belfry, even though his mother had washed them. He was also not sure if he wanted to go up again, whilst some people were claustrophobic Barry was not sure if he liked heights very much. Richard suppressed a smirk whilst the curate fumbled in his cassock pocket. "Now where did I put that key? Ah, here it is." Producing the key he gave it to Richard who took it and put it in his cassock pocket. "Thank you very much," said the curate, walking off to the Vicar's vestry-cum-office. "See you after the wedding."

Barry shook his head, "Not if we see you first," he added under his breath but was nevertheless resigned to helping the curate, then followed after Richard, who had walked out of the vestry to the corridor that led to the church.

Clasping the copies of the anthem in their hands, Richard and Barry walked along the corridor and entered the church. Walking part way along the aisle, which ran at right angles to the nave, they turned left, up the north aisle, passed the choir stalls and then right, walking out in front of the altar rails at the top of the chancel. They both stopped at the centre and bowed to the altar. Separating, they walked down the chancel, sat down in the choir stalls and began to lay out the books.

As it was a wedding there was very little to do. Taking out a prayer book Richard opened it to the page for the 'Solemnization of Matrimony'. Next he opened the hymn book to number 184, 'Dear Lord and Father of Mankind'. Richard sat and hummed through the first verse. He quite liked this hymn and was pleased it had been chosen for the wedding. Richard then stuck the printed order of service in the page of the second hymn, number 463, 'O Perfect Love, all human thought transcending'. He particularly liked this hymn and sat in the stall humming the turn to himself as he sang the words in his head, oblivious to his surrounding or those guests who were gradually beginning to drift into the church now that the bridegroom had come out of the pub.

The sound of Barry clearing his throat brought him back to the present. Smiling sheepishly Richard continued opening the books whilst Barry, who had finished, waited patiently in his seat for Richard to do so too. When he had finished Richard then got up and went to the vicar's stall and opened his prayer and hymn books at the correct places. Leaving also a copy of the order of service and the anthem 'O Praise the Lord' by Sir John Goss. Having done that he went and joined Barry. "Anything else?" asked Barry as he put down the copy of the anthem he was looking at.

Richard looked around him. Everything appeared to be in order. "Only the lights and the altar rail," he whispered in reply. Barry nodded, got up and walked into the men's stalls and flicked the several switches down to turn on the lights whilst Richard, pausing as he crossed the aisle to bow, did the same for his side of the choir stalls. Reaching the altar rail together they both walked to the centre and eased the central part of the rail apart, which they then slid carefully into the fixed section, thus allowing access to the altar. Standing erect for a moment they bowed together then walked back the way they had come to the vestry.

On entering the vestry they were noisily greeted by their fellow choristers, who seemed to be shouting altogether in their combined efforts to tell Richard something. After a few moments of this Barry could stand it no longer and shouted for quiet, allowing Richard to ask, "What's it all about Jim?"

Jim looked around, pleased he had been singled out as spokesman. "The best man came in and wanted to know who was in charge. I said that you were Head Chorister but were in church so he said for me to tell you that he wanted to speak to you and would wait outside the vestry."

Richard looked at Barry who returned his puzzled stare before looking back at him. "What for?" he asked.

Jim, who could only shrug, said, "He didn't say."

Richard looked up at the church clock; it was now almost five minutes to three. "Come on Barry, let's go and find out." He looked back at the others. "Better get your surplices on; we'll be going out in a minute." With that he walked with Barry to the vestry door and stepped outside.

Pacing up and down, whilst smoking a cigarette, was one of the men Richard and Barry had seen coming out of the pub. He continued to pace, their presence going unnoticed, until he stopped to look at his watch, then realised he was being observed. Throwing his cigarette to the ground he stamped on it and rushed up to Richard and Barry. "Which one of you is the head choirboy?"

"Chorister," said Richard, drawing attention to himself. The man looked at the large silver badge with the legend, 'Head Chorister', which hung from a wide blue ribbon around his neck and then at the small bronze badge and narrow red ribbon Barry wore.

"Sorry, chorister," he smiled weakly. "I'm the best man and I just want to say, er, er, ask, if you and your mates will sing extra well today at my friend's wedding," he paused for a few seconds before adding prosaically, "I'll make it worth your while." Taking a wallet from his jacket pocket he started to take out a ten shilling note then, seeing the odd look on Richard's face, changed his mind and took out a pound note instead, which he held out to Richard.

Richard was nonplussed. He was already being paid for singing at the wedding and would have been happy to do so even if he was not paid. It was not necessary to be paid extra for doing something he loved. He was going to sing as best he could anyway. Extra money would not make him sing any better. These thoughts flashed through Richard's mind as the man held the pound note in front of him like a partially withered leaf. He was about to say it wasn't necessary when Barry, knowing what was going through Richard's mind, stepped forward and took the money.

"Thanks very much. Don't worry today we'll sing extra special for you." The man looked relieved and, muttering his thanks, hurried off. Barry pulled on Richard's arm to return to the vestry but Richard remained where he was.

Looking oddly at Barry he said, "What do you mean, 'we'll sing extra special'; we always do our best even if it is a funeral."

Barry looked at his unworldly friend and sighed out loud. This was probably going to be a long haul. "I know that, and you know that, but he doesn't. So if he thinks that by giving us extra money we will make more of an effort what difference does it make?" He paused, "we don't get much anyway. It's all right for you, you get extra as a soloist, the rest of us don't."

Richard had to agree with Barry's last statement but it was still not right, and he felt compelled to say so even though Barry was looking worriedly up at the church clock, which now said two minutes to three. "But it's dishonest. He thinks he's paying for something extra when he's not going to get it."

Barry looked again at the clock and back at Richard. "Look, that's not important. If he thinks he paid extra for something and we sing well, that's all that matters. He'll be happy that he paid the extra and we'll be happy to receive it." The set of Richard's jaw warned him that he was getting nowhere with his argument. "Look there's no time to argue now, if you don't want a share of the money don't take it. OK?"

Richard was still vexed but didn't have either the time or will to argue further and he saw the logic that the other choristers would like this sudden windfall. "OK" he finally said. Relieved, Barry dragged Richard reluctantly into the vestry. Whilst Richard put on his surplice and combed his hair Barry announced the good news to the others – an additional half crown each. All the choristers promised to make an extra effort to earn this unexpected windfall, just as the vicar emerged from his vestry.

The boys lined up with Richard in front as Barry rushed to get his surplice, which he dragged over his head. Running his fingers quickly through his hair he walked quickly to the front to stand beside Richard. The vicar opened his book. "Good afternoon, boys." He beamed at them all. "Good afternoon, sir," they chorused in reply.

The vicar smiled and looked at the two rows of choristers; with their newly starched ruffs and surplices, the complexion of their faces, as if freshly scrubbed, they appeared the epitome of choristers. He looked through the vestry window up at the clock on the tower. It was almost three. "Before we go in, a short prayer." The boys, clasping their hands in front, bowed their heads whilst the vicar, after adjusting his spectacles, read from his prayer book. Barry inclined his head in Richard's direction to give him a conspiratorial wink but Richard failed to respond. "Amen," said the vicar, quickly followed by the boys. The vicar looked at Richard. "Will you send one of the boys back when the bride arrives?"

Richard nodded, "Yes sir." To be answered by a smile.

"Right, off you go then."

Richard opened the door to the corridor, which led out of the vestry then, with Barry at his side and followed by the others, he walked along the stone corridor until they appeared at the door to the north entrance to the church. He stopped. Turning his head he looked at the others. "Ready?" he asked and waited until they had all nodded then pulled open the large carved oak door. As if at a signal the congregation turned and watched at the boys filed part way into the north aisle and waited.

The clock then struck three as Richard looked across the church to the south door where the verger stood and caught his eye. The verger shook his head from side to side: the bride had not arrived yet. Richard turned to Barry standing beside him. "I'll go and wait by the organ; you let me know when the bride arrives."

Barry looked at his watch. "OK," he said easily.

Richard, looking to the back of the queue of boys, said "Jim you go and tell the vicar when we're ready to go." Jim just nodded he'd done this before.

Richard left his place and walked up the north aisle to stand by the side of the organ where he could see both Barry and the organist. Reaching his post he turned around and by merely raising his eyebrows asked the question: 'Has the bride arrived yet?' Barry shook his head. The bride had not, as had sometimes happened, arrived in the short time it had taken him to walk up to the organ.

Richard turned to Mr Bowen who was, as usual, chewing a piece of gum as he played music in the interlude, whilst waiting for the bride to arrive. He felt Richard's gaze on him and turned his head, watched whilst Richard shook his, then turned back to read the music as he continued to play. Richard leant against the panelled woodwork, which lined the organ, then straightened and taking a tin of Meloids from his cassock pocket, he put one in his mouth. Replacing the tin he again settled down to wait. He tried to remember what was the longest he had had to wait, all the time keeping one eye on Barry and the other on Mr Bowen.

After a few minutes Mr Bowen finished playing, ending with a crescendo, pulling out various stops with such speed and verve that Richard never failed to be amazed. Mr Bowen twisted around on his bench. "Not arrived yet?" he enquired.

"No sir," replied Richard. Mr Bowen sucked on a tooth for a second then pulled his watch out of his waistcoat pocket, looked at it, then put it to his ear just to make sure it was working. Giving the winder a few turns he replaced it in his pocket. "Oh well," he said to Richard, "I had better play something else then."

Richard wasn't listening. Barry had just then raised his hand but was moving his forefinger up and down. Richard turned to Mr Bowen. "The bride has just arrived sir, but they are having pictures taken."

Mr Bowen smiled. "Good, now where's the bridal march – I've got it here somewhere." He searched amongst the sheets of music on the stand until he found it and placed it on top of the other sheets. "Better improvise for a bit, I suppose, you never know how long photographs will take." He commenced playing.

Richard smiled, watching Barry all the while. The seconds ticked by until at last Barry raised his hand again as Jim, at the other end of the row, went off to collect the vicar from the vestry. Richard leaned forward. "Ready sir."

Mr Bowen nodded. "Right, I'll give you twenty seconds." Off Richard went back the way he had come, along the north aisle, counting in his head and arrived back at his place at the same time as Jim and the vicar appeared from the vestry.

The organ music faded to be replaced after a few second's silence by the bridal march. As one, Richard and Barry stepped forward, followed by the others at a leisurely pace. At first in ones and twos, then the remainder together, the congregation stood. Richard and Barry turned left into the nave where, at the verger's behest, the bride and her father joined the procession. Careful to avoid the white silk cushions on the step of the chancel, Richard and Barry led the choristers up to the altar rail, bowed together then divided, walking back in the direction they had travelled, through the choir stalls, until they had reached their respective places.

The vicar stood at the chancel step waiting for the bride and her father to reach him. The bridal march carried on for a few more bars then came to a crescendo, dwindled and died. One of the bridesmaids straightened the bride's train, whilst another took the bride's flowers for the duration of the ceremony. Richard looked at the four people standing there: best man, bridegroom, bride and the bride's father. Every wedding was the same: nervous smiles, uncontrollable hands, ghastly grimaces. The best man caught Richard's eye and gave him a 'thumbs up' sign. Richard nodded and half smiled in reply then turned and looked across at Barry who had noted the exchange and so winked in response.

The vicar looked about him noticing that the congregation were beginning to settle down after the arrival of the bride. After a short dry cough he announced, "We sing the first hymn in the order of service, 'Dear Lord and Father of Mankind'." Having made the announcement he gave a copy of the order of service to the bride and groom. As the organ played the introduction to the hymn Richard picked up his hymn book as did the other choristers. He looked across at Barry who, as usual, irreverently mouthed 'here we go again', making him smile. The introductory music drew to an end; with a crescendo as a warning.

Taking a deep breath Richard began singing. Warming to the tune and words after a few bars, he gave himself up solely to the music. It was so easy to do so. The wedding might not have existed. He was so happy just to be given the opportunity to sing again, to hear the notes ring high and clear, to hang in the air then tumble over one another before dissipating to make room for the others. He revelled in his singing. It was his first love. As the hymn progressed he warmed to it more, singing each verse with extra enthusiasm in an effort to make it sound even better than the previous one. For the present singing was everything to him.

The final notes of the last verse faded as the vicar, putting his hymn book down, moved from his place to stand in front of the bride and groom. With only occasional glances at his prayer book for reference he began to read the order of service. "Dearly beloved, we are gathered together here in the sight of God, and in the face of this congregation…"

Richard left half an ear listening to the vicar's words whilst he arranged his music for the rest of the service. His ears only pricked up when the vicar said, "Therefore if any man can shew any just cause why they may not lawfully be joined together, let him now speak, or else hereafter for ever hold his peace." There was a short pause but, as usual, no-one spoke up. He looked across at Barry, who shrugged as if to say 'Ah well, perhaps next time' then both resumed following the service in their prayer books as the vicar continued with the marriage ceremony. Richard had often speculated what would happen if someone did object. Although he had been to lots of weddings as a chorister no-one had ever objected and he was beginning to wonder if anyone ever did except in films and stories.

He paid attention again to the vicar as he intoned, "Who giveth this woman to be married to this man?" The father of the bride gave his daughter's right hand to the charge of the vicar who in turn passed it on to the bridegroom, who giggled at this little ceremony. The vicar looked oddly at him for a moment but then resumed the next part of the service.

As the bride finished saying her part Richard moved soundlessly out of his stall to stand beside the vicar who turned and gave him his prayer book. Richard held it open horizontally, his fingers underneath and his thumbs on top. Richard stood there solemnly waiting for what he felt was the most significant and symbolic part of the wedding service the giving of the ring.

The vicar having obtained the ring from the best man placed it on the prayer book and began the blessing. "Bless O Lord this ring, which we bless in thy name..." He hesitated for a moment as the bridegroom having elbowed the bride began to giggle as he pointed to Richard's thumb, which held the book open. With both the bride and groom trying to suppress giggles the vicar, frowning, continued with the blessing. Richard tried to see what was so funny and looked hard at the book.

Not noticing anything out of the ordinary he then looked sideways back at Barry for help, who wiggled his left thumb.

Richard looked back at his left thumb. It had been covered with gentian violet by his mother after he had cut it. He was used to the sight but now it suddenly looked a very bright purple against the pure white of the page. Quickly, and he hoped, surreptitiously, Richard moved his thumb from sight under the book as the vicar, having finished the blessing with an Amen, took the book from Richard. He offered the ring to the bridegroom who, still giggling, lifted it from the prayer book.

Suddenly feeling very self-conscious Richard moved back to his place, looking across at Barry as he did so. Barry gave a sympathetic shrug of his shoulders, which Richard acknowledged with a weak smile before he resumed following the service in his prayer book. But his heart was not in it. He took a surreptitious glance at the bride and groom; the latter interspersing the words he was speaking with barely suppressed giggles. Richard was troubled with two things; he couldn't see what was so funny about a thumb covered with gentian violet. It was always used in his house for cuts and grazes. It was rare indeed for one of his friends not to be covered with the purple liquid especially hands and knees. It was such a normal part of his and his friends' lives that they didn't give it a second thought. But what disturbed him even more was the fact that the bridegroom had found it so funny at what he considered was a particularly solemn moment of a significant service.

As the marriage service progressed Richard followed it automatically but only partially, as if by so doing he would be able to divorce himself from these people and their ideas. He more firmly resolved not to take any part of the additional money given to them by the best man before the service. Mechanically he said the prayers and responses, sat through the vicar's short sermon, sang the anthem and then the final hymn and with a great internal sigh said the Amen to the Blessing. Feeling more than a little dispirited he and the other choristers led the bride and groom to the vestry for the signing of the register, usually a time of high spirits and tomfoolery born of relief at having got the formal service over with. This time, however, he doubted if he would be properly able to join in.

* * *

Round and round they went, climbing higher and higher with each step, their feet often slipping on the worn stone. Some way back they had passed the entrance to the belfry, which they knew was just over half way up but it seemed too long ago to Barry so he wondered if he had imagined it. He looked up at his friend Richard disappearing for the hundredth time around what seemed to him to be an endless corner. He pulled hard on the rope which served as a hand rail and, stopping for a moment, peered out of one of the small narrow dust and cobweb covered windows. Little light was let in and he was comforted by the naked bulb hanging from its socket above him. Brushing away the dirt he looked down at the graveyard spread out below. It looked a long way down, even from here. For some reason he suddenly felt isolated and alone. He looked up as with a start he realised that Richard, not knowing he had stopped, had carried on. Hurrying to catch up he stumbled and fell, causing him to involuntarily cry out.

Up ahead Richard obviously heard him as his voice reverberated down the stairway. "What's up?"

He sounded miles away thought Barry as he rubbed his skinned knee for a moment before continuing on his way a little more slowly. "Nothing! I just tripped on a bleedin' step that's all." He then hurried round a few more corners with his head bowed down and almost ran into Richard who waiting for him to catch up. Not expecting him to be there, Barry's heart leapt for a moment, wondering who or what is was and forced himself to a sudden halt. He gasped for breath. "What a fright!" He finally managed to get out as Richard stood there grinning at him.

"Come on, we must be nearly at the top," said Richard and continued on his way. Barry stood there for a moment catching his breath.

"I'll believe it when I see it." He followed after, counting each step as if by so doing it would make the climb less arduous and hence easier to bear as, with aching calf muscles, he pulled himself round and round until suddenly there was Richard standing at the top stair before moving across to the narrow wooden door.

Fumbling in his back trouser pocket, Richard pulled out the key the end of which had somehow got tangled in a thread of the pocket lining, which all came out with it. Grimacing, he pulled the key until the thread finally snapped, then stuffed the lining back into his pocket. "Ready?" he asked Barry who, having sat on the step to rest and watch the drama of the emerging key unfold with wry amusement, was now keen to get out into the fresh air. He nodded. Richard turned around and inserted the large key into the lock and as it was on the right hand side of the door turned it anti-clockwise. It didn't move. He tried turning it clockwise but it still would not budge. "It won't move," he said to Barry.

"Here, let me have a go," replied Barry, standing up. He tried as well but without success. He stepped back and frowned for a moment. "It won't budge," he finally said, then stared down the stairwell. He did not want to go down all that way to get some oil from the vestry – if there was any in the first place – and then come all the way back up again. He couldn't possibly come up all those stairs twice in one day. He looked up as Richard was rattling the key back and forth in an effort to loosen the rusted mechanism, his face beginning to turn red from the effort.

"Here, give us a hand. I think it moved slightly just then." He made way for Barry who took hold of the key and together they turned it anti-clockwise. Straining and grunting with the effort, nothing seemed to happen until, with a loud cracking sound, the lock finally gave way with a sudden jerk then slowly, under their continued pressure, it unlocked all the way. Both Richard and Barry let go of the key and looked at their red hands and fingers with stark white indentations from the pressure of turning the key. Both massaged their hands for minute then Richard seized hold of the iron ring. "OK?" he asked.

Barry looked up from rubbing his hands and said sourly, "just get on with it." Richard smiled at Barry's tone and turned the iron ring, releasing the door then stepped back and down as he pulled it open.

Barry stamped through first onto the lead covered roof followed closely by Richard. A seagull, which had been walking around the roof rushed into the air with a screech of indignation as both of them ran to the castellated parapet, which made it look, from where they stood, like the wall of a mediaeval castle. Both peered down to the ground then along the High Street and finally out to sea. "Fantastic," said Barry at last.

"Beautiful," said Richard, pointing to the sea which seemed to almost totally surround the land like a pale blue ribbon. He ran quickly looking over each side in turn and on all, save the west side, could he see the sea. It sparkled and twinkled like a frieze of pale blue sapphires. Here and there were ships and coasters, like toy boats, moving in either direction, their wakes a brilliant white in the azure sea. He returned to the wall facing east to rejoin Barry, who pointed with his finger. This was the side nearest the sea. Only a mile as the crow flies, he thought.

"Look over there," Barry pointed again with his finger, "that red ship, what is it?" Richard followed the direction of his friend's finger.

"That's the North Foreland Lightship anchored at the top end of the Goodwin Sands; you can see it from the cliffs at Viking Bay." Barry nodded his understanding as Richard went on, exhilarated by what he saw. "It's amazing; you could imagine that the Isle of Thanet really was an island from up here."

Barry nodded, looked down to the ground again and blinked his eyes as it seemed to move as he watched it. He shook his head violently to clear it but this seemed to make his sudden disorientation and associated nausea worse. He gulped, and then swallowed the bitter juices, which had come unbidden into his mouth. He stuck out his tongue at the sour taste whilst fumbling in his trouser pocket for an aniseed ball. He was tempted to look of the edge again but finally decided against it. Finding the sweet, he put it in his mouth and sucked viciously to remove the bitter taste from his tongue. It was funny; he thought to himself, whilst going up to the top of the tower seemed exciting now he was up here he couldn't wait to get down again. He watched Richard still pointing out objects and places he knew and went wild when he saw his house on the council estate where he lived. Barry smiled weakly and sat down. It wasn't getting any better; he decided he didn't like it up here after all. Admittedly he had looked over cliff tops, which might have seemed higher than this but this was different. At the top of a cliff you were on solid ground whereas here he was standing on what felt like a none too safe roof of a tower that seemed, by the movement of the clouds, to be swaying back and forth. He plucked up courage to speak up. Torn between getting back down as soon as possible but not wishing to spoil Richard's fun or letting it be known that he was scared of heights. "Hey, Ricky, we'd better get this flag down." He had to call out twice before getting Richard's attention.

Richard tore himself away from looking down alternately at the people in the High Street and then out to sea: the pale blue water looking unreal from that height and distance. He had only really seen blue seas in films. Up near it was always green or gray or even murky brown. Perhaps once in a while, on a clear day in summer, it was a deep blue far out at sea, but today it was a beautiful pale blue colour that he wished he could just stare at forever. He had never seen it like this before and probably never would again. "OK," he said at last, looking up at the flagpole where the ragged dirty grey white ensign flew. "Do you want to do it or shall I?"

Barry started to stand up but suddenly found that he couldn't. The thought of being able to look over the edge of the parapet sent a cold shiver down his spine. He sat down quickly and waved a negligent hand. "No, you go ahead, I'll watch." Richard, not noticing Barry's demeanour, took hold of the thin rope and untied it from the retaining cleats then very slowly pulled down the flag. There was hardly any wind today and after two half-hearted flaps, in protest, the flag resigned itself to being brought down. As it got closer Richard marvelled at how big it was until finally it billowed like a giant sheet around his feet.

Barry, on his hands and knees on the lead roof, gathered up the rippling mass, which to him resembled a parachute, making him feel like a wartime commando, although he had to admit to himself he didn't feel very brave at the moment. Richard carefully released the flag from the rope and having done that successfully, he secured the rope firmly to the metal cleats on the pole. Taking hold of the flag from Barry he stretched it out so that it covered the whole of the roof. "Fantastic!" he said. With its large red cross and Union Jack in once corner it looked just like a flag used by the knights in ancient times. Barry watched him for a few seconds then, his patience beginning to wear a bit thin, he snapped at Richard, "Bleedin' hurry up or we'll be up here all day!"

Richard looked at his friend sitting resolutely on the roof. Barry's cheeks were not as ruddy as they usually were. "All right, all right, if you'd give me a hand instead of just sitting there it'll be done quicker."

Acknowledging the sense in this suggestion Barry took hold of one end of the flag and, hurrying Richard all the time, quickly folded it up so that it could be carried by one person.

"Well I suppose we had better get down or the curate will be wondering if we have fallen over the edge." Barry laughed weakly and made speedily for the doorway, returning quickly to take the flag out of Richard's grasp.

"Hold on a minute," said Richard hurriedly, "I want to look some more!"

Barry smiled. "That's all right; I'll see you at the bottom." With that he ducked through the doorway and, with a final wave, started slowly and carefully down the worn steps. Immediately he was surrounded by the stone walls and roof he felt better. Barry hesitated, wondering whether he should return to the roof but at the last moment, almost as he took the first step upwards, his courage deserted him. He inclined his head and shouted up the stairwell, "Don't forget to lock the door after you." He waited until he heard Richard's 'OK' then carried on his way; feeling happier with every step he took; every now and then pausing to look quickly through one of the narrow dusty leaded windows to see the extent of his progress.

Richard watched as Barry disappeared; only slightly puzzled by Barry's eagerness to leave. He listened intently to Barry's muffled reminder then shouted 'OK'. Hearing nothing more, he went back to the parapet and had a last look at the sea. It was still just as beautiful. He rested his elbows on the flint wall and watched the white edged ships move majestically through the sea. Overhead a light aeroplane flew into Ramsgate Airport, momentarily distracting him from his vision of the sea. He stood there mesmerised by the sight. The effect of what had happened at the wedding service was gradually being dispelled by both the air and beauty of what he saw. In the vestry he had felt a bit of a fraud when the best man had thanked him profusely for, 'The best singing he had ever heard.' He had been so embarrassed he could only smile weakly and nod his head. In the noise and humour of the moment the best man had not noticed and having thanked Barry as well, to a more enthusiastic response, went to join the others for photographs. Suddenly the service, which had at the time seemed interminable, was over. Richard felt, if only for a short while, free of all worries. He lifted his arms wide, feeling as he did so that he was being cleansed physically and spiritually by the action of the wind on his face and body.

The moment ended suddenly when he heard a voice calling his name. Moving from his position at the east end of the tower he looked first over the edge of the south and north and then finally the west, which overlooked the old part of the churchyard. Standing on the grass, his arms still clutching the flag, was Barry, who waved at him. Richard waved back and then he listened intently, as Barry cried out again, cupping his hands around his ears. "Hurry up," cried Barry, "the curate wants the key back so he can go home."

As if on cue the curate appeared and waved up at Richard, then beckoned him down. Richard nodded, though doubted if he could be seen properly, then drew back from the wall and moved to look once more over the east side of the tower at the sea. With a final look all around, and after checking the rope was securely tied to the pole, for he did not know when he would be able to come up here again, if ever, he moved to the doorway and shut it behind him. With a savage flick of the wrist he locked the door and, after checking it, moved slowly down the spiral stairs to the ground.

Up on the roof all was peace and quiet again until the seagull, which had been disturbed by unknowing visitors, landed on the tower and resumed its pacing once more.

Chapter 3: **Porridge for breakfast**

The sunbeam, lancing through the gaps in the threadbare curtains, which barely covered the window, gradually moved down from the ceiling to settle on Richard's face. The light, heat and finally the angry buzzing of a trapped wasp against the window pane combined to seep into his unconscious mind to waken him.

Richard opened his eyes, slowly. Dust motes drifted back and forth in the dull yellow sunbeams as he looked around the room. Over to his right, on the marble-topped small cupboard lay his clothes, in a more or less tidy heap. Whilst up above, in the top bunk; the indentation that represented his brother Robin, seemed to move in time with his brother's breathing. Despite the sun beginning to heat the room it still felt cold, even for an October morning. Owing to the cold Richard pulled the meagre blankets more tightly around his head, like a monk's cowl and breathed out, watching his breath float like mist in the cool air before quickly dissipating. Whilst originally unnoticed, he became aware of the soreness on his scalp, caused by the hairgrips his mother had forced into his hair after it had been washed to make his straight hair look wavy: mirroring the hair of some film star she favoured. Richard shuddered as he relived the moments when his mother pushed the metal hair grips hard into place. Especially when the sharp points scraped along his skull; seeming in his mind to have not only pierced the skin but also gone right through to the bone.

Slowly Richard withdrew a hand from the blanket and ran his fingertips lightly along the undulating contours made from the waves in his hair. As he did so a hairgrip fell, with a soft sound, to the pillow. He groped for it with his hand. Having retrieved the hairgrip he held it back from his face in order to study it as his father burst into the bedroom saying loudly, "Rise and shine." Drawing back the curtains to let in more light, he paused for a moment to look out of the window, his weather-beaten face; from the time he spent in the navy, coming to life as with a smile his eyes crinkled shut under the sudden onslaught of the sun. He turned, looked down and then shook Richard by the shoulder.

"Come on, show a leg." Suddenly noticing the hairgrip in Richard's hand he frowned, and pursed his lips. "You'd better say that fell out in the night, or you'll be in trouble." Richard smiled and nodded sleepily. His father, satisfied, looked up and then gave Robin, on the top bunk, a shaking. "Come on, come on, show a leg." Their father walked out of the room with the final admonition, "Come on Ricky, its half past nine, you'll be late for church."

Richard nodded his head and started to get out of bed whilst he heard his father enter his sister Marilyn's bedroom and call out, "Come on, show a leg," before he hurried downstairs to the kitchen.

Richard got out of his bed and gave Robin a shove, smiling at his mumbled response that he was awake. Getting Robin fully awake and out of bed was like trying to bring a dead man back to life. Taking off his father's old shirt, which served as a nightgown, Richard threw it onto the bed, dressed hurriedly and went into the bathroom to wash. As expected there was no hot water, that would have to await the fire being lit in the back room. He washed slowly putting his hand gingerly under the cold water that ran from the hot tap, hoping that if he left it running long enough some hot, or at least warm water left over from the night before, would somehow magically appear.

He had almost finished washing when Robin, half dressed, blundered into the bathroom, ricocheted off Richard, almost pitching him into the sink, and used the toilet, giving great sighs of relief. Having finished peeing, he pulled the rusting, damp chain and sat down on the toilet lid watching Richard dry his face.

"Who's been a naughty boy then?"

Richard paused, looked at his brother quizzically for a moment and then continued to dry his hands and face on the tattered towel, taking care not to dislodge any more pins from his hair.

Robin grinned, "Who's been taking their hairgrips out, then?" he said with relish, and then suddenly yawned mightily and noisily.

Richard eyed him sourly. "They come out in the night when I'm asleep," he replied to his disbelieving young brother, who nodded his head sagely in reply. Richard smiled and threw the towel at Robin, "Here, catch," then he walked out of the bathroom.

Running lightly down the stairs he went into the kitchen and sat in his place. His father, at the sound of the door closing, turned round from the hob, looked at Richard, sighed and said, "Its porridge this morning." At the look of dismay on Richard's face he continued hurriedly. "Your mother said to have porridge from now on," he paused before adding quietly, "now that 'winter's' here."

Richard slumped in his chair. Whilst he did not mind porridge too much, Robin hated it. It made him sick. Both he and Robin had hoped that because, up until recently the weather had been warm, the start of this winter ordeal would be delayed. He gazed out of the partly steamed up kitchen window, wondering what Robin's reaction would be when he came down to breakfast.

He was broken from this reverie by his father placing a large bowl of porridge in front of him. Trying to make light of it, his father smiled weakly, "Come on, it's not so bad, it will do you good."

Richard picked up his spoon, dug it into the rapidly congealing grey mass and spooned some of the porridge into his mouth. It was very hot and although tempted at first to spit it out he cooled the porridge by breathing fast, in and out, through his mouth before swallowing it. His father watched him for a few seconds before turning back to the hob and ladling another, though slightly smaller, amount into a bowl for Robin, whose footsteps could be heard on the stairs.

Robin suddenly crashed through the door into the kitchen, the door banging into Richard's chair, making him jump.

"Don't you ever turn the handle?" his father said annoyed.

Robin looked up at him. "No" he replied with a grin on his face, which slowly faded as he spotted the bowl of porridge in his father's hand. His father, noticing the dejection in Robin's face, forgot his annoyance and gently pushed Robin to his seat.

"Come on, it won't bite you." Placing the bowl in front of Robin he gave him a spoon. "Don't worry, you can have some milk and sugar on it." He paused, reaching for the sugar bowl. "That will make it taste better."

Robin's spirits rose as he watched his father dip a spoon into the sugar bowl and begin to sprinkle it over his bowl of porridge. He was so engrossed in watching this, as were the others, that his mother's voice, when it sounded, broke the stillness of the room as would a clap of thunder.

"No, he won't!"

Richard at first started, and then cringed. His mother stood by the open door, which Robin had forgotten to shut properly, thereby allowing his mother to enter the room soundlessly. Closing the door behind her, she looked down, first at Richard, her searching eyes resting for a long moment on the pins in his hair as if counting them, and then at Robin before turning finally to their father and taking the sugar bowl from his hands.

"Sit down and eat your breakfast," she said to him, then turned on Robin, "and you!"

Their father started to sit down, then hesitated, saying, "Would you like some porridge, Mum."

Their mother paused and then stared at him for a moment, her face a mixture of disdain and puzzlement, before turning and walking the few steps to the hob. Taking a spoon from the drawer nearby she carefully tasted a very little of the porridge, smacking her lips artificially loud in appreciation. "Delicious," she said, then tasted a little more. "No," she finally added in a voice heavy with false disappointment, "I'll just have some toast, the boys will probably want seconds, and I don't want to deprive them."

Robin looked at Richard, who returned his gaze and shook his head from side to side negatively as his mother, after taking a piece of bread from the wrapped, sliced loaf on the table and putting it under the grill, continued, "They come first in this house," she intoned, her voice laden with martyrdom. After checking the toast she stood by the side of the table and eyed Robin intently as he very slowly skirted the edge of the bowl with his spoon. Noticing her gaze he stopped, dipped the spoon beneath the surface skin, lifted it up and very tentatively put the congealed grey mass into his mouth, which he then proceeded to chew vigorously. His mother then looked at Richard, who was already eating, then moved to the grill and turned the bread over to toast the other side.

Returning to the table she paused, watching the others eat then leaning forward with a practised motion she scoop a long fingernail into the butter and carried a globule to her mouth: then, with a satisfied look on her face and making sucking and slurping noises, proceeded to lick the nail clean.

Richard felt nauseous; he hated the way his mother dug her long nails into the butter – even subsequently just thinking about it made him feel sick. They did not have butter very often but whenever they did, their mother always picked at it with her nails. He closed his eyes, while his mother smacked her lips, and tried to concentrate on eating his porridge, pausing only to glance across at Robin whom he knew also disliked this habit of their mothers and had stuck his tongue out, as a gesture of distaste, before hastily pretending to eat his porridge.

Meanwhile their mother, having licked her fingernail clean, removed and buttered the toast and poured herself a cup of tea, then moved to the back room adjoining the kitchen but not before fixing Robin with her eyes. "Go on, eat your porridge." She paused for effect then added, "Or else."

Robin needed no further encouragement: the "or else" held a threatening note, which from experience he knew was best not to ignore. Very slowly he began to spoon the porridge into his mouth and with great difficulty, since he did not wish to chew it, swallowed. His father watching from across the table gave him a menacing look and mouthed "Eat up." His eyes moved warningly towards the back room and back again, from where the two boys could hear the rustle of a newspaper, and slowly drew his finger across his throat. Both Richard and Robin smiled at this gesture but knew equally well that it was not just a joke.

Richard finished his porridge first and then, under the careful eyes of his father ate a few spoonfuls of Robin's porridge, thus enabling his brother to clear his bowl, which he did with panache, offset somewhat by giving a great sigh, now that his ordeal was over. Their father smiled and, with the relief evident in his voice, turned to face the back room, saying, "They've both finished their porridge, Mum."

Robin wiping away the cold sheen of perspiration, which had collected on his face and holding his mug of tea with the other hand, froze as his mother replied, the voice, though very quiet, was laden with malice, "Good." There was a pause accompanied by further rustling of the newspaper and noise from the wonky springs of the settee moving, followed by, "Then they can both have second helpings."

Robin looked up, his mouth open; disbelief flooding his features. Richard, not able to look his brother in the eye turned his face away as their mother marched into the room. He watched, inwardly aghast, as his mother ladled a large helping of porridge into his bowl and then Robin's, scraping the pot to ensure she removed the last remaining scraps. Having finished, she patted Robin on the head and affecting a broad Dundonian accent, put the pot down on the stove and returned to the back room, saying, "It'll do you guid, you're both growing laddies."

Robin stared uncomprehendingly at the now cold lumpy congealed mass in his bowl. He rubbed his eyes hard, hoping that it was an illusion, which would vanish when he opened his eyes again; but the porridge was still there when he finally had the courage to look. Raising his head he looked at his father who could only shrug his shoulders, then inclined his head in Richard's direction, making him pause from eating his second helping of porridge. Seeing the mute appeal for help in his brother's face, his eyes beginning to glisten with unshed tears, Richard leaned across the table, took his brother's bowl and, although his stomach felt to him as tight as an inflated football bladder, ladled half of it into his own. He returned the bowl to Robin, who smiled gratefully as he wiped a fresh sheen of sweat of his forehead.

Robin looked down at the bowl. Despite Richard's assistance there was still more porridge in it than he could possibly eat. He looked up at his father and down at the bowl again then, having made his mind up, took out his handkerchief and ladled a couple of spoonfuls of porridge into it. His father looked on in silence, first amazement then resignation flooding his features. Though at first tempted to say something he finally shrugged, knowing in his heart that it was not fair to expect either of his sons to eat so much porridge when they didn't like it. Robin, looking up, shrugged back. Putting the spoon down he very carefully tied up the handkerchief and slowly eased the bulging, already damp mass into his trouser pocket. Having done this, he picked up the spoon and resumed slowly eating.

Hastened by the rustling sound of the newspaper from the back room, Richard bolted down the porridge he had taken from Robin's bowl, washing it down with great gulps of lukewarm tea from his mug, knowing he had to hurry in case their mother returned to the kitchen and saw the evidence of his helping Robin. His stomach was now so taut against his trouser belt that the elastic seemed stretched to breaking point. Richard decided to undo it and as he did so, the snake's head buckle leaping out of his hand, said in a stage whisper, knowing it would get a laugh in response, "Let go a shackle."

His father grinned. He was the one who usually said this on the rare occasions that his sons had over-eaten: a hangover from his navy days. Having eaten the porridge taken from his brother and the bulk of his own, Richard slowed his pace just as the noise from the settee springs warned him that his mother was returning to the kitchen.

She entered the room with the newspaper tucked under her arm which, without a word being spoken, she gave to their father, who took it gratefully and began reading. Sitting down next to Richard she poured herself another cup of tea, added milk and, as she was trying to lose some weight, two saccharin from the small cardboard packet, which lay on the table. Richard watched as the saccharin dissolved, churning up the surface of the tea; thinking of his father, who always referred to them jokingly as depth charges. When they had finally dissolved, his mother took the spoon from the sugar bowl and slowly stirred the tea, all the time eyeing Richard and Robin.

Robin was rapidly reaching crisis point. His bowl of porridge, despite the help given to him by Richard and his own valiant efforts, including the cold damp lump of porridge in his pocket, did not seem to be getting any smaller. Also with having eaten so much he wanted desperately to be allowed to go to the toilet and, coupled with this, he had an almost unbearable urge to fart. It was only knowing his mother's attitude to breaking wind and the consequences that kept him from doing so. But even as he suppressed yet another build-up of wind in his gut, causing it to protest loudly, he wondered for how much longer he could hold out.

He watched enviously as Richard, with a great sigh, finished his own porridge and placed his spoon in the empty bowl. At this, his mother's eyes left Richard and began to concentrate on Robin. Conscious of the scrutiny Robin put another small spoonful of porridge in his mouth, chewed it hurriedly and let it slip down his throat. Under his mother's unflinching gaze he did this a few more times and then stopped: he just couldn't eat any more, he was already full fit to bust and he just knew that if this carried on he would either be sick or make a horrible mess in his trousers. Already he could feel the bitter juices at the back of his throat and his back felt clammy under his rough shirt as another wave of nausea washed over him.

"Can I leave the rest please?" he asked his mother, who was now looking at Richard's hair. She turned to look at him as he added, "I've almost finished," and as an afterthought continued, "It is my second bowl."

"No!" replied his mother, "you're not leaving the table until it is all gone." Turning to Richard, who looked as if he was about to leave his seat, she said, "Sit down; I want to do your hair." Richard sat down, looked across to Robin and then raised his eyes to the ceiling. A clout around the head from his mother, followed by the admonishment, "Keep still!" riveted him to his seat whilst his mother pulled the pins, she had inserted the night before, roughly from his hair. Richard looked across the table at his brother, willing him to finish the porridge, noticing that Robin was merely staring into the bowl whilst his spoon moved listlessly to and fro.

"Have you been taking these pins out?" The sinister note in his mother's voice dragged him out of his reverie causing him to become very alert.

"No." Richard replied and then added as an afterthought, "They come out when I'm sleeping." His mother gave a non-committal "Hm" as she continued to comb Richard's hair, making the front as wavy as possible by a combination of continual combing, pressing his hair between her fingers and patting. Richard's head was suddenly pulled to one side as the comb caught in a snag at the back of his head. His involuntary cry of pain was quickly followed by a hard smack across the side of his cheek. His head ringing from the blow, he barely heard his mother as she bent forward and in a menacing tone, hissed, slowly accentuating every syllable.

"If you don't sit still and stop messing up your hair I will hit you so hard you won't know if you're coming or going."

Richard sat whilst his father stirred uneasily behind his newspaper. Their mother looked up at the noise and then glanced across at Robin who was still staring at his bowl hoping for a miracle that would make the porridge disappear. He too was broken from his daydreaming by his mother's voice. "Eat!"

The single word of command galvanised Robin to put another spoonful into his mouth and then under his mother's watchful gaze he ate another. "Go on – finish it up." When he failed to respond quickly enough his mother added, "Or else."

Robin dipped his spoon into what little remained of the porridge and put some more into his mouth. Sweat was starting to pop out onto his face so fast you would have thought he was standing in the rain. It was also running down his back. He reached a shaky hand for his mug and took a sip of tea, hoping that it would help him to swallow the porridge, but he couldn't move it. He realised he had had enough; his stomach was churning with a combination of nausea and fear; the latter worsened under his mother's penetrating gaze and he was holding back so much wind he felt sure he would soon explode.

Without any warning he suddenly vomited into his bowl the last few spoonfuls of porridge, mixed with stomach juices, the tea, and something else he didn't remember eating and, by the look of it, would not have done if he had been given the choice. For a brief moment after he had finished being sick, Robin stared, horrified at his bowl, now full again, then raised his head slowly to look at the others' faces, his eyes starting to fill with tears.

His father, moved sufficiently by the sight of Robin with porridge and saliva sliding down his chin onto the table, put down his newspaper and cleared his throat uneasily. He looked up at his wife who was motionless but staring uncomprehendingly at Robin. "I think he's had enough, Mum."

His wife whirled round at his words. "Oh, you do, do you?" The menacing chill in this statement sent a shiver down Richard's spine as his mother moved across to Robin. She stared at him for a moment, looked away and then back, and then in a voice heavy with disgust said, "You ungrateful dirty little bastard." She paused for a moment noting with satisfaction the way Robin cringed as the words hit home, as if they were physical blows. "We make sacrifices to make sure you get proper food to eat and this is all the thanks we get." She paused for breath. "All over the world people are starving whilst what little money we have goes on food for you and what do you do?" She stopped again for a moment as stared down at Robin. "Well – I'm waiting," she added.

Robin looked up at the unyielding face and started to speak, "But I've already eaten one ..." He wasn't allowed to finish the sentence as his mother hit him hard across his face, making his head jerk back violently. She leaned forward and stared Robin in the eye malevolently.

"You'll eat every bit of what's in your bowl if it takes you all day – right?" Robin, his head beginning to ache from the blow, nodded slowly nodded yes.

"Right", his mother added with a note of finality and returned to combing Richard's hair with extra vigour and viciousness, keeping her eyes on Robin who continued to eye his bowl. Lifting up his spoon he slowly dipped it into the bowl and very carefully chose a discernable piece of porridge out of the mess in the bowl. Chewing it slowly, watched closely by his mother, he swallowed it with great difficulty. The relief had had felt when he had been sick was beginning to fade: just looking at the mess in the bowl made him feel ill. Again without warning he was suddenly sick into the bowl.

His mother slammed the comb down and leapt across the table and grabbed Robin by the hair, pulling his head back violently so that he now looked up at her. With her face mere inches from Robin's she whispered "Just what do you think you are doing eh?" The latter accompanied by a sudden jerk backwards of the head.

Robin gazed into her eyes, his face pale, the nausea and fear threatening to overwhelm him. "I can't eat any more," his eyes moved across in the direction of the bowl, "I don't feel well."

His mother looked him up and down and in doing so noticed the damp mark on his trousers. She released Robin's hair and stood back. "What have you got in your pocket?" she asked, noticing with satisfaction, Robin go even paler than before.

Robin looked down at his corduroy trousers, the damp mark from the hidden porridge for all to see. He couldn't speak and looked across at his brother in a mute appeal for help. Richard opened his mouth to speak, but a warning glance from his father made him shut it again. Looking at his brother, however, he felt compelled to say something. "Mum, I..."

"Be quiet!" his mother said and Robin's shoulders slumped. His mother leaned forward and dipped a long fingernail into the butter and then licked it clean. "Well," she said in between licks, "I'm waiting." Robin just sat, it was taking all his concentration trying not to be sick. With a swiftness that left them all breathless, his mother moved across the table, grabbed Robin by his hair and pulled him upright, whilst with her other hand delved into his trouser pocket and took out the sodden handkerchief. Opening it she noted with satisfaction the cold porridge. "Well, and how did that get there?" she commented with a smirk and great satisfaction.

Robin decided to confess all – he didn't have either the strength or willpower to resist any longer. "I put it there," he stopped for a moment before adding, "I don't like porridge it makes me ill."

His mother carefully dropped the once concealed lump of congealed porridge back into Robin's bowl and then slapped him across the back of the head and then grabbed hold of his hair. Pulling Robin's face close to hers, "Don't talk to me like that," she turned his head viciously so he could see his bowl. "There's nothing wrong with porridge. I ate it as a girl and my father before me and his before that, so you will eat it, RIGHT!"

Robin couldn't stand the suspense; his mother's voice had gradually built up to a crescendo so that the last word had been screamed into his ear. He looked down at the mess in the bowl and, unable to speak, very slowly shook his head negatively from side to side. His mother's face went white as it drained of blood from her anger. Looking at Robin for a moment she took firmer hold of his hair and pushed his face into the bowl, moving it from side to side, shouting out, "When I say you will eat, you will eat – go on eat your porridge. Eat!"

Richard looked aghast. "Mum he can't breathe." His father added his voice."

That's enough; you've made your point but if he can't eat it, that's all there is to it."

Their mother stopped and released Robin's head, which he slowly removed from the bowl, wiping the mess from his face as he did so and being careful not to drop any on the floor. Tears began to form in his eyes and he looked up. "I can't eat it, Mum, it makes me sick."

Richard's heart went out to his young brother. Spontaneously he went to get up to help him but was pushed back into his seat by his mother. "Where do you think you're going? I haven't finished your hair!"

Richard gestured helplessly with his hand. He knew he was asking for trouble but was prepared to do anything to help his brother who sat miserably in front of his bowl, his face covered with slime and porridge down which ran two tracks of tears. "He's going to be sick again in a moment," Robin nodded wordlessly in confirmation, "so I thought I would take him up to the bathroom."

As he finished speaking, Richard stood up again as if to go and help his brother. His mother, momentarily taken aback by Richard's intervention, recovered to thrust him back into his chair. In doing so Richard automatically raised his arms as if to protect himself from a blow. His mother became infuriated by this and, whilst she had not originally intend to hit him, decided that he must have known about Robin hiding the porridge in his trouser pocket, and hit Richard hard around the head. Richard gritted his teeth and did not resist the blows, making only a half-hearted attempt to protect himself. He had achieved his objective and succeeded in drawing his mother's anger away from his brother to himself. Tired of hitting an object, which offered no resistance, his mother picked up the comb from the table. Jerking Richard's head, still ringing from the blows, upright, she finished combing his hair with a few short, vicious strokes.

Punching him in the back to make him stand up, she said, "Right, you go and get ready for church, and you," turning to Robin, "had better finish that porridge." What that she stomped out of the kitchen into the back room, slamming the door shut behind her.

Richard, Robin and their father let out sighs of relief. All of them knew that this episode was over. Walking over to Robin, Richard took his bowl and emptied it into the sink, pushing the porridge down the plug hole, using water from the cold tap. Leaving the bowl on the draining board he went and helped his brother out of his seat. "Come on, I'll give you a hand to clean up."

Robin smiled his thanks weakly. He hated porridge since it did make him feel unwell but now that he had eaten it once, was resigned to do so again for the rest of the winter. "I'd have been alright if she hadn't made us eat two bowls." Richard nodded, opened the door and holding his brother's arm, walked through the hall to the stairs just as their sister, Marilyn, came down and stopped on the bottom stair. She looked at Robin's besmeared face before speaking.

"The porridge season's started again, has it?" Robin had to smile as his sister, squeezing his arm, walked round them into the kitchen, saying "Lead me to it!"

"Come on, let's go," said Richard as he and his brother climbed the stairs together. Helping his brother into the bathroom Richard sat Robin on the toilet seat. Taking the towel from the bath he soaked one end under the tap then wiped his brother's face. Rinsing out the end of the towel, he did this again until Robin's face was clean. Rinsing the towel out a last time, he turned and placed the dry end in Robin's outstretched hand, then watched as he dried his face.

Robin looked up at his brother. "Thanks." Richard shrugged and sat on the bath as Robin continued; gently rubbing his forehead, "No wonder we all get headaches from all the slapping we have to take."

Richard snorted then laughed; his brother was getting back to his usual self again. "Are you alright?" he asked. Robin nodded and smiled. "Well, I'd better get ready for church." He got up as Robin waved him away and went into their bedroom. Taking off his old jersey and shirt, he took his Sunday shirt from the airing cupboard and pulled it on over his head, trying not to mess up his hair. After buttoning it he then tied his school tie, making sure the knot was tight and would not come loose, but more especially pass inspection by his mother. Letting his corduroy trousers slip to the floor, he dropped them onto the bunk bed with his other clothes, and then took his grey flannel shorts out of the wardrobe and a clean pair of socks. Having finished dressing, he sat on his bunk and fumbled underneath for his black shoes, which his father kept clean and polished for him, and put them on. He left his only jersey where it was and took instead the blazer he wore to school. Having finished dressing he walked out of the bedroom back into the bathroom where Robin still sat on the toilet seat, leaning backwards to rest awkwardly on the large iron pipe which ran down from the cistern.

Richard looked concernedly at his brother for a moment. "Are you sure you're alright?"

Robin nodded. "You had better go."

Richard smiled. "See you later," and left the bathroom and ran lightly downstairs, through the hall into the kitchen. Marilyn was reading the paper whilst sipping tea. Richard walked passed and stood in the now open door to the back room. Clearing his throat nervously he spoke. "I'm off now, Mum." His mother looked up from reading her magazine and looked him closely up and down, trying to find flaws in his appearance, whilst Richard stood there anxiously, unable to control his twitching right kneecap.

"Hm," said his mother, "straighten your tie." Richard did so as quickly as he could, even though he knew there was probably nothing wrong with it, and then stood rigid whilst she cast another sceptical eye over his appearance. "Got your comb?" Richard nodded and patted his blazer pocket, being reassured by the feel of the shape of his comb. His mother resumed looking at the paper. "OK, off you go." Then turning back to him as he turned away, making him freeze in a partially completed turn, and added "And make sure you're not late back."

"No, Mum," said Richard without a pause, turning the door handle and with a quick glance at the kitchen clock on the window still, stepping outside to the porch where he sighed with relief. His bicycle was not in its usual place and looking outside, he saw his father leaning on the wall at the side of the house. His eyes seemed to be gazing across the fields to Margate but as Richard stepped closer he saw that they were glazed over as if his father were gazing at something further away, which he was, the cold wind off the fields bringing back memories of the days when he had stood on the deck of an Anti-Aircraft Armed Merchant Carrier during the Russian Convoys in the second world war.

He started at Richard's approach and then relaxed again as he gradually drew himself back to the present. He smiled a slow lazy smile. Putting his hand into his pocket, he withdrew a tobacco tin, opened it easily with his strong hands and took out a cigarette, which he had previously rolled. Putting the cigarette into his mouth, he replaced the tin into his pocket and took out a box of matches. With his right hand holding the matches he took the cigarette from his mouth and pointed with it at Richard's bicycle. He was a taciturn man and spoke slowly, as if savouring each word.

"I got your bike out, Ricky, to save you time, what with Rob an 'all." Richard looked in the direction indicated by his father – he had already noticed the bicycle leaning against the wall, and smiled whilst his father lit his cigarette and flicked the match away into the 'green', a small plot of land, which had been grassed over at the corner of Northdown Hill and Pearson's Way.

"Thanks, Dad, I'd better get going." He walked the few steps to his bicycle but his father's voice detained him.

"How's Robin, is he alright?" He had really wanted to go and see for himself but had been reluctant to do so because of his wife. Not that he was afraid of her; it was just that he preferred a quiet life.

Richard, noticing the concern in his father's voice and aware that he cared about them, even though he tried to hide it by acting gruffly, made light of it. "Yes, Dad, he's OK. He was sitting on the toilet when I left him." He paused, watching his father's face before adding, "He'll be OK." He got on his bicycle. "I'd better go now, see you later, Dad."

He waved a quick goodbye and cycled off along the path down the side of the house, bumped hard onto the pavement across the short grass verge and then over the kerb onto the road. He cycled for a moment and then freewheeled down Northdown Hill. In the distance he could hear the church bells ringing, drawing him like a magnet to church. The wind, added to the speed he was cycling, soon ruffled his carefully combed hair.

Richard exalted in his freedom as he turned into Northdown Road and began the hard cycle ride up the short but steep hill. Trying to maintain his momentum he pedalled furiously but laboriously, standing on his pedals as he neared the crown of the hill, which was topped by the hump-back bridge over the railway line. Pausing there only for a moment to look up and down the line, he pushed himself off the wall and continued cycling to church, the bells that much louder now he was getting nearer.

Richard travelled along Northdown Road until he came to the piece of waste ground, which led to the track that was a short cut to church via the graveyard. He hesitated for a moment, wondering whether to take that route, but since it had rained the night before it was bound to be muddy and as he was wearing his Sunday best clothes he decided against it. He pedalled off with renewed vigour, the sun and rain-washed wind blowing away the tenseness in his body, which had built up over breakfast. He hoped that it would be better when he got back home from church as it usually, but not always, was. He turned into Church Street, his heart beating a little faster as he neared his destination. Along the narrow pavement people walked towards the church, some clutching prayer books, others newspapers, old men with sticks attempting to stand a little straighter, Richard thought, as they too felt the magnetism of the lodestone that was St. Peter's Church.

As the church tower came into view he looked up at the clock. "Twenty to eleven," he muttered to himself. He was not late but had hoped to arrive a little earlier this morning. He leaned heavier on his pedals, passing other cyclists and being passed in turn by a large black car, which glided to a halt at the church gates to deposit its passengers. The old barn and piggery on his right disappeared seemingly in a flash and immediately he had to pull on his brakes as he reached Vye & Son, the grocers, to squeal to a halt outside the entrance to the vestry.

His friends, Barry, David, Jim and Herbert were all standing there blocking the entrance. As he got off his bicycle and wheeled it onto the pavement, they divided, flanking the entrance with Psalters held high.

"Attention," shouted Barry, "make way for the new Head Chorister." Richard smiled at this impromptu ceremony and waved airily at the mock salutes as he walked past, unperturbed by the anonymous raspberry and leaned his bicycle up against the flint wall. He turned to face his friends, who still stood to attention by the gate as Mr Parker, who was in the men's choir walked through.

"Good morning, boys," he said, looking slightly puzzled, "good morning Richard," he said looking back at the others.

"Good morning Mr Parker," replied Richard. Mr Parker hesitated for a moment and was going to ask what was going on, but then thought better of it, being distracted by the clock chiming the three-quarter hour and so walked on to disappear into the vestry.

"Come on then, what are you waiting for?" said Richard. His friends broke ranks at these words and with large grins on their faces clustered round him and clapped him on the back. Then Barry took hold of his right arm and Jim his left, and together propelled him towards the vestry door.

"Let's get the lamb to the slaughter," laughed Barry. Richard grinned with the others, the troubles of his home forgotten for the moment as, happy in the companionship of his friends he allowed himself to be led into the dark coolness of the vestry, there to be greeted by the rest of the choir.

Chapter 4: **An unexpected event**

Richard followed Barry out of the vestry, pulling on his school blazer as he did so. He stopped for a moment then bent down to pull up his socks, which were drifting towards his ankles. As he did so he felt the money from yesterday's wedding heavy in his trouser pocket.

Barry, meanwhile, had retrieved his bicycle from the pile against the wall and wheeled it over to where Richard was now tying up his shoe laces. He leant over his saddle, the horn digging into his stomach and whispered, "Look."

Richard looked up, his eyes squinting into the sunlight, a questioning expression on his face. "What?" he asked. Barry looked sideways and then back to Richard.

"Out there," he indicated the entrance to the vestry yard with his head. Richard stood up and looked towards the iron gate in the wall. There standing on the pavement were three girls from the local boarding school, one of whom had a small dog on a lead. On seeing Richard looking at them, the girls all broke into giggles and one walked off, but returned when called back by another of the girls.

Richard stood up and extricated his bicycle from amongst those leaning against the wall. He was about to speak but Herbert and David walked out of the vestry and with a couple of "See you tonight" wheeled their bicycles out onto the road and with only a passing glance at the girls, cycled off.

"What do you think they want?" enquired Richard. Barry looked again at the girls and then back at Richard and shrugged his shoulders in a dismissive gesture.

"I don't know, anyway I'm off home, coming?" With that he got on his cycle and rode through the open gate, bouncing hard down the steps to cycle slowly down Church Street.

Richard wheeled his bicycle to the vestry gate and down the steps. He was about to cross the pavement to the road when he suddenly found himself surrounded by the three girls, and the small dog. He stopped momentarily taken aback.

The girls looked at each other and then one said, "Excuse me, is your name Richard Luckhurst?" Richard felt from the way the girl asked the question and the expectant look on the other girls' faces, that they already knew the answer. He decided to play along with the game, whatever it was.

"Yes, it is," he replied, nodding his head at the same time, "how did you know that?"

The girls all looked at each other again and then all giggled together whilst Richard, looking around, noticed that Barry had stopped down the road and was looking back at him. The girl who had first spoken held out her hand. There was a letter in it. "I've been asked to give this to you," then added as an afterthought, "it's from Emma." As Richard took the letter another girl added, "Emma Wesley." With that the girls all giggled again before turning on their heels and running off across the road and around the corner of the chemist's shop, and thence down the High Street where Richard knew lay the entrance to their school grounds.

Richard looked at the letter for a moment, reading his name several times. Then wheeling his bicycle across the pavement and onto the road he got on, keeping one foot on the pedal and the other on the pavement to maintain his balance. Having examined the letter again he opened it, noticing as he did so that Barry was cycling back towards him. Richard had just started to open the letter when Barry reached him, his bicycle brakes bringing him to a shuddering halt. He looked at Barry, who returned his gaze, asking, "What have you got there?"

Richard put the letter into his pocket, "Nothing, just a letter."

His curiosity getting the better of his normally good manners, Barry persisted, "What does it say?"

Richard still hesitated. He was loath to let Barry see it before he had had the opportunity to read it alone first, but couldn't think why. Not wishing to share the letter with his friend was only part of it; he was also slightly confused by a feeling of warmth, coupled with that of tingling expectation, which he only usually experienced at times like Christmas.

Barry sat on his cycle, which he was moving slowly back and forth, continuing to look at Richard but without saying anything else. Richard sighed inwardly, then reluctantly took the envelope out of his pocket, looked at it for a moment and then slowly tore it gently open. Taking the letter from within he opened it out and began to read it to himself.

Dear Richard,

My name is Emma Wesley and I am 11 years old. I have been watching you for weeks and would like to meet you. Please tell one of my friends if you will, please.

Love Emma x

Richard read the letter through again, slowly this time, and would have read it a third time, only Barry was showing signs of impatience. He held the letter out to his friend who snatched at it eagerly. Barry too read the letter through twice and handed it back, then stared at Richard for a moment before speaking. "Well, well, well," he finally said, "some stupid girl has fallen for you." He paused for a moment then added, "You've got a girlfriend!"

Richard could not help but blush a little at this remark but still managed to blurt out, "No, I haven't, I don't even know what she looks like." Whilst trying to ignore Barry's grinning face and knowing nods of disbelief. He thought for a moment before adding, "There's always lots of girls from that school at Matins and Evensong; it could be anyone of them."

Barry paused from nodding and leant on his handlebars, gazing into the sky before saying wistfully, "You're right, it might be one of those sexy sixth former, like in the St. Trinian's films," and feigned a shudder of delight.

Richard laughed, "What sexy sixth formers? They all look the same in their grey belted raincoats and hats. Anyway, she's the same age as us."

Barry considered the matter for a moment. "Yes, you're right, I suppose," he added reluctantly. "On the other hand, she might be fat and ugly." Richard tried to dismiss such thoughts from his mind but read the letter through again, expecting it somehow to dispel such fears, before putting it back in his pocket. No, she couldn't be ugly, he thought as he cycled off along Church Street, followed by Barry, who shouted, "Wait a minute!"

"What?" Richard replied, still cycling but slower, until his friend caught up.

"Well, tell us what you are going to do?"

Richard thought for a moment. "I'm going home and then..."he was stopped by the growing look of exasperation on Barry's face and so started again. "What is there for me to do? You've read the letter. I suppose one of her friends will be one of the girls who gave me the letter. Perhaps I'll see her tonight, who knows – who cares, I don't." He lied to himself. "Look, I'll see you tonight." With that he waved and cycled off along Northdown Road, which led to the council estate where he lived.

Barry stood watching his friend gradually disappearing into the distance. He was at once slightly envious and worried by this new factor in his friend's life. More to the point, how it would affect him. He had heard tales of how, once some girl got her hooks into you, you were done for – there was that Patricia Laslett for a start, who always wanted to play 'kiss chase' round the back of the ambulance station at the end of Northdown Road. "Ugh," unconsciously he wiped his lips with the back of his hand, as if that would be enough to erase the memory. Then seeing Richard disappear over the hump back bridge, which crossed over the railway line he sighed and cycled slowly home, feeling – he didn't really know why – slightly sorry for himself.

Cycling over the hump back bridge, Richard was too excited to see if any trains would pass by. He freewheeled down the hill, the wind driving away any remnants of the troubles of the morning. Hopefully his mother would be in a better mood by now after this morning's episode over the porridge. He reached the bottom of the hill of Northdown Road and automatically guided his bicycle up Northdown Hill. Resuming pedalling, he continued on his way home. For some reason, everything seemed so much clearer now: his every sense more alert to his surroundings.

As he pedalled his movements caused the letter in his pocket to crackle. He ran the words, which he already knew by heart, over again in his mind, wondering what Emma Wesley would look like. Suddenly he pulled to a halt, a pang of fear coursing through his body. What on earth would he do with the letter? His mother must never find it. For some reason that Richard was unable to fathom, his mother had forbidden him and Robin to have anything to do with girls. She never said why and Richard had found it safer not to mention the subject, and more to the point, never mention the fact that he had ever spoken to any. That he should even consider taking into the house a letter from a girl was, he thought, a form of sacrilege. Richard faltered; he was unable to decide what to do. Should he leave the letter with Barry to look after? He was his best friend and could be trusted. Richard rejected the idea. Why should he? It was his letter and he should be allowed to keep it.

Richard took the letter out of his trouser pocket, opened the envelope carefully and took out the letter.

He read it through quickly, holding it tightly against the gusts of wind, which threatened to tear it from his grasp, then carefully put it back into the envelope, and then back into his pocket. Reading it through again had firmed his resolve. He was determined to keep it with him, whilst keeping the knowledge of its existence from his mother. At least, he told himself, for the time being. If it turns out that I don't like her then it doesn't matter and I can throw the letter away. But just supposing he did, then it was even more important that his mother should not find out. Having made up his mind, Richard resumed cycling the last few hundred yards up the hill to his house. Although the sky was beginning to darken with clouds, and a few heavy spots were starting to fall, spattering the pavement, the sun was shining in his heart as he arrived home.

Humming to himself he reached the front gate, got off his bicycle and walked it along the path to the back where his brother Robin sat on the concrete step of the porch. Richard leaned his bicycle on the wall and sat down next to Robin, who moved up slightly to give him some room. Richard felt his brother still looked a bit ill. His usually rosy cheeks were pale and though his blond hair blew about in the wind it had an air of lifelessness about it. He patted his silent brother on the knee.

"How are you feeling, Rob?" he asked. Robin smiled weakly in response to this question but did not reply immediately. He had been sick a few more times in the toilet before being able to finally wash his face properly and go and lie down in their bedroom. Although he had hoped for a bit of peace and quiet his mother had come upstairs and told him to get outside. He had now been sitting on the step for the best part of an hour watching the clouds drift by, although the sun had kept him warm and he was sheltered from the wind, but not the coming rain.

Without thinking Richard asked the question uppermost in his mind. "What's for dinner?" then immediately regretted it as Robin involuntarily flinched.

Robin smiled ruefully. "That's OK." He paused for a moment. "Scrag end stew with plenty of slimy fat," he made a face – "smell it?" Richard sniffed the air a few times, nodded, and then stretched his legs out in front of himself, hearing the letter crackle in his pocket. He looked surreptitiously at Robin but he was too absorbed in his own thoughts to notice the noise. Richard let the sun play on his face as he looked up into the sky, with his eyes closed, his eyelids turning a bright red then a darker browny-red as the sun, at first clear, was obscured momentarily by a passing cloud. He looked down again as Robin began talking.

"She's going to drive me mad one day. I know it." Richard has to smile a little, although he understood and could accept the reasons for his brother feeling the way he did, as Robin continued, "I reckon she is mad anyway. I mean, who in their right mind, would make someone eat two great big bowls of porridge for breakfast?" He paused again, taking a deep breath. "Especially when they know I hate the stuff 'cos it always makes me feel ill. It's not just that, though, she's always hitting us. It doesn't matter what we do, we always get shouted at and hit – it's not fair!"

Richard, noticing that his brother's eyes were getting rather watery, put his arm round him and gave him a hug, then released him. Richard understood and agreed with everything his brother had said. He knew other families were not like this. Although his friends got punished whenever they did something wrong they did not have to creep around the house like mice for fear of being noticed. It wasn't just that they were frequently being hit but that their mother seemed to enjoy having power over them and seeing them cower as she went by. Richard admitted to himself he was scared of his mother since she was so unpredictable and could lash out for no reason. He hated it when they were all downstairs and she was up in their bedroom looking around for something to complain about. The sound of her shoes clumping on the lino as she stomped about made each thud seem like a physical blow to his head. Then her hurrying down the stairs demanding why this or that wasn't right or as it should be. She only had to raise a finger to make him or his brother flinch. It was such an automatic defence reflex of his body that he no longer consciously attempted to avoid blows knowing that his body had conditioned itself to move at the slightest hint of violence in order to lessen the force of an impending blow. He knew that it was a result of their bad nerves that himself and his brother and sister all bit their nails. Not only that, Richard also gnawed the knuckles of his little and first finger so that they were permanently covered with thick chewed scar tissue.

He looked down and rubbed the tough skin lightly with the fingers of his other hand and was about to reply. Robin, however, had started to speak again so Richard decided to let him run on to get it off his chest. Although this morning's episode had been bad, the receipt of the letter from Emma Wesley had somehow opened up a whole new aspect of life, which although he had yet to fully explore it, he felt in his heart it could only be good.

"She'll be sorry when we get older," said Robin, his voice assuming a threatening tone. "She won't be able to hit me then, or if she does, I'll hit her back." He stopped for a second, clearing his mind. "I won't forget anything she's ever done to us, never!" He added adamantly, "And when I grow up and have a house of my own, if she ever wants to speak to me or visit, I'll tell her no and when she asks why, I'll just say all the cruel things she's done to us."

Richard had opened his mouth to speak when through the kitchen window there came a piercing whistle. Automatically, Robin and he stood up. They both knew that when their mother whistled they had better come running or else. "Just like dogs, we are," said Robin, "woof, woof."

Richard smiled. He was glad that his brother was coming out of his black mood and getting back to his normal cheerful self again. Whilst he shared Robin's thoughts and feelings he did not seem to feel them as deeply as his brother. Besides, for him, being able to go to church and sing was a form of escapism – not only because it got him out of the house and away from his mother, but more especially because he enjoyed singing so much since he was able to lose himself – if only for a short time – in the music. He wished Robin could share this with him, and then it might make things easier for him to bear. Robin was, unfortunately, tone deaf and after a few tries he had had to leave the choir. Perhaps if he could sing, things might have been different, thought Richard, clapping his brother on the shoulder. "Come on, Rob, let's go and eat the Scrag end stew." Robin looked at his smiling brother and made a face but allowed himself to be led into the kitchen, but not before he had released a great sigh of resignation.

* * *

Richard lay on his bunk bed looking up at the wire support for the top bunk where Robin slept, whilst his mind wandered over the events of the day. It had started off fairly normally; Robin was never one for eating breakfast even when it wasn't porridge. At least the worst was over now. Robin might complain bitterly but at least he would eat the porridge as best he could from now on. Provided, of course, he didn't have to eat two bowls. Richard's gaze wandered on to his model of the Sunderland Flying Boat, used in the Second World War, which hung by string from the ceiling. He had bought the Airfix kit from money he had earned from singing in the choir. Although he had made it himself, his father had helped with the painting of the camouflage. On top it was a wavy green and khaki brown, whilst underneath it was all white. It hung there at an angle so you could see the top of the large wing. Richard had bought it because he liked its graceful lines, even though it was so large, and because it was at home in the air and on the sea. He had seen them on films and hoped one day to see a real one, and perhaps even fly in it.

His mind jerked back suddenly to what he had been consciously avoiding. Slipping his hand under the pillow he felt for the letter, which lay there, but resisted the impulse to pull it out and read it when he touched it. He knew the words off by heart but re-reading them somehow made them seem fresh and new, and as if they were actually being spoken. He had wondered at his reaction to his receipt of this letter. As he had never really had a special girl friend, as some of his friends had, it somehow seemed more precious. He told himself not to be so stupid. Suppose she was, as Barry had said, fat and ugly? Or was thin and spotty with glasses? Richard didn't actually think that girls with glasses were ugly, because they weren't. Whenever he looked at a girl with glasses he always imagined the glasses weren't there. More often than not they were very pretty, in fact prettier than girls who did not wear glasses.

Richard sighed. He was still unable to fathom out why one short letter should suddenly mean so much to him. He had never really bothered with girls before, partly, he had to admit, because he knew his mother would probably kill him if she ever found out. Abruptly Richard sat up. It was getting dark outside and soon he would be on his way to church. Perhaps tonight one of Emma's friends would be at Evensong to arrange a meeting. Whatever happened, there was nothing he could do, so he might as well stop worrying about it all. With that last thought uppermost in his mind, but with others still lurking in the background, Richard went into the bathroom to get washed in preparation for Evensong.

PART TWO: **ADVENT**

Chapter 5: **It's brown water!**

The dry, sometimes cool though not cold winds of October had given way by late November to those more damp and chill. This change was brought home to Richard as he bicycled back to his house from Friday night choir practice. Although his face constantly streamed with rain occasional gusts of wind peppered his face with rain drops each time making him flinch momentarily as he peered through half closed eyes before bending his neck even further to afford his battered face some small relief from the storm. He could feel the rain seeping down inside his coat collar, driven by the wind, despite his sou'wester draining most of the water, which fell on his head, down the back of his raincoat. As he crossed the small hump-back bridge over the railway line another, stronger gust of wind caught him, causing him to wobble whilst he fought to retain his balance. Then suddenly he was over the top careering down the other side sheltered from the icy blast of the wind and rain by the high wall that was one side of the large bus depot.

Richard relaxed his grip on the handlebars and sat up, easing the ache in his back caused by bending almost double to escape the worst of the storm. Freewheeling down the short hill he was able to look about him, seeing, in the light of the dim street lamp, the rain being hurled here and there by the wind. In the light it looked like snow, whilst in the distance up Northdown Hill the rain seemed to rage even fiercer than it had before since nothing stood in the wind's way as it blew across the open fields from Margate. Richard shuddered involuntarily as he pulled his raincoat collar tighter round his neck in an attempt to give himself some greater protection from the elements. He also jammed his fingers tighter into the stout leather gauntlets, which covered his hands.

Gritting his teeth he began to pedal hard as he neared the bottom of the hill and the last bit of protection afforded by the brick wall. Without any thought of possible traffic appearing from his left, since the road was a dead end and only led to the rubbish dump, which was closed at night, he launched himself across Dane Valley Road and up Northdown Hill. The force of the wind and rain combined, as he left the temporary shelter of the wall, caused him to lurch sideways for a moment, then pushed him from behind as he, and the wind, rounded 'The Cabin' – a small shop-cum-cafe made out of corrugated iron. Determined he would not walk the rest of the way home, since although easier it would be much slower and hence he would get wetter, Richard continued on his way. Leaning on his pedals, cursing himself for going out tonight in such foul weather then immediately taking back such thoughts, knowing that he would have gone to choir practice regardless of what the weather was like. Richard knew that after this morning's incident he was lucky to have been allowed out at all. Richard thought back to this morning when Robin and he had stood in front of his mother as all three of them had crowded into the small bathroom whilst their mother pointed to the splashes of brown on the green painted walls.

* * *

"Well, I want to know who did that." Richard and Robin looked at each other nonplussed, unable to understand what their mother was talking about. "Well?" their mother demanded looking at them both but most of all at Richard, "I'm waiting."

Richard looked at his mother's face and then at the dirty brown marks on the wall. He hadn't noticed them before. They didn't use to be there since he had helped to paint the bathroom. He just hadn't noticed when they had started or where they came from, it was a mystery to him but his mother seemed to know. The only thing to do was to tell the truth – he didn't know. "I don't know," he replied.

His mother straightened and sighed that world-weary sigh with which Robin and himself we both so over-familiar. "You don't know, don't you," said their mother, bending forward to both of them to accentuate her words, "Well, I do." Inwardly Richard sighed with relief. He knew that they were nothing to do with him and from the puzzled look on his brother's face Robin wasn't involved either. Both waited to see what their mother would say as she looked again at the marks and then back again at them both. "These marks are caused by one of you coming into the bathroom and having a sit down toilet and then instead of pulling the chain like any civilised person it is left there and then another one of you comes along and does a 'wee-wee' on it, splashing bits of brown on the wall." Their mother finished on a triumphant note.

Richard and Robin looked at each other in amazement. The idea was so outrageous that unable to control themselves, they simultaneously burst into laughter, immediately to regret it as their mother lashed out at them both, hitting them round the head, causing them to reel back where, tripping over themselves in an attempt to get away from her blows, they fell against the bath then to the floor, the laughter dying on their lips.

"Don't you dare ever laugh at me again!" screamed their mother, looking at them both, her eyes moving back and forth like a cat about to pounce on a bird, her lips twitching involuntarily. "Ever! Do you hear me?" Richard, lying on the floor was reluctant to get up with his mother hovering over them like a predatory animal and nodded an affirmative, accompanied by a barely audible "Yes." Switching her eyes to Robin who did likewise, she bared her teeth in a wicked smile of satisfaction. "Right, well you made this mess so you two can clean it up and Heaven help you if you ever make such a mess again." With that she stormed out of the bathroom and stomped downstairs.

* * *

A car suddenly shot passed him, bringing him back to the present, covering him in a fine mist of dirty water making him close his mouth quickly as he felt the taste of the muddy particles on his tongue. Finally reaching the sanctuary of his house he cycled along the path. Stopping only to open the door to the porch he dragged his bicycle inside and leaned it against Robin's, which lay against the wall. Taking off his Sou'wester he shook it a few times to remove the excess water before placing it on his saddle to dry. Whilst watching the rain outside he unbuttoned his coat and then slowly closed the door to the porch. Unlacing and leaving his very wet shoes on the small mat in the porch, he opened the door to the kitchen and stepped inside.

His father, sitting in the back room, looked round and said gruffly, "Eat you supper and then straight to bed." Although his voice was fierce his face was not and his eyes belied the tone of his voice. Richard smiled quickly, in case it was noticed by his mother who was also sitting in the room, and suitably subdued, replied, "Yes, Dad."

Taking off his coat he went and hung it on a hook in the hall then returned to the kitchen where on the table his father had left the bread, butter and cheese. Taking the knife, Richard hurriedly made himself a sandwich then poured a cup of milk from the bottle, which was also on the table and sat down to eat. With his brother and sister upstairs it was very quiet. Richard was anxious to eat his supper quickly and join them. Apart from the silence, he felt he could feel the tension in the air, like a tangible force emanating from his mother in the back room, which made him feel uneasy. He had barely finished the thought when his mother glided through the door and watched him eating. Richard carried on biting a piece of his sandwich but his mouth had gone dry and he found it difficult to chew. With a tremulous hand he reached out and picked up the cup of milk, took a sip and then swallowed the partly chewed cheese sandwich, which was in his mouth.

Without warning, his mother suddenly leaned forward and scooped a globule of butter into one of her long nails and conveyed it to her mouth. Unconsciously

Richard had flinched as his mother had leant over him, since he had expected a blow. He now straightened as, with a smile playing around her lips, his mother started to return to the back room. "When you've finished that get straight up to bed." Richard paused in his eating and hurriedly moved the partly chewed bread and cheese in his mouth to one side with his tongue so he could reply. "Yes, Mum," he said hurriedly to his mother's back as she disappeared into the back room where he heard her sit down with a great sigh.

Richard resumed eating with renewed vigour until he finally finished the last bite of sandwich and drained the milk from the cup. Still chewing he cleared away the food into the larder then washed up, leaving the crockery and knife to dry on the wooden draining board. He stood by the sink for a moment wondering whether to say goodnight or go straight upstairs. Without too much deliberation he decided it would be wiser to do the former in order to avoid being charged with being deliberately rude. Soundlessly, in his stockinged feet, he walked across the lino and stood by the open door to the back room. Hurriedly, as if afraid his courage would desert him, he spoke.

"Goodnight, Mum, goodnight, Dad." His mother made no response but his father looked at him and with an urgent incline of his head indicated that he had better get going. Turning quickly Richard walked through the kitchen into the hall, closing the door quietly behind him. Pausing only to take his hymn book out of his raincoat pocket he ran lightly upstairs and into the bathroom.

* * *

Richard sat on the toilet reading his hymn book. It was one of the few places he knew he was guaranteed peace and quiet, if only for a few minutes. He stopped reading for a moment and warmed his hands over the paraffin fire standing next to the sink, massaging his finger still feeling stiff from the cycle ride, and then resumed reading. A short knock sounded on the door.

"I'm in here," came the automatic response from Richard who, thinking nothing of it, carried on reading. It was a standard phrase in the house whenever anyone was in the toilet. Usually it was sufficient for the person on the outside to go away for five minutes; but not this time.

"How long are you going to be?" came the insistent voice of his sister, Marilyn, through the wooden door. "I want to clean my teeth," then as an afterthought, "now." Richard didn't even bother to look up as he turned over a page. "Out in a minute," he said with absolutely no intention whatever of fulfilling this promise and resumed his reading.

Marilyn had presumably had the same thought, for without another word she forced the rather shaky lock on the door and barged in. Paying no attention whatsoever to Richard she picked out her toothbrush from the collection in the cracked glass mug on the window sill, put toothpaste on it and started to clean her teeth.

Richard looked up, his mouth gaping and for a few seconds he could think of nothing to say. Then he found his voice. "Hey, you can't come in here, I'm in here – get out!"

Marilyn continued to clean her teeth, putting her mouth under the running cold tap to wash away the toothpaste. "Shut up. I can't be expected to wait for you before I clean my teeth. Anyway it's your own fault; you'd spend all day in here if you could."

"No, I wouldn't," said Richard, feeling a need to justify himself. "I don't spend any more time in here than you do, now get out," he finished as forcibly as he could.

Marilyn finished cleaning her teeth and rinsing out her toothbrush she dropped it back into the glass mug. Taking a final mouthful of water she swilled it round and round and had a quick gargle before spitting it into the sink. Turning off the tap she picked up the towel lying on the bath to dry her face and hands and turned round to look at Richard. "Don't worry, I'm going. This place smells like a pigsty anyway. Poo," and marched out of the room slamming the door behind her.

Richard sighed and tried to relax as indignation flooded through him. Everyone knew that the lock on the door could be forced but once someone was in the bathroom it was a sacrilege to go in. It was unheard of. Richard tried to resume his reading but he was unsettled. He sniffed loudly, drawing air in through his nostrils and out through his mouth. It couldn't smell in here, the thought to himself, I haven't really done anything, yet. He sniffed again. Turning over another page he sang a hymn quietly to himself but was soon interrupted; this time by a drop of water that fell heavily on his forearm.

Richard looked at the moisture spreading through the cotton of his shirt sleeve until it stopped, then resumed singing. Consciously he thought nothing more of it until his sub-conscious mind shrieked at him that the water was not clean but had a brown centre. Richard looked again at the damp patch on his sleeve, pulling at his cuff to get rid of the creases. At the very centre of where the drop had landed was what looked like some fine reddish brown dust. He rubbed it with his fingers and it adhered to his fingertips. Richard was elated. Like, he imagined a boffin would feel at having solved a knotty problem.

Deciding he had, after all, finished, Richard put his hymn book on the window sill, stood up, pulled the chain to flush the toilet and then buttoned up his shorts. He washed his hands and cleaned his teeth whilst looking at the cistern, which was fixed to the wall above the toilet. It was dirty green in colour and made of cast iron and had probably been there since the house was built. He now noticed that the cistern was covered with condensation whilst the corner edges were rusty brown on which large drops of water were hanging just waiting to fall. He finished cleaning his teeth, dried his face and hands with the towel, replacing it on the bath.

Richard then went and stood by the toilet and watched the water from the condensation on the rusty cistern collect until it formed a droplet, which hung precariously for a moment before suddenly dropping. To quickly for Richard to follow its fall but he saw it land on the dirty cracked and chipped linoleum with a plop, causing fragments of dirty brown water to land at random on the floor and wall. Richard looked up again and watched as yet another drop of rusty water began to coalesce, after a while, on the cistern further along. It too hung for a short time, swaying to and fro, seeming to revel in its newfound strength before plunging down to ricochet off the toilet seat to spatter the wall with rusty brown water.

Yet again Richard looked up at another drop beginning to form and waited until it was ready to drop, then held out his hand. Wavering to and fro as if reluctant to make this final leap, the drop of water suddenly fell hard into the palm of his hand. Automatically he closed his fingers over it, trying to prevent losing any of the precious liquid. Turning to the light, he opened his hand and looked at the water, which had begun to spread over his palm leaving a residue of fine brown dust, which he knew was rust from the cistern. Richard exalted: he had solved the mystery of the dirty brown marks on the wall and toilet seat that his mother had accused him and Robin of being responsible for. Richard smiled ruefully to himself as he heard someone coming upstairs. He tensed, listening for a moment until he realised it was his father. He walked a few paces to the bathroom door and watched his father emerge from the corner of the stairs. "Dad, come here a moment."

His father smiled. "Why?" Not saying another word, Richard beckoned him into the bathroom and stood by the toilet as his father followed him in. "Look, Dad, these brown marks are caused by the rusty brown water on the cistern falling down onto the floor and toilet seat, look."

Richard's father looked and together they watched the drops coalesce from the sides of the cistern, form into large drops and then fall to either the lino or the toilet seat, some of which then splashed onto the wall. After a number of drops had fallen Richard's father held out his hand, caught a few and then examined them under the light bulb. "You're right; it's only rust from the cistern." Then turning to his son he added "Why didn't you explain this to Mum, Ricky, instead of laughing at her?"

Richard looked up at the cistern and then back at his father. "We weren't laughing at her and anyway that cistern wasn't wet on the outside as it is now, so no rusty drops of water were falling." His father looked at the condensation on the cistern and on the windows, probably caused by the small paraffin heater kept there to take the chill off the air. "OK Ricky, I'll take care of it and tell Mum." Thankfully, Richard smiled at his father and left the bathroom, leaving his father staring at the drops of rusty water on the cistern.

Reaching his bedroom he opened the door and stepped inside. It was dark but a faint light was coming in through the curtains and from the light round the edge of the door. Richard waited a second or two to allow his eyes to adjust to the darkness then walked the few steps to his bunk bed. He could tell from the quiet that Robin wasn't asleep yet. He started to get undressed, leaving his clothes on the cracked marble top of the small cupboard, his pile mingling with those of Robin's. When he was down to his underpants he felt under his pillow for the old shirt of his father's, which he used as a nightgown. Having put it on he leaned forward until his head was only a few inches away from his brother.

"Hey, Rob, I solved the mystery of the dirty brown marks." Robin raised his head suddenly almost banging into Richard's.

"How?" he asked. Richard told him, leaving out the prelude of Marilyn invading the bathroom, which still rankled with him. Robin was amazed at the simplicity of it all but at the same time annoyed that he and Richard had been punished for a 'crime' of which they had been totally innocent. He thought about it some more. "Thank Gawd, perhaps tomorrow she'll take it easy on us for a bit."

Richard nodded in the dark. "I hope so because I agreed to go pungering with Barry on Saturday. Want to come?"

Robin shook his head from side to side. He had other plans and was not too keen on digging crabs out of their lairs. He didn't mind that so much as having to get hold of them and tie them up whilst at the same time trying to stop them from nipping you. "No, thanks, I told Eric that I'd play football with him down the rec, if I could get away."

"That's OK said Richard and got into bed and pulled the blanket up round his chest. Putting his hands together he said a quick prayer then just lay there, finally being left alone with his thoughts. With his head cradled by his hands he watched the curtain blow gently in, driven by the wind and then just as easily fall back into place. Although he could hear the occasional patter of raindrops the storm, through which he had recently battled, had moved on, bringing a quiet stillness to the night. He was glad the weekend had finally arrived. Last weekend he had met a friend of Emma's and had been told that she had been ill with flu and had been kept in, but was well now and would meet him after Matins on Sunday, if he still wanted to. Richard had agreed readily. Although he had got over the disappointment of not hearing from her friends soon after he had received the letter, this fresh contact had revived his interest. Now that he knew the reason for their not meeting, he had thought Emma had changed her mind, he was very eager to meet. At the back of his mind was a slight wariness caused by a nagging doubt that she might be ugly or stupid or any one of a number of things. Or even worse, suppose she was very nice but decided that she did not like him: fears which Barry had done little to allay. He sighed deeply. Whatever happened, it would all be over by Sunday. With these thoughts uppermost in his mind, coupled with the fact that he and his brother had survived another skirmish with their mother, Richard turned over and promptly, if a little restlessly, fell asleep.

Chapter 6: Lamb for the dog and a haircut

Richard cycled lazily down the High Street free-wheeling part of the way. Looking straight ahead he could see clearly the dark green sea, framed on either side by the shops and above by the endless blue sky, with occasional white horses asserting themselves by frothing into life for a few moments before seeking the anonymity of the sea. Although it was a mild day for November, the speed at which he was travelling down the hill made a cold wind, which cut straight through his worn jersey. Richard shivered once as he looked quickly over his shoulder to see if the road was clear and then hurried into Belvedere Road to stop almost immediately. Getting off his bicycle he lifted it onto the pavement then across to the wall, which was one side of the wool shop that nestled next to Woolworth's. Resting his bicycle on the wall he took hold of the wickerwork basket, made by his father when he was in hospital, and lifted it free of the handlebars. Crossing Belvedere Road, he lingered for a moment by the greengrocer's shop on the corner; savouring the smells of oranges and apples until becoming aware of the watchful gaze of the shopkeeper he moved the few steps up the High Street to David Greig's.

Richard pushed the door open and walked through, letting it close gently behind him. The shop was busy so without looking round he moved straight to the butcher's counter and took his place in the queue. The smell of cheeses and hams from an adjacent counter assailed Richard's nostrils as he gazed idly around, watching shoppers on less crowded counter, whilst others came in, walked around, before queuing to make their purchases, sometimes changing their mind about what they had asked for and then paying before walking out again. An old woman complained about the price of eggs whilst her husband looked suspiciously at an aging Stilton cheese mouldering on a shelf.

"Thank you, madam, that'll be 5/6d," said the ruddy faced butcher to the woman in front of Richard jolting him out of his reverie. The woman gave him the money, smiled and with a cheery "Good Morning" left the shop. The butcher gave the money to a passing assistant to put in the till. Noticing Richard was next; he rested his hands on the counter and leaned forward.

"Right, son, what can I do for you?" he enquired.

Richard looked up, swallowed and spoke quietly. "M-m," he stammered for a moment then caught himself, "may I have five breast of lamb pl-please."

The butcher smiled in a kindly way, turned and repeated the order to his assistant in a loud voice, "Five breast of lamb from the cold store for this young man, Billy." Turning back to Richard and seeking to put him at his ease, he winked and said in a confidential, though very loud whisper, "You must have a big dog at home to eat all that lamb, eh?" and poked Richard in the ribs with one of his large red sausage-like fingers. The woman who had been complaining about the price of eggs and her suspicious-looking husband who were now standing behind Richard tittered.

Richard tried but could not prevent the crimson rushing to his face, while his ears burned like two coals, which had somehow been stuck on either side of his head. "N-no," he finally replied in a quiet voice, "they are for us."

The woman and her husband laughed outright at this, whilst Richard stood there, his red cheeks threatening to consume him. The butcher seeing that he had unwittingly embarrassed Richard was deeply sorry that his attempt at camaraderie had misfired. He turned away, muttering "Can't think what's keeping my lad," and walked off quickly towards the cold store.

Richard stood there quietly, wishing the butcher would hurry up. Behind him he could hear the old woman and her husband repeating the conversation and then laughing anew. Richard felt mortified. He wanted to run out of the shop but knew that if he did so he would be in even more trouble when he reached home. He envisaged the scene his mother would make if he returned home without the breasts of lamb for tonight's meal and shuddered. The butcher finally hurried out of the cold store with the lamb already wrapped. Leaning over the counter he put it into Richard's basket, which rested on the shelf, whispering, "That'll be four shillings, son."

Richard counted the money out from the bag of change given to him by his mother and handed it to the butcher, giving him a weak smile, which was all he could muster at that time. "Thank you," he said, turning away as the butcher having taken the money with his left hand touched his straw hat with his right forefinger.

The walk to the door seemed endless. Richard felt as if the eyes of all those in the shop were on him. With the shrill laugh of the old woman still ringing in his ears he reached the door, opened it, then in a rush he hurried out narrowly missing two old ladies who were trying to get in. With a hurried "Excuse me, please" he slipped passed and ran up the High Street. Crossing the road he resolved never to go to David Greig's ever again; knowing in his heart that he probably would have to but hoping it would not be too soon before he had to do so.

Richard's pace slowed as he neared his destination, 'Cupit's the barber. After the mess his mother had yet again made of his hair, when trying to cut it herself, he needed it to be cut properly. As he approached the door Richard hoped he would not get the bad tempered barber who was always too rough and never failed to nick the mole at the back of his neck. Either with the electric clippers or, if not then, he did it when he used the cut-throat razor. Not only was it painful when the barber tried to stem the bleeding with a styptic pencil but his mother usually slapped him hard for getting blood on his shirt collar.

Richard took a deep breath and clutching his heavy shopping basket with one hand pushed open the door with the other. A bell clanged loudly as the door opened, which made a boy who was sitting down awaiting his turn look up from reading his comic. It was Barry. Although he was his best friend Richard almost turned round and walked out again. Only the thought of having to walk around much longer with his pudding basin haircut deterred him. Closing the door he walked over to Barry, who was the only one waiting, and sat down.

Barry having resumed reading his comic looked up, a quick glance at his friend's hair confirming what he first thought when Richard had entered – that his mother had cut his hair again. Knowing how sensitive his friend was he decided not to mention it. Having also noticed how heavy the basket was by the way Richard had been carrying it and by the solid thump it made when Richard dropped it to the floor, he looked down at it and grinning mischievously, asked, "Is that the usual half ton of meat for the Luckhurst family?"

Richard looked round quickly, at first put out, but seeing the grin on his friend's face and the glint in his eye, merely punched him, none too gently, on the arm. "Yes it is and if you don't shut up I'll ask my mum to invite you round to help eat it!"

Barry snorted, then rubbed his arm and laughed. "I wouldn't mind," he replied, "as long as she doesn't give me a great big plate of chips to eat. You must love chips in your house as you're always eating them." He thought for a moment then continued, "It doesn't matter what time of day I come round your house but I only have to be there for five minutes or so before your mother shoves a great big plate of chips under my nose and is telling me to eat up and grow up to be a big boy. I wouldn't mind but I don't really like chips all that much." He paused again before continuing, "Your chip pan must be red hot from all the use it gets."

Richard laughed out loud at his friend's past discomfiture, which he quickly stifled when the barber, who was known to be in a perpetual bad mood, turned around and glared at him. The other barber also turned round, winked and smiled before resuming cutting his customer's hair. Barry lowered his head and indicated to

Richard that he should do likewise. Taking a letter out of his pocket he waved it in front of Richard, whose eyes followed it back and forth. "I'm going to get a 'Boston' haircut today – this note from my mother says I can."

Richard sighed in envy at his friend no longer having to suffer the indignity of a short back and sides. The electric clippers starting at the neck and running almost to the crown of your head before the barber – seeming reluctantly – stopping, only to start again at another point further along. "Really, your mother is going to …" he trailed off although if he had continued he was going to say 'let you have a Boston' but Barry's po-faced expression warned him that something was up.

Barry looked over in the direction of the two Barbers and then inclined his head closer to Richard's before whispering, "Not really." He stopped to make sure they were not being overheard but both of the Barbers were talking to their respective customers. "I wrote it myself" then as if seeking to justify his actions, "I'm fed up having short back and sides especially in winter, its cold." He feigned a shiver.

Richard shook his head in wonder, especially at his friend's nerve to try such a thing in the first place. There was of course only one drawback and both of them knew what it was. Would Barry get his hair cut by the bad tempered barber or the other one, Mr Knightly? If the former, Barry would not stand a chance of having a Boston; if the latter, then he might just get away with it. Everything hinged on who finished first. Richard had just reached this conclusion when Barry leaned closer, whispering. "Look, I know I got here before you but if old grouchy finishes first will you take my turn?" he stopped before adding, "please".

Richard looked up at the barber in question. He did not seem to be in too bad a mood today, still.... He turned and seeing the look of mute appeal in his friend's face could only nod an affirmative. Barry heaved a noiseless sigh of relief and resumed reading his comic. Richard too began to relax as his encounter with the butcher in David Greig's began to fade. If he did have to have the grouchy barber cut his hair at least it would look better than it did now. He gazed idly around the shop. The sun shining weakly through the net curtain reflected off the green colour of the advertisement for 7 O'clock razor blades hanging off the opposite wall: the shop being alternately darkened and then lightened at the whim of every passing cloud floating across the sun. Around each of the sinks and in front of the mirrors facing each chair stood a variety of bottles and jars including a giant jar of Brylcreem. On either side of the mirror were shelves, which carried an even greater variety of hairdressings or shampoos whilst on the walls were hung various combs held fast to the cardboard backing by elastic. On the left wall were two steps, which led up to a back room. Through the half drawn curtain Richard could see a kettle gently boiling on a single gas ring; a teapot, mugs, tea, milk and sugar were nearby. Every now and then the grouchy barber would look in through the curtain, waiting to see if the kettle had fully boiled. Suddenly, with a murmured 'Excuse me a moment, sir," he walked up the two steps and quickly made a pot of tea, which he left to brew as he hurried out to continue his work.

After a few minutes, much to Barry's chagrin, he had finished with that customer. As soon as the man had paid and left, the grouchy barber went up into the back room and poured out two cups of tea. Having added milk and sugar he brought them out into the shop and placed one on the shelf near his colleague, who just nodded his thanks since he was attempting to listen to what his customer was saying.

"Right, who's next," said the grouchy barber looking at the two boys whilst he drank great gulps of his tea. Barry gripped the comic he was holding tighter and tried to pretend to be immersed in what he was reading. Richard got slowly out of his seat and walked towards the barber's chair. The barber stopped drinking his tea and shook his head, saying, "No, not you, he pointed towards Barry, 'him, he's next"

Richard hesitated momentarily nonplussed. Then in a rush he said, "No, I'm next." The barber turned to Richard and gave him a withering look. "Go and sit down." He returned his gaze to Barry, "Come on, you're next, up on the chair. I haven't got all day." With that he put his mug down and reached for the cover used to protect customer's clothes from the cut hair.

Barry stood up clutching his comic. "It's not my turn, mister, it's his," pointing to Richard who nodded in agreement.

The barber had had enough of this charade. He looked Barry straight in the eye, saying, "You came in before this lad so it's your turn now, right? Right! Now if you have changed your mind and don't want a haircut kindly leave the shop, otherwise get up on this chair."

The last few words were spoken in a voice of command. Barry knew when he was beaten. There was no question of him not having a haircut. As Richard resumed his seat, accompanied by a shrug of his shoulders, Barry dropped the comic on a seat, walked to the barber's chair and sat down slowly. The barber floated the cover over him and fixed it tight, too tight, at the back of his neck, at the same time asking in a perfunctory manner. "What will it be then, short back and sides?"

Barry's mind was in turmoil – should he produce the letter or wait until the next, and perhaps more favourable time when he got the other barber? That would be preferable and perhaps more sensible, and in the long run successful course to follow. On the other hand he had been planning this for weeks – ever since his last haircut in fact – and to be thwarted at the last moment was almost too much to bear. He was still trying to decide what to do when the barber said, not too quietly, with his mouth very close to Barry's ear, "Well?" Barry decided. "Not a short back and sides. My mother says that I can have a 'Boston'.

The barber, who was already reaching for his electric clippers paused, turned to look Barry in the eye, disbelief and amazement vying with each other as they flooded over his features. "Your mother says you can have a what?!" The last word almost being shouted made the other barber turn around.

"A 'Boston' replied Barry.

"Well," replied the barber, "I don't give them to boys your age unless I have a letter from one of their parents giving permission," he turned to his partner. Jerking his thumb in Barry's direction, "He wants a 'Boston'!"

Barry took the letter he had written out of his pocket and without a word handed it to the barber, who took it also without speaking, his lips a thin line and grey-flecked moustache bristling. He opened the envelope and took out the letter, which he unfolded carefully.

Then, settling his glasses more firmly on his nose he began to read. He read it through, looked at Barry over the top of his glasses and then read it again. Satisfied, he turned to his partner and in an assumed jocular voice said, "Listen to this." His partner stopped cutting the customer's hair and with comb and scissors poised he – and the others in the shop listened. The barber, relishing the moment, held the letter at arm's length, cleared his throat theatrically and pausing only to give Barry a glance, read aloud to the whole shop.

'*To whom it may consern.*' 'Spelt with an 'S'.' said the Barber. *Please give barry a boston haircut. He don't like a short back and siddes cos it makes his neck cold in winter.*
> *Sinned*
> *Mrs Mitchell*'

As he read it, complete with mistakes and in a high pitched voice both his partner and the customer burst into laughter, when he had finished. Gratified by this response he turned to Barry. "Your mother didn't write this, you did."

Barry tried to brazen it out. "Yes, she did," he replied, adding earnestly, hoping to give some credibility to his statement, "only this morning."

The barber looked back at the letter and then at Barry. "You say your mother wrote this?" When Barry nodded his head he said, "Well it's easy to prove – I'll get a pencil and paper so you can write it out and we'll compare the handwriting of the two, OK?"

Barry surprised and dismayed at the speed at which his plan was already unravelling, knew he was beaten but still tried to bluff it out to the very end. "My mum's writing is like mine," he declared. Richard looked on, admiring his friend's nerve, as the barber held out a pencil and paper without saying another word. Barry looked at the writing implements, at the barber and then back to the pencil and paper. He finally admitted to himself that he had misjudged this campaign. In a voice so quiet that only the barber could hear him he said, "OK, I wrote it."

The barber, triumphant, tossed the pencil and paper to one side, picked up and switched on the electric clippers, murmuring, "Short back and sides it is then." It may have been his imagination but it seemed to Richard, as this drama he had seen unfold concluded, that the clippers were going just that little bit higher than usual.

Meanwhile Mr Knightly had finished with his customer and turning to Richard indicated that he was ready to cut Richard's hair. Richard got up from his wooden seat, moved across to the barber's chair and sat down. As he did so he looked across at Barry who did not look up but merely sat gazing at the sink, his face a picture of defeat.

Mr Knightly having fixed the cover around Richard's neck, looked at his badly cut hair. "Your mother, again?" he enquired. Richard merely nodded. "Never mind," sighed Mr Knightly, "let's see what we can do." With that he very carefully proceeded to make something out of the mess Richard's mother had made of his hair.

Barry's own haircut was soon finished. Stepping down, he paid the barber, who smirked at him and going to Richard whispered "I'll wait for you outside."

Richard nodded his agreement as Barry with a final sour glance at his own barber, opened the door and left the shop. There being no-one else waiting for a haircut, the other barber left the shop and moved into the back room.

Mr Knightly continued to tidy up Richard's hair as best he could. Tutting every now and then as he came across an awkward piece, which had been cut particularly badly. "You really ought to tell your mother not to bother to cut your hair, you know." Richard nodded his agreement as Mr Knightly continued, "You always end up here anyway so I can tidy up the mess she makes, so where is the saving?"

Richard could not agree more. The trouble was in trying to tell his mother this. Who would dare? As there were two boys in the family she was determined to save money on haircuts by doing it herself. Every now and then she took out the hand clippers she had bought from a neighbour's catalogue and cut their hair. It was only because Richard sang in the choir that he subsequently came to the barber's to have it cut properly. His brother Robin was keen to point out that he, "Had to walk around like a right berk for a couple of weeks" until his hair started to grown out again.

Before long Mr Knightly finished cutting and whilst combing Richard's hair said, "Well, that's the best I can do I'm afraid."

Richard looked at himself in the large mirror on the wall behind the sink and at the back of his head as Mr Knightly held up a square mirror behind him. He was very relieved to see that it looked alright again. Beaming a smile at Mr Knightly he expressed his grateful thanks. "Thanks very much Mr Knightly."

Mr Knightly made a deprecatory gesture with his face and hands. After he had brushed away the cut hair from around Richard's shirt collar and removed the cover Richard stepped down and dug into his pocket for some money. His mother had told him to pay for his haircut from the change from the shopping. He gave it to Mr Knightly who walked with it over to the wooden draw, which was used as a till. Dropping the half crown in, he took out a shilling and held it out to Richard who, having retrieved his shopping, was in the process of walking passed the counter on his way out of the shop.

"Here's your change, Richard." At his puzzled look he continued, "I can't charge you for a full haircut when I've only given you a tidy-up. Here" he added, thrusting his hand out further.

At first reluctant to take it, knowing that having to tidy up his mother's mistakes was probably more difficult and time consuming than cutting it in the first place, but at Mr Knightly's insistence he reached out and took the proffered shilling and put it in his pocket. "Thanks very much, Mr Knightly."

"That's alright. And remember, the next time you mother wants to cut your hair, tell her that it doesn't cost that much more to have it done properly." He smiled and Richard did likewise.

"I will," he replied. Although he knew that he had no intention of doing so, at least not in that way since it was probably the quickest way to get a belt around the ear. "Thank you. Goodbye," he said and opening the door stepped outside leaving the door open to allow someone else to enter.

Outside he looked around and saw Barry about a hundred yards down the High Street outside the fishing and bait shop. He was using the window as a mirror to look at his hair. Frowning at what he saw, occasionally brushing the hair on the back of his neck upwards and then down again. Richard stopped beside his friend and waited until Barry noticed him. "Just look what that maniac did to my hair. He did it on purpose just because I wanted a 'Boston'." He turned around so that Richard could see the back. "Look, it's shorter than yours is and you look half scalped.

Richard laughed at this comment whilst pulling on his friend's arm. "Come on, let's go and look at the sea." Moving the heavy bag from his right to his left hand he began to walk down the High Street towards the cliff top. Barry, with one final look at his hair in the shop window, shook his head in disgust and disbelief, then turning up the collar of his jacket, in the vain hope of hiding his scalped neck, ran to catch up with Richard.

"Can you come pungering this afternoon then?" he asked Richard, who nodded affirmation. "Great!" cried Barry, clapping him on the back, "Come on, I'll race you to the railings," and started off.

Richard stood there shaking his head in disbelief and shouted after Barry, "How can I you idiot, when I've got this lot to carry?" Barry slowed down and stopped as the words reached him, then back-pedalled until he met up with Richard who was walking towards him. Then taking hold of one of the handles he started off again, dragging Richard, the wickerwork basket stretched between them, off down the hill. Resisting only for a moment, then with a 'what the hell' gesture, Richard raced off as well. The two of them whooping and shouting as dodging pedestrians and cars and with the large packet containing the breasts of lamb threatening to bounce right out of the basket, they ran down the remainder of the High Street, along Sea Approach then hurtled across the Promenade to crash breathless into the railings, which lined the top of the cliff.

Richard and Barry hung there with their arms dangling over the railings, taking in great gulps of air. Richard's eyes roved around whilst he caught his breath. On the right the sea still lapped the cliff's edge so you could not get round to Louisa Bay without getting wet. In front of him, in Viking Bay, the glistening sand, where the sea had been, told him that the tide was on the ebb. Dotted here and there, children played, both they and their parents well wrapped up to protect themselves from the cold wind blowing in from the sea, some sitting on metal and wooden chairs seeking heat from the weak rays of the sun, others merely standing and gazing out to sea. Along the water's edge ran a dog, happy to get his paws wet but, this late in the year nothing else. First racing ahead of its owner then back again, staying with him for a few moments then racing off to repeat the process over again. Stopping occasionally to savage a piece of seaweed, dragging it with him for a space then just as easily dropping it to turn and bark at the incoming waves.

Richard's eyes moved on to the jetty. The old wooden boat house, covered with sea and salt-stained dirty cream paint, stood on the end near the shore. On the right-hand side of the building, by the top of the steps, which led up to the first floor of the boat house stood his old friend the wooden Scottish soldier, which he assumed was once a figurehead of an old sailing ship. Whilst over the double doorway, leading into the room where the fishermen kept their nets, hung another ship's figure-head, of a man, thought to be Hercules, flanked by two whalebones. On the other end of the jetty was a covered area on the roof of which was the outline of a Viking ship. In the summer this was lit up at night by coloured bulbs. Richard had fond memories of that ship since he had often used it as a model in sandcastle competitions and had won prizes. He sighed at the memory of last summer and this seemed to serve as a signal to break the silence between them.

"The tide's going out," said Barry, knowing it was unnecessary to say it but needing to do so all the same. Richard nodded, so Barry continued, "Should be just right for pungering this afternoon."

Richard nodded again, still lost in his thoughts and then reluctantly dragged himself back to the present. He turned to look at Barry, "Well I'd better get going." He lifted the shopping bag. "What time shall I see you down Joss Bay then?"

Barry shrugged; he had been hoping that they would go down and look round the jetty but knowing Richard's mother he had better not detain his friend. "How about two o'clock?" he suggested.

Richard nodded his agreement, and then had an idea, "I know, I'll call for you just before two – OK?"

This time it was Barry's turn to nod. "OK, see you," and clapped Richard on the shoulder.

Richard was reluctant to go, knowing that Barry would rather he'd been able to stay a little longer but if he didn't go soon he'd get into trouble. He didn't want that. Not only because he wanted to go pungering with Barry that afternoon but also because he was going to meet Emma on Sunday. If once his mother got it into her head that he was being 'difficult', as she called it, she might not let him go to church on Sunday. She had done it before and would probably do it again, but he hoped not this Sunday. Giving Barry a smile and a quick wave, Richard turned and walked back up the way, which a few minutes before, they had run down together. Reaching the top of the small road, 'Sea Approach', Richard turned around to wave a final goodbye to Barry but his friend had already gone. Richard turned back and resumed his trudge up the High Street, moving the heavy bag from hand to hand, mingling with the other Saturday morning shoppers as he made his way back to where he had left his bicycle, thence home.

Chapter 7: Pungering and sticky pink paint

Laying their bicycles down on the grass at the top of the cliff, Richard and Barry untied their pungering irons from the crossbars. Richard examined his critically for a few moments. His Dad had helped him make the pungering iron using a piece of three eighths of an inch iron rod, which was about three feet long. One end had been pushed right through a thick piece of wood – the centre of which had been laboriously drilled and then burned out by heating the end of the iron in the coke fire at home – which served as a handle. The end of the iron rod had then been bent at right angles to prevent it slipping out. The other end of the iron rod had been sharpened to a rough point and then bent round in a semi-circle so as to form a hook.

Richard tried the handle then swished the iron rod back and forth a few times, listening to the sound it made as it cut through the air. Satisfied, he walked the few paces to where Barry stood, at the top edge of the cliff, gazing out to sea. He eyes scanned over the beach, the wet sand and flat rocks making up the wave-cut platform, until his eyes reached the sea where gently foaming waves tumbled in over the rocks that were covered with thick brown and green seaweed. It was a real spring tide. The sea was out the farthest either of them had ever seen it at Joss Bay and they looked at each other in wonder. Barry was the first to break the silence: he whistled in amazement. "I don't think I've ever seen the sea so far out before."

Richard nodded his head in agreement. "I'll bet there are lots of crabs out there!" He turned. "Come on let's go." As one they walked the short distance across the grass until they came to the concrete slope that led down to Joss Bay beach. It was as wide, deep bay with a large beach, packed with holidaymakers in the summer but now, except for one or two people walking out of sight with a dog, it was deserted. The bay was surrounded on all sides by steep white chalk cliffs, through which, at intervals, ran horizontal bands of flint, topped by a thin covering of earth and a layer of scrubby grass.

Reaching the sand Richard and Barry walked across the beach to the high tide mark where the sand was hard and smooth; making their progress easier. Moving to the right of the bay they aimed for the point of the cliff, which marked the right hand edge of the bay where it met the sea at high tide. Avoiding clumps of evil smelling seaweed, left by the last high tide and hazardous lumps of flint jutting out of the sand, they reached the side of the bay. Large rounded boulders of chalk, the last remnants of a cliff fall, lay strewn about like giant marbles, whilst up against the cliff were piled hundreds of flints, some as large as footballs, angular and jagged, others like pebbles, weathered and smoothed by years of action by the sea.

Richard stepped up onto a large chalk boulder in order to get a better view, lifting his hand to shield his eyes from the sun. Looking down at Barry he said. "Well, where shall we go, straight ahead?" He looked out to sea again. "I've never seen the tide out so far before." Then shaking his head from side to side, he repeated his earlier statement and added, "I bet there are tons of large crabs out there."

"Let's have a look," said Barry, holding out his hand for Richard to pull him up. Richard pulled, jumping down onto the sand to make room as with a big heave Barry appeared for a moment up beside him. Squinting against the glare of the sun from the white chalk cliff, Barry looked around especially in the direction indicated by Richard. After looking elsewhere for a few moments he looked back and then down at Richard. "OK, let's try there first." Jumping down he fell in beside Richard at first walking over the damp sand, the imprints left by their shoes filling up with water as they passed by, then onto the flat rocks, covered here and there with seaweed, winkles, cockles and limpets but most of all by thousands of mussels. Richard reflected as he walked easily over the mussel beds that it was not so simple in summer when they ran over them in bare feet. But by the end of the summer season his feet were toughened to the touch of mussels and he had frequently been amused by the amazed looks of holiday makers as he ran swiftly over the mussels in bare feet. It was even funnier when they tried to copy his antics and usually ended up just hopping about.

Pausing here and there, occasionally slipping on the clumps of seaweed, to look into rock pools left by the retreating tide, Richard and Barry gradually reached the sea and stood for a moment on a pinnacle of rock, watching the waves endlessly breaking. After a few minutes Barry broke the silence. "In or out," he asked.

Richard studied the waves for a moment, watching the seaweed swirl about as each wave, after breaking withdrew with a sigh, before replying. "In," he said emphatically. Barry too had been watching the waves. "Yes, you're right, it's definitely on the turn, we had better get started."

Gripping his pungering iron in one hand Barry took the cork, which he had placed there to stop accidentally puncturing himself, off the pointed hook with the other. Putting the cork in his pocket he swished the iron back and forth for a moment then pulled on the iron to make sure it was firmly fixed in the handle. Satisfied, he clambered off and started in search of edible crabs.

Richard, looking at the chalk rocks and seeing no suitable crevices as hiding places for the edible crabs he was after, moved off along the edge of the tide away from Barry, probing here and there with the iron without success. The sea swirled and sucked around his wellington boots, loose stones threatened to topple him as he moved on farther until he came to a small inlet, which had been cut into the chalk by retreating tides. Already the sea was threatening to cover the horizontal crevice, which had been cut into the chalk by the action of the waves and sand. He crouched down, the water – when a wave came in – almost level with the top of his wellingtons. Carefully Richard inserted the pungering iron deep into the crevice and moved it from side to side until, encountering an obstacle, he moved the hook around it and pulled hard. The iron stuck for a moment and then suddenly came free, bringing with it a lump of flint, which had been embedded in the chalk. Richard dropped it into the sea then tried again. He felt something, another obstruction, which appeared to move. Richard pushed the iron rod deeper into the crevice so that the hook was now behind the object Richard pulled hard and was rewarded by the sight of an edible crab emerging reluctantly from the darkness. A cry from Barry exulting over a find distracted him for a moment – making him look up. The crab, as if aware of this reprieve and needing no further encouragement, dropped off the ledge into the murky water, where it scuttled off to safety. Richard turned at the noise, as the crab with a splosh dropped into the sea, in time to see the crab disappear. Futilely hitting the water with the pungering iron in an attempt to stop the crab, which was now far away, he succeeded only in splashing himself. Snorting with disgust at his stupidity, and annoyed at Barry for crying out, he turned back to the crevice in the chalk moving into deeper water as he did so.

The sea now slopped dangerously close to the top of his wellington boots, a few drops succeeding in getting over the top of them. Richard looked up, noticing the wind was a little fresher and the waves more pronounced. Although reluctant to move on to another spot, since it would be a long time before the tide went out this far again, he turned in order to walk back a couple of yards into shallower water. As he did so he noticed a large crevice partly obscured by seaweed. Stepping over to it, he pushed his pungering iron in deep until, to his surprise, the handle almost reached the overhanging seaweed: it was deep. Moving the iron to and fro he gradually pulled the iron out but nothing was pushed before the point. Masking his disappointment Richard tried again, probing far to the left and right. The point suddenly caught on something, as he tried to pull it out the second time, and then just as suddenly slipped free easily.

Richard tried again in the same place but this time there was no obstruction, it had gone. 'A crab,' though Richard excitedly. Crouching low in an attempt to see into the crevice he move the hook of the iron on the 'roof' of the crevice with the point on the right, and then gripping the handle extra tightly suddenly, and with a viciousness, which surprised even himself, thrust the iron into the crevice and in a single sweeping motion to the right, pulled. The iron stuck at first and then reluctantly and, with what seemed agonising slowness, it began to come free. Richard kept the pressure on and gradually a large claw emerged, quickly followed by another.

Richard, in a crouching position, was transfixed, his eyes almost level with those of the largest crab he had ever seen. With the crab appearing to eye him warily, he judged that it must have been at least twelve inches across, pink-brown in colour with giant claws, which had black pinchers. For several moments he didn't know what to do. The hook of his pungering iron was curved over the back of the crab so as long as he kept the pressure on it the crab could not retreat or move sideways in order to escape. On the other hand Richard did not want to pull the crab out any further in case, like the other one, it fell into the sea. Given the size of its claws Richard did not fancy trying to either catch it or look for it with his hands if it fell into the sea. Judging from its size his fingers would easily be crushed by the serrated claws.

Richard looked up to see if Barry was nearby to give him a hand. Although he had ready in his pocket the looped string to put around the claws, he felt that any movement he made might cause him to slip, so allowing the crab to escape. He was undecided what would be the best thing to do and had started to reach into his pocket with his left hand, having decided to get the string out when the crab, making a move, caused him to grasp the pungering iron with two hands in order to hold the big crab in its present position. As he struggled with the crab, trying to maintain a precarious status quo, Richard again marvelled at its size. Its colouring was perfect, as was its shape and pincers. The look of it proclaimed it to be a crab among crabs. The crab stopped moving as quickly as it had begun and, thought Richard, eyed him with a baleful expression. Richard's feelings towards his adversary were beginning to change. Although he had caught lots of crabs before, and had no qualms about cooking them in a pot of boiling water, he began to have doubts about such an inglorious end befalling such a magnificent specimen. Not releasing the pressure of the iron for a moment, he looked around; still no sign of Barry. Simultaneously he decided to let the crab go and released the pressure in the pungering iron, sliding it across the crab's back to its legs until it was no longer restrained. Instead of either rushing back into the crevice or falling into the sea to effect an escape, as he would have thought, the crab stayed stock still, then raised itself on its legs as if it were stretching, like a cat, so as to somehow shake off the imposition of the pressure of the pungering iron. Having done this, Richard imagined it eyed him again finally for a moment, before slowly edging back into the crevice.

Richard raised the iron in a mock salute as he watched it disappear. It had all happened in a few minutes but at the same time seemed to have gone on forever. The sun now seemed to shine a little brighter as if a cloud, real or imagined, had hesitated to watch the drama unfold and had now moved on. The water which had slopped unheeded over the top of his boots now impinged on his consciousness and his toes moved squelching in his boots. Richard stepped up onto a rock opposite the crevice and took off his wellington boots to shake out the water, which had accumulated there. As he sat down to do so, the first large wave from the incoming tide lapped at the entrance to the crevice where a few moments ago he had, for the first time, he admitted to himself, really met a member of the animal kingdom on its own level and had been forced to come to terms with it. Richard sat for a few moments, wondering. That crab was not only big it must be very old. He looked quietly about him. He had got to know this bay and these rocks very well over the years and knew he had never seen the tide out this far before and probably would not again for a few years at least. He put his arms round his shins and with his chin touching his knees, hugged himself as he thought; I'll probably never see that giant crab again but will always know that it is here. He looked again at the rock but the rapidly incoming tide had almost reached the top of the crevice. Sighing to himself, he picked up his pungering iron and with a final backward glance, resumed his search for crabs, conscious of the encroaching tide, which served as a spur to greater effort.

* * *

Richard brought his gaze further in. The tide had been coming in for over two hours. The spot where he had had his tussle with the giant crab was now covered with deep water and he knew that the flat rocks remaining were not likely to yield any crabs, as least not the edible variety. He banged his pungering iron against a limpet to dislodge it as food for the crabs they had caught, and then left it when it clung tighter to the rock on which it was perched and hit the rock instead; spattering pieces of chalk about whilst some adhered to the iron. With a final look at the sea and the sky he spoke.

"I think we'd better get going, we won't catch any more crabs today." Barry looked around as Richard walked over to the pool where the captured crabs lay tied up. "Do you know which ones are yours?" he asked Barry as he walked over.

Barry crouched down and looked at the crabs, which despite being tied had all moved from their original positions. He frowned. "I think so," and putting his pungering iron into the pool, he lifted onto it four of the crabs. Richard waited until Barry had got his four crabs and then did likewise until the three remaining crabs were strung along the iron like washing on a line. "Right, let's go," said Barry and set off over the seaweed and mussel-covered rocks, careful not to dislodge the wriggling crabs from their precarious perch. Soon they reached the hard wet sand strewn with boulders, which had been worn smooth by the sea.

Richard and Barry made their way towards the concrete slope to the top of the cliff. Reaching their bicycles Richard picked up his bicycle and lifting up the flap emptied the crabs into the saddlebag then hooked his pungering iron onto the crossbar and got on his bicycle.

Barry, having loaded his saddlebag with his four crabs, got on his bicycle and stared out to sea. "It's been a nice day really," he finally said, "apart from this awful haircut." Richard smiled. "Never mind, it'll grow again." He paused for a moment. "Next time you want a Boston you'd better go somewhere else."

Barry nodded his agreement then with both of them giving a last look at the sea and without a word being spoken; they cycled off by common consent. Across the grass at the top of the cliff, thence onto the road leading back to their various homes. Reaching the road where they would have to separate, they both stopped. Barry was the first to speak. "Big day tomorrow, eh?"

Richard smiled back and nodded. "What do you think she'll look like?" he asked.

Barry's face took on a sage-like appearance, frowning, he pursed his lips before giving a considered reply. "It's been my experience..."

But he got no farther as Richard burst out laughing. "What experience?" but stopped when he saw Barry's look as he made to cycle off.

"Do you want my opinion or don't you?"

Richard bit his lip and restrained himself. "Yes," he replied.

After nodding, Barry started again. "It's been my experience that when girls say their friends are pretty it usually means they're plug ugly," and laughed.

It was Richard's turn to look sour now, but, "You're only jealous" was all he could think to say.

Barry stopped laughing and thought about it for a moment. "Yes, I will be if she's pretty. Ah well we'll all find out tomorrow."

Richard's heart sank at this and the words were out of his mouth even before he had thought of them. "What do you mean 'we'll all'?"

Barry smiled. "Well you are meeting her after Matins, aren't you?" Richard nodded. "Well then, we'll all be there as well." Richard's face fell so Barry quickly added. "Only joking, but you don't mind if I'm there, do you?"

Richard did, but couldn't think of a way to say so without either hurting his friend's feelings or saying something stupid he might regret later. He valued Barry's friendship and would not willingly do anything, which might jeopardise it. Although still young and not having had time to formulate any specific reasons for thinking so, he knew friendship was a fragile relationship, which like a flower or plant, could if properly nurtured grow into something strong and be able to withstand any amount of difficulties. Although if too much is asked for, or taken, too soon, or even through neglect forgotten; then like a flower or plant it will only wither and die. He was certainly not prepared to hazard his friendship with Barry, unless he really had to, and certainly not someone who he had yet to meet and might not even like when he had met her. He contented himself with merely shrugging his shoulders, which Barry took to be an affirmative.

He visibly brightened. "Great, I look forward to it. Well better get these crabs home before they walk back to the sea." With a cheery wave of farewell he cycled off in the direction of his house. After watching him for a second or two, Richard cycled off to his own house, wishing, in one sense, tomorrow was over and done with, so that he could relax again and get on with living.

* * *

Reaching home Richard leaned his bicycle against the wall of the porch. Undoing his saddlebag he carefully lifted out the three crabs that were inside. His other cares temporarily forgotten, he thought of that fourth giant crab he could have caught but instead had left it where it was. He was not sentimental when it came to things like lambs, rabbits, chickens or even crabs. They were food and there was not time for sentiment. For a moment he bathed himself in the expected hero's welcome he would receive when he brought the crabs in: if he said so himself, they were fairly big and everyone in his family liked crab – even his mother. With these thoughts overriding any others he opened the back door to the kitchen and with the crabs dangling from his left hand he used his right, as he often did, to get hold of the kitchen wall and pull himself up into the kitchen.

Richard froze as his put his feet down on the kitchen floor. He couldn't move his fingers away from the wall. The smell of new paint now assailed his nostrils and a quick look around told him that the kitchen had been freshly painted with glossy pink paint. He now remembered that as he had been leaving the house, his mother had started to paint the kitchen. The crabs moved restlessly in his left hand so he very slowly lowered them to the floor just as the door from the back room opened and Robin walked in.

He espied the crabs immediately and came over and knelt down beside them, "Crabs, lovely." He remained kneeling for a moment, looking at them and occasionally giving them a prod. Then it dawned on him that Richard hadn't moved. He looked up. "What are you standing there for, why..." he trailed off as he saw Richard's fingers stuck to the paint. "Oh no," said Robin as he stood up next to his brother.

Richard looked at Robin and back at his fingers. "Well, I can't stand here all day," he said. "If I pull them away slowly perhaps the paint won't come away?" Robin stared oddly at his brother and Richard had to agree that it was not very likely; the paint felt like glue. He took a deep breath. "Here goes," and slowly and with great care eased his fingers away from the shiny, pink sticky wall.

Unfortunately the paint had been on the wall sufficiently long enough for it to have adhered properly to the layer of paint underneath and in so doing it had made the thick layers of all the previous paints soft and tacky – the fact that the pink paint used was a gloss and not an emulsion only increased this tackiness – so as Richard moved his fingers away he did not just lift off the top layer of pink paint but all the other gloss layers as well, right down to the plaster.

Robin looked on in wide-eyed horror as the full extent of the damage was revealed. Richard merely groaned and stared for a few seconds at the grey plaster finger marks, willing them to go away. His next thoughts were to try and paint over the marks. Moving quickly he picked the crabs up from the floor and dropped them into the large deep sink by the window, then went back out to the porch and soaking a rag in paraffin scrubbed the paint of his fingers. Having done that he returned quickly to the kitchen where Robin still stood viewing the mark with morbid fascination.

Robin looked away from the grey 'scar' on the wall as Richard returned. "I think I'll run away from home," said Robin. He paused whilst he scrutinised the mark closely. "I don't think I can stand it."

Richard grimaced. It was too awful to contemplate. He had had a quick look around the porch whilst he had been cleaning his fingers but had been unable to find the paint or the paint brush. He took hold of his brother's arm to get his attention. "Rob, quickly, where's the paint she's been using?"

Robin looked at his brother, fear and pity mingled in his eyes. He swallowed convulsively. "There isn't any. I think she used it all up and put the tin in the dustbin."

"What's in the dustbin?" Unseen by either of them their mother had entered the kitchen from the hall and had caught the last few words, which she now repeated, making them both jump. "What's in the dustbin?"

She moved into the kitchen, looking around at the painting she had done that afternoon, humming to herself in satisfaction. Richard found himself suddenly standing alone, as Robin faded into the back room, and was desperately trying to decide whether to stay there or go upstairs. Robin had suddenly felt an urgent and overwhelming need to go to the toilet. Richard looked around at Robin, aware of and appreciating his brother's dilemma; being torn between loyalty to his brother and staying out of the firing line. Unobtrusively Richard waved Robin away as he spoke to his mother. "I've had a bit of an accident." He stopped, and then added quietly, "I didn't mean to do it."

His mother looked quickly around but seeing nothing obviously amiss, asked, "Accident – what accident?"

Richard moved aside and merely pointed at the bald patch of grey plaster amid the sea of pink paint. He started to explain what had happened. "I came in the door and..." Expecting the blow he had begun to take action to avoid it and in doing so managed to lessen its force. But not the second and third, which was a closed fist to the crown of his head that made him fall to the floor. In doing so he wondered, in an idle moment, before the blow began to take effect, whether his neck was a little bit shorter now. From his position on the floor Richard looked up, not daring to move in case it provoked his mother to further violence but knowing in his heart that it hadn't really started yet. More importantly he was wondering whether he would be allowed to go to church tomorrow. He was prepared to accept any amount of punishment from his mother's hand provided he was not kept at home.

He watched his mother's face as she minutely scrutinised the damage, her mouth twitching as she spoke to herself, fingers hovering over the damaged paintwork but not daring to touch it. She looked down at Richard, her face a ghastly red and purple colour. Richard cringed as his body prepared itself for another series of blows. Instead, after a few attempts to speak his mother spat out the words, "Get out of my sight."

Richard turned over to scrabble off from the kitchen floor into the back room but was unable to avoid a kick his mother had aimed at his ankle. Hobbling into the room he began to make his way to the door to the hall, hoping to escape to the bedroom for a while to allow his mother's temper to cool down. "Where do you think you're going?" His mother's voice cut across the room as his outstretched hand was only a few inches from the door handle. Richard turned to look at his mother and pointed with his hand upstairs as a prelude to his explanation. "You told me to get..." he never finished as his mother punctuated her statement with a slap to his head. "Stay here."

Richard nodded, not daring to speak, and remained rooted to the spot, as his mother turned on her heels and left the room and went outside. After a few seconds Richard heard the sound of the dustbin lid being dropped noisily to the ground. He waited, the seconds' ticking off in his head in time with the throbbing in his ankle, as the muscles in his body relaxed now that his mother, not in the room, was unable to hit him. The sound of his mother returning to and rummaging around in the porch caused Richard to stand a little straighter with each passing second until he was virtually at attention by the time she burst back into the kitchen clutching a tin of paint in one hand and a paint brush in the other.

Richard quaked under his mother's gaze and watched with trepidation as she dipped the paint brush into the tin and scraped it around the bottom before applying the paint to the wall. Relief flooded through Richard as he watched the grey area begin to blend with the surrounding pink, until from where he stood it looked as if his accident had never happened. Richard smiled. That had not been too bad, he thought to himself; he'd had a lucky escape. Richard looked from the wall to his mother's face, expecting to see her pleased with the result of the painting and was dismayed not only to see that she was still angry but that her features had a quizzical look as she contemplated the rapidly fading smile on his face.

Richard blenched as his mother stared and then, at his mother's command to "Come here!" he slowly and reluctantly willed his legs forward. Richard was still wondering why his mother was still upset when, as he got closer, he saw that although the grey patch was now pink, but because he had taken off so many layers of paint, when he had touched it, it was uneven and looked just as bad close up, if not worse, than it had when it had been grey. Richard swallowed convulsively as his mother continued to contemplate the wall. He knew he was much too close for when, as he knew it would, his mother's anger finally erupted. He thought about moving backwards but his mother spoke before he had the opportunity to make up his mind. "Do you see what you've done you stupid, stupid boy?" She waited as did Richard, who was trying to decide whether or not this was a rhetorical question. "Do you!" his mother shouted out.

Richard nodded convulsively. "Yes," then added in order to lessen his acceptance of his guilt, "It was an accident." His mother seemed to have forgotten him as she applied some more paint, which she had managed to scrape up from the bottom of the tin, onto the patch on the wall in an attempt to build up the paint on a level with that on the rest of the wall. All the time she was muttering to herself as the futility of what she was trying to attempt began to dawn on her. Finally she flung the now empty tin to the floor in exasperation. Richard jerked to one side to avoid the tin as he watched it bounce on the lino. His mother just stood there looking at the wall. "Just look at it. I've tried so hard to make this place look nice and look what happens. You come along and without any thought for me or anyone else, just wipe your stupid hands all over it.

Richard felt only partly aggrieved over this. It wasn't that he didn't care, or was deliberately careless; but just that he had a lot on his mind when he had entered the kitchen with the crabs, which he could hear scrabbling around in the sink. He had already said he was sorry – and he really was – what more could he do? There had been no malicious intent on his part, it had just happened that something he normally did ever day had had some unforeseen consequences. "I'm sorry," he repeated, trying to put into those two words the fact that he really regretted what had happened. Not because he knew further punishment was to come but because he really hadn't meant to have done it.

His mother turned as he spoke those words, which brought her out of her reverie. "Sorry? Sorry! Oh yes, you'll be sorry all right." Getting hold of Richard with her left hand she slapped him hard round the head, back and forth. Richard closed his eyes, as with his back forced against the door jamb, his head jerked first one way and then the other as each blow landed. After a few times he mother stopped since her hand was beginning to hurt. She shook Richard until he opened his eyes. "Don't you dare move." Richard could only nod in response as he tried to reorientate himself, watching dimly as his mother left the kitchen and went into the porch to reappear almost immediately brandishing a cricket stump in her hand.

"Right, take your trousers down and bend over that settee." Richard backed into the back room, a tear finally erupting from his eye. He hated being beaten with his trousers and underpants down – it was so humiliating. It was not that it hurt more, he could bear that, he just found it degrading. He shook his head. "Not that, please, I'm sorry, I won't do it again. His mother smiled evilly, pleased that the extent of his punishment was beginning to dawn on him. She poked him hard in the stomach with the cricket stump. "Come on hurry up!"

Richard hesitated for a moment then prepared to do as he had been told, but his mother, noticing the hesitation decided to speed him up. Her anger, far from dissipating, now that the initial shock of seeing the paint was over, was in fact growing and in slapping Richard she had only succeeded in making her hand sore. This coupled with Richard's hesitation finally made the anger, which had been building up, swell up and burst. With a shout of "Do as you are told" she swung the cricket stump backwards and in a slapping motion, using the stump instead of her hand, she brought it forward to land with all her strength on the back of Richard's head. Richard, his hands busy uncoupling the snake buckle on his trousers, staggered sideways under the blow. White spots flashed before his eyes heralding unconsciousness as, before he could anything to prevent it, he fell to the floor, landing in an untidy heap amid the furniture.

* * *

Richard opened his eyes and looked about. Above him, very close, was a man whilst in the background he sensed others hovering. Voices muted, seeming purposely so. He stared as a wave of panic built up, then swept through him. He didn't know who he was, what or where he was. As the seconds ticked by with no enlightenment forthcoming a bubble of fear began to well up inside him. He tried to get away from the man who was leaning over him; but the surface against which his body pressed was unyielding. He began to struggle but seemed to have lost the ability to know how properly to move his limbs. Above all was the overriding thought, 'who am I? Where am I?' going round and round in his head. He knew that the person in front of him was a man but if he knew that, why didn't he know anything else? He felt that the knowledge he was seeking was lurking at the back of his mind but somehow it eluded him whenever he tried to grasp hold of it. The bubble of fear was getting larger with each passing second and was about to erupt from his mouth as a scream, when the man leaned closer and spoke. "Are you alright Ricky?"

The bubble that was about to be a scream burst and for the second time in as many minutes, it seemed, relief flooded through Richard like a torrent as he suddenly remembered who and where he was. The man in front of him was his father, whilst he could hear his brother and sister talking in the background. Richard made an attempt to smile and tried to swallow but found his throat was too dry, to reassure his father, then contented himself with merely nodding. His father smiled in return and looked across at his wife sitting unconcernedly on the settee, still holding the cricket stump. "I think he's going to be alright." When she made no response to these words he shrugged and turned back to Richard. Putting his arm underneath Richard he lifted him effortlessly. "Come on; let's get you up to bed."

Richard allowed himself to be carried upstairs and deposited on his bunk where, after removing his shoes, trouser and shirt his father put him into bed. "Just you rest there for a bit." Richard smiled again in response. He head was beginning to throb and he could feel a bump on the back of his head as it touched the pillow. His father eyed him for a moment. "Do you want anything?"

Richard nodded again and tried to swallow before speaking but found his throat still too dry. He spoke. "Water," he paused, trying to swallow again before adding "please."

His father turned to comply with the request but Robin, who had followed them upstairs spoke quickly. "I'll get it," and rushed downstairs and in a minute was back with a mug of water.

Their father took it from Robin and holding Richard up with one arm held the cup with the other so that he could drink. Richard felt better almost immediately as he drank the cold water then lay back on the pillow. Now that his immediate fears were over the throbbing pain in his head was becoming unbearable. Although he just wanted to close his eyes and sleep, he still worried about tomorrow. He looked up at his father. "I'm alright, Dad," he paused to swallow properly, "honest." Then let it out in a rush. "I will be able to go to church tomorrow, won't I?"

He watched his father frown, as he considered the matter, and noticed the beginning of a negative shake of his head so added hurriedly, hoping that he wouldn't be asked to explain why but at the same time knowing that his father did not share his mother's insatiable curiosity to know what they were doing every minute of the day. That he was, in his own way, prepared to treat them if not as adults, then almost so, "It's important."

His father stopped frowning and nodded. "I'll see what I can do." Noting the look of relief, which washed across his son's face, he knew he would make it possible somehow, if he was able, and provided Richard was well enough, that his son would go to church. He knew how important his singing and the church was to his son who, he felt, had been punished enough for what he had done. Richard had not done it deliberately – he was not that sort of boy. It was only that he was either too busy trying to enjoy himself or perpetually daydreaming, which sometimes made him forget that he, like all of them, was living, in respect of their mother, on a knife-edge. "Don't worry," he finally said, "I'll see to it, now try to get some sleep."

Richard nodded; his eyelids were already partially closed as his father turned to go downstairs, noticing Robin still standing by the door. "Oi," he pointed, "you downstairs," he said, prodding him with a large forefinger.

Robin stood his ground, his face set. "I want to speak to Ricky."

His father, to weary by events to argue, reluctantly agreed, as Robin knew he would. "Alright, one minute – no more or I'll send your mother up."

He left the bedroom.

Robin waited whilst his father walked downstairs then he heard the kitchen door open and shut before creeping up to the bunk bed. He knelt down on the floor beside his brother's bunk so that his head was on the same level as Richard's. Laying his hand on his brother's shoulder he spoke. "Ricky, are you sure you are all right?"

Richard now almost asleep, slowly moved his arm out from under the bedclothes and took hold of his brother's hand. "Yes, I'm okay Rob, just very sleepy, that's all. I'll see you tomorrow." With those words his last reserves of energy left him and he fell promptly asleep.

Robin remained where he was for a moment and with a few tears beginning to run down his face, spoke to himself as much as to his sleeping brother. "It's not fair, Ricky. She shouldn't be allowed to treat us the way she does. It's not right." He waited for a few moments then releasing Richard's hand and putting it back under the bedclothes he stood up wiping his eyes with the back of his hand. He walked towards the door. "I'll get my own back, you wait and see." With his words hanging in the air like a malevolent mist he left the room and closed the door quietly behind him.

Chapter 8: **A meeting – at last**

Richard sat in his place in the choir wishing that the Vicar would hurry up and finish his sermon, which seemed to have been going on forever. He cast a fleeting eye over the congregation sitting in the darkened church since most of the lights had been switched off for the sermon. Some were paying attention; others assumed attentive poses but were in fact obviously dozing, giving themselves away by sudden starts as they realised they'd almost dropped off. Dotted here and there the hardened few had long since given up such pretensions and lightly slept.

His eyes continued to roam until they rested on a group of girls from the local boarding school. Richard turned his head away quickly, shivering in anticipation. He turned his attention to the coloured lights on the opposite wall, caused by the sun shining through the stained glass windows in the chancel as he recounted the events since he had received the letter from Emma. It has been weeks since he had first met that group of giggling girls. Then after Evensong last Sunday he had met the girl with the dog who had said Emma had not been well but would he like to meet her next Sunday after Matins. He shivered involuntarily again and wiped the sheen of sweat that was beginning to form on his forehead. Whatever had possessed him, he thought. The girl with the dog, whose name he could not remember, or perhaps she had not given one, had said that Emma had been watching him for weeks and loved him very much. He wondered, was it true? Would I love her? He remembered again asking what Emma looked like and was told she was very pretty. What if she wasn't? He couldn't just run away or should he? His friend, Barry was no help when he asked him for an opinion before the service. Putting his arm across Richard's shoulder in a fatherly gesture he had said,

"Girls always say their friends are pretty," he pauses for a second before finishing off the sentence quickly, "especially if they are plug ugly."

Richard had walked angrily away, followed by his friend's laughter. Richard now looked across the aisle at Barry who winked, tapped his watch and mouthed 'Not long now.' He looked away, not liking the relish with which Barry was looking forward to this rendezvous.

Richard jumped to his feet slightly slower than the others, as the Vicar intoned, signally the end of the sermon. "In the name of the Father, and of the Son and of the Holy Ghost. Amen."

"Amen." Said Richard quietly.

"Hymn 45, Creator of the Starry Height," said the Vicar before he turned and climbed down from the pulpit and resumed his place next to the choir. Mr Owen played the first line of the hymn and Richard was again able to forget his worries temporarily as he concentrated on singing the hymn, one of his favourites. Even though the service was drawing rapidly to a close he forgot his fears and worries and gave himself up to the music.

The taking of the collection and the blessing followed quickly upon one another and the organ sounded the first note of the music with which the choir would process out of the church to the vestry. The server took the processional cross from its place by the altar, bowed, then turned and walked slowly down the chancel stopping momentarily by Richard and Barry who, now standing, left their places, faced the altar, bowed, and turned on their heels to walk behind the server. The other boys and the men followed in sequence with the curate, churchwardens with the collection plate and the Vicar bringing up the rear. Richard felt, more than ever this Sunday, that everyone's eyes were on him as if they too know of his meeting. Passing a group of girls from Landen Hall he was certain they giggled. Too embarrassed to look, Richard kept his face and eyes fixed on the floor until he saw with relief the steps leading up to the vestry.

Reaching the vestry the curate said a short prayer after which the usual pandemonium broke out as the choristers took off their ruffs, surplices and cassocks, the men just the latter two. Everyone talking at once, voicing their opinion of the service, especially any mistakes in the singing. Meanwhile the two church wardens, having negotiated their way through the seething mass of choristers, sat down at the table and began to count the collection. Richard having disrobed put on his blazer and started to walk to the door, but hesitated reluctantly when Barry cried out, "Wait for me!" as he disentangled himself from his cassock and hung it on Herbert's peg in his rush to join Richard, much to the formers annoyance.

"Do you mind," complained Herbert as he went to hang up his own cassock, but Barry had already moved away to join Richard.

Richard was wondering how to get rid of Barry when they both bumped into the curate who beamed down at them. "Ah, Richard and Barry, the terrible twins, how fortunate. I wonder if you would mind doing a little job for me. No, of course you wouldn't."

Richard, unable to properly believe his good luck, immediately saw a way out of his dilemma. Quickly he blurted out, "I'm afraid I have an appointment to keep, but Mitchell hasn't sir."

The curate looked oddly at him for a moment, then smiled and waved Richard out of the vestry, placing his hand firmly on Barry's shoulder restraining him. Barry scowled at Richard leaving, as the curate turned to him, smiling. He was about to say he had an appointment too but somehow the words seemed stuck at the back of his throat.

As he made his exit, Richard heard the curate speaking. "Now, Barry, I want you and one of your friends to go to the belfry and....?" the words faded when the door closed behind him.

A breeze ruffled his hair as he walked to the gate and stepped down to the pavement. He leaned against the window of the grocers, which was embossed in gold lettering with the words 'Vye and Son' and watched the parishioners coming out of the church. Saying goodbye to their friends and then wending their separate ways home. He stiffened as a group of girls from Landen Hall appeared and then relaxed as they crossed the road to walk down the High Street. He looked up as some of the men from the choir came out of the vestry; some nodded to him then all strolled across the road to the Red Lion pub. In dribs and drabs other boys and men came out, said good morning and went off, some walking others cycling whilst a favoured few got into their cars and drove off, leaving the street empty and quiet again.

The clock on the tower chimed a quarter past twelve, bringing Richard out of a reverie. Only a few stragglers remained, talking to the Vicar by the gate, his surplice blowing in the wind. After a few minutes they too left and the vicar returned to walk back up the path to the south entrance of the church. The disappointment, which had been growing with each passing second, now seemed a tangible weight. Richard stood up straight. He was now willing to admit to himself that he had been looking forward to this moment all week and now nothing had happened. He sighed loudly and looked up at the church clock, the big hand of which had begun the leisurely journey to twenty minutes passed the hour. Walking slowly up the steps he took his bicycle from the wall and wheeled it out onto the road and then stood it upright by leaning the pedal on the kerb. Seeing that one of his shoelaces was undone he knelt down to tie it up. As the other one seemed a bit loose he began to tie that up as well. Richard had almost finished when a shadow fell across him and he noticed that his eyes were almost level with those of a small dog, which he recognised as belonging to the girls from the school. Next to it was a small pair of black laced shoes and knee length grey socks with a blue trim. "Hello," said the girl.

Richard froze for a second then stood up, shakily. Although he didn't wish to, he stared for a moment without saying a word. This couldn't be Emma Wesley, he thought, she was – well beautiful. Not quite as tall as himself, he could see that she had, under her hat, blond hair in a pony tail. Her eyes were bright blue, and seemed to sparkle with a life of their own, as he looked. "Hallo," he replied, then feeling the need to elaborate, "I'm Richard Luckhurst." Not knowing what else to do he stuck out his hand.

The girl smiled nervously and took it lightly in her own. "I know, I'm Emma Wesley."

Richard's mind was reeling both from excitement and nausea brought on by worry, what should he do and say next? He was terribly aware that he did not know what to do or how to act and desperately did not want to make a fool of himself. His problem was solved by the dog tugging at its lead. Emma looked down at it for a moment and then said. "I'm supposed to be taking Marmaduke for a walk," then added in explanation, "it's the only way I would be allowed out so I could get to see you. I hope you like dogs."

Richard nodded an emphatic yes as he looked around. There were only one or two people about but he wished to avoid bumping into Barry. "How about a walk in the churchyard," he suggested lamely. To his surprise Emma agreed straightaway. Side by side with the dog Marmaduke pulling ahead and then stopping just as suddenly to sniff the curb, they made their way up the path alongside the south side of the church, passed the grave of the Kentish Samson, which Richard pointed out to Emma and was gratified by the response of a warm smile. Emma had seen it a hundred times but she was happy just to be with Richard. Across the south entrance of the church and along the length of the church to the west gate and tower until they reached the entrance to the Garden of Remembrance, all without saying another word to each other.

Seeing his first suggestion had not been met with ridicule, Richard was emboldened to make another. "Shall we sit here?" he said pointing to the wooden seat in the Garden. Emma looked dubiously at the seat and then at the dog. Noticing her look, which he took for disapproval, he added quickly, "Or shall we walk on for a bit?"

"Oh no, this is lovely, only Marmy probably won't get any exercise if we stay here."

Richard looked at the small dog, thinking that he wouldn't need much: then pushed such thoughts to the back of his mind. "What would happen if you let him off his lead – would he run away?" he asked.

"I don't think so," replied Emma cautiously.

"Anyway, he's not a very big dog," said Richard, trying not to be disparaging, "if he does run away, I'll be able to catch him. I'm a fast runner at school."

"Are you?" said Emma, who after looking at Richard for a moment, until he began to feel embarrassed, bent over and unclipped the dog's lead. Marmaduke, relishing his freedom, ran round and around the Garden of Remembrance, stopping every now and then to sniff a gravestone or flower. Emma and Richard watched him for a moment or two in case he ran off but when this seemed unlikely Emma relaxed and sat down on the seat.

Richard looked about for a few seconds and then sat down beside her, but not too close, wondering what to say next. He had never spoken to a girl before in this sort of situation and wasn't quite sure what he should say or do. For the moment Emma seemed quite happy just to watch the antics of the dog and this enabled Richard to steal a few side glances at her, thinking how pretty she looked. It was whilst he was doing this that she turned slightly and looked back at him.

Richard, embarrassed by her directness, turned away slightly then looked back. Discomfited by the silence and taking his courage into his hands, he said haltingly the first thing that came into his head. "Haven't you got beautiful blue eyes?"

Emma looked away for a second and began to blush, as for one horrible moment Richard thought he had gone too far, then turning back she said "Thank you and impetuously took his hand in hers.

The ice had been broken and soon Richard was telling Emma all about how much he loved singing in the choir and where he went to school, and then listened in turn as Emma told him about her family and school. The reason why she was at boarding school was because her father was in the Foreign Office and had been posted to the Embassy in India. Richard listened, fascinated, but more than the flow of conversation was the feeling beginning to well up uncontrollably inside him that he was falling in love. The emotion was so strong that he could almost feel it. He had met lots of other girls, mostly his friend's sisters, but they were not like this. This was something special and even though it was difficult, his body being suffused with such a feeling of total well-being, he took great pains to try and remember everything Emma said so he could recall it later on. He also thought carefully before making any response to a question to make sure he didn't say anything too stupid as they laughed together at only something only very slightly funny. But most important, the way her hand rested in his; being held by him as if it were so fragile it might break at the merest touch.

As the thought occurred to him he gave a gentle squeeze and was rewarded by the slightest return in pressure of her hand to his. It was one of those moments he wished would go on forever but if not, as he knew it would not, he would remember it always.

The sound of the church clock striking the three-quarter hour shattered the dream-like quality of the moment. Now, suddenly, all the sounds and the smells of the churchyard assailed Richard's senses; as if somehow resentful that they had been kept away from his awareness.

Noticing Richard's troubled expression Emma asked what was suddenly wrong. She too was happy. After weeks of looking at Richard in church and trying to attract his attention she was pleased that he was just as nice as she had hoped and imagined he would be. "Nothing," replied Richard, "except that I had better get home or my mother will be wondering where I am."

Emma looked at her watch then jumped out of the seat, still managing to keep hold of Richard's hand as she did so. "I must get back to school, as well. Where is Marmaduke?" and she began to call out his name, turning her head from side to side as she did so, since he was not in sight. "Marmy, Marmy." Richard did think about calling out as well, even though he though he thought it was a ridiculous name for a dog, however, his dilemma was solved by Marmaduke appearing from behind a gravestone and running up to Emma who quickly clipped his lead on.

Marmaduke seemed to realise he was on his way home as he led them both out of the Garden of Remembrance along the path at the side of the church and back to the road. Richard, whilst attempting to talk about nothing in particular, was painfully torn between wanting to prolong this first meeting and an increasing awareness that he had better hurry home.

On reaching the gate Emma stopped. Pulling on the lead Marmaduke promptly sat down, waiting, not too patiently, to be told to move on so that he could go home and hopefully get something to eat. "Well," said Emma pausing slightly, "can I see you next week after Matins?"

"Yes, of course," Richard replied, perhaps too hurriedly in his eagerness to see Emma again. Gazing into her eyes he felt compelled to add sheepishly, "I'm afraid that I am not allowed out much, except to go to church, or," he added quickly, "unless I have a good reason for doing so." He paused whilst Emma stood waiting, just happy to look at Richard whilst he continued. "It's just that my mother doesn't like the boys where we live and refuses to let my brother and me play with them, or have anything to do with them." He daren't mention what his mother thought about girls. "So I don't get allowed out much," he finished rather lamely.

"That's all right," replied Emma, "I'm in the same boat so I hope you like dogs because I'll usually have Marmy with me."

"Oh, yes," said Richard, reaching down to pat Marmaduke on the head. He's a lovely dog." Even though he didn't really think so and would have preferred a 'real' dog, something like an Alsatian.

Emma smiled and then frowned as she looked at her watch again. "I really must go, see you next Sunday." Richard had hardly time to nod before she took off, running down the High Street with Marmaduke racing ahead, barking spasmodically. Before she turned into the driveway, which led to the school, she slowed sufficiently to look back and wave before disappearing into the grounds. Richard too raised his arm but since Emma vanished so quickly he doubted whether she saw it.

Richard turned and walked hurriedly to where his bicycle still leaned on the kerb. Everything had gone off much better than he had hoped or expected. Emma was really lovely, but more important, he really liked her. It couldn't have gone better if he had arranged it all himself. Added to that he was filled with elation at the prospect of seeing Emma again next Sunday and who knows, perhaps the Sunday after that; the future, like his happiness, seemed endless. As he sat on his bicycle he repeated her name over and over in his mind, just letting it roll round and around as he relived moments, in the last half hour, of their meeting, again and again.

"That's the last bleedin' time that stupid curate gets me to go up in that belfry for him." Richard turned his head slowly as Barry's words broke into his daydreaming. He looked to see his friend brushing dust and cobwebs off his trousers and jersey as he walked out of the vestry, closely followed by Jim who was grinning broadly. Richard sat on his bicycle and smiled as Barry came up to him. "Just look at the state of me." He paused for a moment to brush off some more dust and cobwebs, which seemed glued to his clothes. "My Mum'll go mad when she sees me."

Richard smiled again. "What happened?" he asked, trying not to grin too widely.

Barry seemed not to hear, so Jim answered for him, "We climbed up the tower to the belfry to get some old church records and when Barry pushed the door, because it was very stiff, he tripped and fell into the dust and dirt on the floor." Jim stopped for a moment, laughed out loud and then, gripping his stomach, continued, "And when he got up he tripped over a bell rope and fell over again into another load of cobwebs and dirt." Jim stopped talking, unable to continue because of his laughter over the incident as he thought about it all over again.

Barry scowled at Jim angrily for a moment then turned suddenly to Richard as he remembered. "Well, how did it go?" He looked about quickly, "where is she, did she turn up, what does she look like, what happened?"

Richard laughed at the rapidity of the questions but at Barry's look of puzzlement he replied, "Yes, she did turn up, but has now gone back to school. She's," he paused, looking for a suitable adjective, "lovely; and nothing happened."

Barry leaned closer, followed by Jim who asked in a confidential whisper, "What do you mean nothing happened?"

Richard shrugged his shoulders. "Just that, we went for a walk and then sat and talked for a bit." Then unable to stop himself from saying it, added involuntarily, "she's beautiful."

Jim and Barry looked at each other for a moment before Barry sighed heavily. "Oh, Gawd, he's in love."

Richard started to blush as this statement but a quick look at the church clock told him he had better hurry home. "Look, I can't stop now; I'll see you at evensong tonight." With that he cycled off followed by the cries of his two friends, "Ricky's in love," repeated over and over, fading as he left them behind.

As he cycled Richard tried to remember whether his Sunday dinner was at half past twelve or one o'clock. He knew that after yesterday's incident with the paint he had been lucky to get out at all. If only the vicar hadn't talked so much in his sermon he could have been with Emma a little longer or home earlier. A car whizzed by very close to him and he realised that in his effort to cycle faster, by standing on his pedals, he was weaving from side to side and it was slowing him down. He concentrated on cycling home properly as fast as he could and soon reached the front gate. Opening it quickly he entered with his cycle and then closed the gate quietly behind him. There was no-one about, neither his brother, nor sister or father. He was still trying to decide whether this was good or bad, when he opened the kitchen door and stepped inside, noticing as he did so that everyone was sitting at the table eating their Sunday dinner.

He looked rapidly at the clock ticking noisily on the window sill. It was just after five minutes past one. Only his brother Robin looked up, whilst the others continued to eat, and rolled his eyes up to the ceiling before tackling anew a massive dough-ball on his plate of minced beef and potatoes. His mother stopped reading the *Sunday Pictorial* for a moment, as she picked a piece of minced beef out of her teeth whilst looking Richard up and down. Having got hold of the piece of mince with her long finger nail she looked at it for a moment then licked it off, turning to Richard as she did so. "So you've decided to grace us with your presence, have you?"

Richard took this as a signal that he could go to his place where his meal was cooling but a look from his mother made him suddenly hesitate even as he lifted his foot. "I'm sorry I'm late but it was a long sermon." The look on his mother's face told him that was not going to be enough. "And afterwards I had to help to tidy up in the Vestry," he lied, knowing it was wrong to do so but better than telling the truth given his mother's attitude when it came to girls. Even if his friends' sisters came round with a message they receive a curt response from his mother and he was always being told off and accused of inviting them round even though he had not done so.

He suddenly realised that his mother was asking him a question but only caught the tail end of it, "... weren't you?" Richard stood paralysed to the spot and cursed himself for daydreaming. Normally it didn't matter but he did it even when he knew that it was important for him to pay attention: like now. He didn't know what was the best thing to do; should he answer 'yes', or 'no', or actually say that he hadn't heard the question?

"Well?" said his mother impatiently, her voice now raised a little. Richard had just decided to say 'yes' when his mother suddenly stood up, stepped over towards him and grabbed hold of his ear and twisted it so that he had to face her, saying maliciously. "You weren't listening to what I was saying, were you?" She paused, expecting a reply and getting none gave Richard's ear a vicious twist that made his eyes water.

"Yes," gasped Richard, "I was."

His mother looked at him, a glint beginning to appear in her eye as she began to enjoy this game of cat and mouse. "Well in that case," she purred, "tell me what I said."

Richard knew he had miscalculated and lost this particular argument. From the corner of his eye he could see his brother Robin moving his head from side to side and decided to own up. "I don't know."

His mother with a triumphant "Ha!" let go of his ear and slapped his face once very hard, making him see spots before his eyes. "Go and stand in the hall. If you can't be bothered to get home in time to eat with the rest of us you can wait, go on, get out!"

His ears ringing from the blow, Richard walked gingerly passed his mother but hurried when she raised her hand as if to hit him again. Reaching the sanctuary of the cold hall he closed the door behind him then breathed a sigh of relief. He crouched down for a moment to ease the ache, which had crept into his leg muscles since his mother, in pulling on his ear, had forced him to stand on tip toes to reduce the strain on his ear. He had crouched down for only a few seconds when his mother's voice came crashing through the door.

"You had better not be sitting down out there or God help you!"

Richard stood up, slowly easing his legs into an upright position. He had to smile ruefully to himself at his mother's sharpness: she always seemed to know what they were going to do before they had properly thought it out for themselves. He rubbed his cheek then carefully felt the bump on his head from the day before. Getting only one slap today was, he knew, to get off very lightly for being late for dinner – his mother was obviously taking it easy on him after yesterday. His only regret about yesterday was that the crabs had been cooked and eaten so he hadn't got any. Robin had told him this morning – without any malicious intent – that they had been delicious, which had made it even worse especially after the trouble he had taken in catching them. He was even more pleased now that he had let the giant crab go.

He sighed and leaned against the wall with his muscles slightly tensed so that he would be able to stand upright at a second's notice should it be necessary for him to do so. Through the door to the kitchen filtered the sounds of his family eating after which he knew would come his turn. For the moment, despite the difficulties he was experiencing, the future now held greater promise than before. Hugging himself against the cold of the hall, which he was beginning to feel, he warmed himself with these thought of the future with Emma, and settled down to wait his turn to eat his mince beef and dough-balls never minding that it would be cold and with congealed fat.

PART THREE: **CHRISTMAS**

Chapter 9: Carol Singing and a VIP visitor

"I've had enough of this," grumbled Jim, "let's go home."

Richard smiled unseen in the dark. It had seemed a good idea when they had discussed it at last night's Evensong. Who could sing better than the choristers in St. Peter's choir? No-one, was the general consensus. Who had been practising carols for the last few weeks? We have. Having established that Richard, Barry, Jim, David and Herbert had agreed that they should go carol singing and two hours ago they had set off in high spirits. Now they were chilled, their faces pinched from the ice cold fog, which seemed to have been following them around all evening. Worst of all, instead of making a lot of money to buy presents for Christmas they had made only a few shillings. It had not occurred to them that in the areas where they had been singing there was little money to spend on carol singers, however good they were.

"It's not fair," continued Jim, having got no response to his earlier complaint, "we've been singing our hearts out and what have we got? Hardly anything!"

The group of boys trudged out of Victoria Avenue and started down Northdown Hill at the bottom of which was the house were Richard lived and the others had left their bicycles. On the right was a field, within which, slightly set back from the road and shielded by trees from the wind that frequently blew over the fields, stood a large house. Originally it had sat in solitary splendour amongst the fields of the nearby farm, until the building of the new council estate after the Second World War. Now one side faced row upon row of identical semi-detached houses. On seeing the large house Barry suddenly stopped walking and as the others, not noticing, carried on leaving him behind, he cried out.

"I know – we'll go and sing carols over there, they must have pots of money living in such a big house." The boys all stopped.

"Over where?" asked David, somewhat querulously. He too was very tired and more to the point, hungry and just wanted to go home.

"Over there," said Barry, again excitedly pointing to where a yellow light flickered through the trees as they swayed slowly and eerily from side to side, as if driven by invisible hands.

Richard looked to where Barry was pointing. Living nearby he knew that the old man in that house was regarded as some sort of Lord of the Manor. Neither he nor his family mixed with their neighbours who had been suddenly forced on them. He shook his head from side to side and walked back to Barry. "We can't go there; they might set the dogs on us. I've heard them barking at night."

Barry, looking at his friend, was not so easily put off. "Have they really got dogs?" he asked innocently.

Richard was prepared to lie, if only to finish the matter, but could not. "I'm not sure," he replied lamely, "but I still think we ought not to go in there."

Barry was not to be put off. He was determined to try one more house. It was his last chance to redeem himself since this carol singing expedition was his idea in the first place. "How much have we got so far tonight, Bert?"

"Eight shillings and sixpence farthing" came the instant response since he had been keeping a running total.

"How much is that each? Asked Barry.

Herbert did a quick calculation in his head. "About one shilling and eight pence." Then ignored by the others started checking, using his fingers to help in his calculations.

"One and eight pence," repeated Barry, "we get more than that singing at a wedding for half an hour" he said disgustedly. "I say we try our luck at the big house and then go home. Who's with me?"

The boys all looked at one another and then at the big house, which seemed a bit spooky with the trees being whipped from side to side as the wind now suddenly sprang up and began to drive away the fog. One by one they put their hands up, Richard doing so last. Without another word being said, Barry crossed over the road followed by the others but even he stopped when they reached the five bar gate, which barred their way. He looked about him before saying, slightly nervously to no-one in particular, "I can't see any notices about dogs, can you?"

Richard, noticing his friend's hesitation, moved forward and lifted the heavy iron lever and then pulled at the gate until with the help of the others, the gate squeaking protestingly, it opened sufficiently to allow them to slip passed. Barry and David pulled the gate shut, whereupon they walked as a group to the imposing front door, their feet crunching noisily on the gravel despite their attempts to try and walk quietly. On reaching the door they all stopped and got out their booklets of carols.

"Which one shall we sing first?" asked Jim, trying to see by the feeble light of his bicycle lamp, whose batteries, after the last two hours' use, had just about given up: being unequal to the task they had been called upon to perform.

"Wait," said Richard, "I've got an idea." He waited for a moment until he was sure that they were all listening. "Instead of singing a few carols and then knocking on the door, why don't we knock first just to see if they would like to hear some carols?" From the dubious looks and glances the others gave him he knew they weren't sure that this was a good idea. Just as it appeared that David was going to dissent he added the most telling argument in favour of his suggestion. Looking about him and pointing to the door, "Besides in a house this big we might sing for an hour without anyone hearing. There are no lights on in the front of the house."

Barry stepped back and looked up at the building, then walked around before returning to the group. "He's right you know." The others agreed that this would be for the best and then all looked at Richard.

Richard looked back. "I didn't mean that I would be the one...." he trailed off, knowing it was useless to try and persuade any of the others to perform the task. Walking the few steps to the door he lifted the knocker and then gently let it down again so that it did not bang too hard.

In exasperation, now that the decision had been made, Barry stepped forward and with a "Harder, you twit!" banged the knocker hard twice on the door. The noise it made surprised even him so that he stepped back a pace. On hearing footsteps from within he stepped back again, leaving Richard isolated by the door.

Someone must have flicked a switch inside the house for suddenly Richard found himself bathed in light. Before he could adjust to this properly, his eyes blinking rapidly, the door opened and he found himself looking into the face of a woman, who looked about the same age as his mother. She looked down at him and smiled.

"Yes, what can I do for you?"

Richard swallowed convulsively but taking his failing courage in both hands replied, "We were wondering if you would like to hear some Christmas carols."

The woman lifted her face and looked over Richard's head, and seeing no-one else, said bemusedly, "Who's we?"

Richard stared at her uncomprehendingly for a moment and then gestured with his arm where he thought his friends were standing. Noticing that not only had she retained her original smile but that it was getting bigger, he turned around and realised that he was alone. Stepping back from the door he saw his friends lined up against the wall of the house trying unsuccessfully to merge with the ivy. With an angry gesture he waved them out and watched as they came reluctantly into the light.

The woman laughed as they emerged one by one. "Hold on a moment, I'll just go and see." And with that she turned on her heel and leaving the door slightly ajar, walked to the back of the house.

When her footsteps had receded sufficiently Richard turned angrily on his friends. "What do you think you're playing at?" he demanded. "I felt a right idiot there for a moment, saying would you like to hear some carols from us with no-one but me there."

They couldn't face him and only Barry said, somewhat sheepishly, "It was just that, well, we didn't know, did we? Anything might have happened." He trailed off then in an effort to justify their action, "They might have set the dogs on us."

Richard turned away, his retort dying on his lips as the sound of footsteps heralded the imminent return of the woman. Opening the door she leaned out and looked at Richard, now surrounded by his friends. "Yes we would." All save Richard sighed with relief. "If you follow the wall of the house round to the back I will meet you there." With that she closed the door with a solid clunk. As quickly as it had come on, the light went out.

Richard turned and led the others around the side of the house until reaching the back they came across a paved area surrounded by a small wall with columns. A few steps led down to a large expanse of lawn, which was surrounded in turn by various shrubs and small trees before this led in turn to the large trees that surrounded the ground and protected the house from the wild winds, which blew across the miles of open fields. Having hesitated at the edge of the paved area Richard now led his contingent of choristers to the French windows set in the wall. Although the curtains were drawn shut some light showed brightly at the top and bottom. There they waited.

Without warning the curtains were drawn back and the woman who had answered the front door unlocked one of the French windows and left it ajar. With a sprightly "Whenever you're ready" she went and sat on one of two armchairs set by the fire, facing them. Giving Richard an encouraging nod she leant forward and spoke to someone in the other chair. Richard looked and noticed that an old man, much older than the woman, sat there. As the chairback was so high he couldn't see much other than thin white hair on a balding head and a tweed-coated right arm with a claw-like hand clutching a pipe.

Richard was drawn from his reverie back to the group by Barry's whispered, "What shall we sing first? How about 'O come all you faithful', or..." he looked through his carol booklet muttering to himself.

In a flash of inspiration Richard knew what they should do. "Listen," he said, "this is going to be the last for tonight, right?"

They all nodded save Jim, who said "for any night."

"OK," replied Richard, "well why don't we just sing all the carols from the Nine Lessons and Carols service, including all the solos and descants?" The others looked around at each other echoing agreement. "Right then, we'll start with 'Once in Royal David City' with me singing the solo for the first, third and fifth verses then we go through the rest as practised." The others nodded their agreement. Taking a tuning-fork out of his pocket he first hit it and then placed it against the wall, where it gave of its faint note. "Hum." They all hummed until they were satisfied they had obtained the right pitch.

Richard cleared his throat, swallowed and began to sing his solo, his voice cutting through the night so perfectly that even the wind appeared to drop and the trees stop swaying as if to hear the carol better.

The yellow light from the room illuminated their faces and carol booklets as the boys strived to achieve the perfection that Mr Owen had been demanding at choir practice these last few weeks. That first carol having ended they sang their way through the list for the service of Nine Lessons and Carols, which was to be sung the first Sunday after Christmas, and a few more; 'Away in a Manger', 'While Shepherds Watched', 'Silent Night', 'Holly and the Ivy', 'Unto us a boy is born'. All these, until after half an hour by common consent the broke into 'We wish you a merry Christmas', finishing on a crescendo, which echoed round their heads until finally fading into the now cloudless sky.

The silence spread and they wondered whether they should have sung a few more. Barry held up his carol booklet questioningly, but Richard, seeing the lady getting up from her seat, taking something from the mantelpiece and then walking towards him, shook his head briefly once. The woman approached the French windows and then stopped. Leaning forward she held her hand out to Richard and put something in it saying, "Thank you that was beautifully sung. A Merry Christmas to you all."

Richard looked up from his hand, his fingers tight around the money. "Thank you very much, Merry Christmas," he replied. His friends too, all chipped in, "Merry Christmas, ma'am," they chorused then turned and walked back the way they had come.

The woman at the window nodded and smiled her thanks to them all as they disappeared around the corner of the house and listened for a moment as their footsteps on the gravel gradually faded. Then with a sigh she closed and locked the French windows and pulled the heavy velvet curtains together. Turning she walked back into the centre of the room and sat on the floor in front of the fire next to the old man in the chair, whose pipe had gone out unnoticed. Reaching up she patted her father's hand, which distracted him from watching the flames in the fire. Turning his watery eyes on his daughter he took his pipe from his mouth with his left hand and spoke in a soft voice, so fragile.

That," he hesitated, wishing and needing, to get it right first time, "that was beautiful." The woman looked up from gazing at the flames in the fire as he continued, "I remember....I remember when Jean and I at Christmas used to...", but he couldn't go on as he thought of his wife, now dead, and returned his gaze to the fire.

The woman taking his right hand in hers said, "I know," and gave his hand a squeeze, which was returned faintly. The woman turned her head to where, if it had not been for the walls of the house, she would have been able to see the boys departing. 'Thank you for calling this night', she thought and repeated to herself, thank you, then turned back and sat quietly with her ailing father and watched the flames in the dying fire.

Outside the boys reached the gate without saying a word to each other. After going through it they shut it quietly and crossed the road. Barry could stand the waiting no longer. "How much did we get then?" he blurted out as Richard stopped under a lamppost surrounded by the others. Without a word Richard opened his hand and the boys could see that he had a pound note. Barry leaned forward and snatched it out of his friend's hand. Opening it to the light he exclaimed, not fully believing it, "A pound, we're rich, a pound".

The boys in turn handled the money before returning it to Richard, whilst Jim said, "a pound, we should have gone there first."

All of them chorused their agreement, and then silence ensued whilst each contemplated what should happen next. "What time is it?" Richard asked no-one in particular, but knowing that Barry was the only one with a watch.

Barry pulled up the sleeve of his coat and squinted at the dial of his watch under the street light. Looking up at the light he frowned, then remarked, "It's about as dim as a Toc H lamp," then looked down at his watch before saying, "It's almost half past seven."

Richard sucked in his breath; he was out later than he said he would be. "I'd better get home," he said, "who wants to hold on to the money until we can divide it up?"

"How much have we got altogether?" asked Jim to Herbert.

Taking the proffered pound note from Richard, Herbert said importantly, "One pound, Eight shillings and sixpence farthing." David sucked in his breath at such wealth as Jim spoke again, "What is that each?" All five did the sum in their heads to work out the exact amount. As expected by the others Herbert came up with the answer first. "Well, it's five shillings and eight pence for all of us, which leaves tuppence farthing so four can have a ha'penny and one the farthing." He stopped, watching their faces. "Well I can't break it down any more than that!"

Richard looked at him. "I'll take the farthing, "he said and noticed the relieved looks on the other's faces. All save Barry, who said,

"No, I'll have it – what's the difference."

Richard grinned at his friend, who smiled back, for a moment before saying, "We can't split the money up now. Herbert, can your dad divide it up for us?" Herbert nodded in reply. "OK, you keep it all and we can share it all out tomorrow when we go carol singing with the choir at Haine Isolation Hospital, OK?" Everyone chorused their agreement and watched carefully whilst Herbert pocketed the money, making sure he did not drop any of it.

Herbert, having done so safely, the boys walked leisurely down the hill to Richard's house to collect their bicycles. There Herbert, Jim and David said goodnight and cycled off to their various homes, leaving Richard and Barry behind.

After a few moments silence Barry sighed, "Oh well, I suppose I had better be going home now," he said, wanting really to stay a bit longer so he could ask Richard what had happened when he had last met Emma but being reluctant to do so knowing that Richard liked to keep such things to himself.

"I'll see you tomorrow," said Richard, closing the gate, and then looked round as Barry exclaimed.

"What on earth is your brother doing?"

Richard turned to see Robin silhouetted against the window making urgent gestures for him to come in. Richard turned back to face the road. He had noticed the large black car parked outside the house, which he vaguely recognised as belonging to Mrs Mackenzie from the local Rotary and WVS.

"I had better go in, see you tomorrow."

With that Richard turned and with a brief wave of his hand jogged quickly along the path, which ran down the side of the house and disappeared into the porch.

Barry watched him go and then waved to Robin who, having waved back, disappeared from view. The light in that room went out, leaving the front of the house in darkness. Taking his gloves from his saddlebag Barry put them on, feeling lonely again. As the only child of elderly parents he missed having his friends around him, even when he knew he would see them again soon. If only I had a brother like Richard, or the others did. Seating himself more securely on the saddle he leaned on the pedals and cycled off down the hill towards St Peter's roundabout and the fish and chip shop where, he had decided, he would buy a saveloy before returning home.

* * *

Even before he had opened the kitchen door Richard could hear his mother's voice, artificially loud with nervousness and faintly fawning. He stepped out of his shoes before entering the kitchen, leaving them behind in the porch for the spiders to nest in.

His arrival being instantly noticed by his mother, who announced his presence, "Ah, here he is the little scallywag." She looked at Mrs Mackenzie who had turned round to smile at Richard who smiled back. "Out all hours singing carols with his friends so he can buy presents for Christmas." She beckoned to Richard to come into the room. "Come and say hullo to Mrs Mackenzie."

Richard moved into the room noticing several things at once. The fact that the best cups and saucers were being used; his father stuck in a corner cradling the delicate china in his large hands raised his eyes to heaven as Richard caught his eye. The box of Christmas delicacies on the sideboard, Mrs McKenzie's snobbish son sitting smug in the uniform of a nearby public school, and finally Mrs Mackenzie herself who smiled at Richard and held out her hand. Richard took the hand in his and shaking it gently said "Good evening, Mrs Mackenzie", as unnoticed Robin slipped back into the room.

Mrs Mackenzie smiled even more broadly at the undue solemnity of Richard's greeting. "Hullo, Richard, how are you?"

Richard, having got the initial meeting out of the way, relaxed slightly and sat down on the vacant pouffe nearby, his cold cheeks tingling from the sudden change in temperature. "I'm very well, thank you." He replied, causing Mrs Mackenzie to smile again at his adult response. His mother too relaxed at her son's perfect performance, which she knew he had acquired from a combination of his going to church, meeting what she considered to be the right sort of people, and her beating it into him.

Having said hullo, Richard sat patiently whilst Mrs Mackenzie quizzed him about school, the choir and all the other things he had been doing. Every now and then his mother interrupting nervously, to Mrs Mackenzie's irritation, when she thought Richard had not made as sufficiently adequate response. Richard, now that he had got started, was happy to answer all her questions since she, at least, seemed to be genuinely interested to see how he was getting on. He also met her occasionally at church. Whenever he did so he had to tell his mother all about the meeting who made him repeat the conversation several times, word for word, until he knew his mother must know it off by heart, in fact better than he did, and probably ran it over and over again in her mind until the next time.

Finally the questions ran out and after consulting her expensive looking watch Mrs Mackenzie brought the visit to an end. As she stood up so did the Luckhurst family en masse, bringing a hint of a smile to Mrs Mackenzie's lips. Saying goodbye in turn to Robin, Marilyn and Richard's father, then after shaking hands with Richard she turned to go: her son smiling and nodding each time echoing his mother's farewell.

When all this had been completed Richard's mother spoke, "I'll just show you out," and stepping hastily by, opened the door to the hall and went out followed by Mrs Mackenzie's son, where she could be heard opening the front door. With a final regal wave and last smile at Richard, Mrs Mackenzie left the room.

Robin moved to the door and shut it quietly then turned round. A collective sigh ran around the room. Robin turned on the television set. Marilyn collapsed on the settee with a, "Thank gawd that's over for another Christmas," whilst their father fumbled for his tobacco tin and pulling it open took out a thin cigarette he had made earlier that day from the last of his tobacco and put it in his mouth. Replacing the tin in his pocket he lit the cigarette, dropping the match into the fire. Drawing hard on the cigarette he inhaled the smoke deeply then blew it out into the room as he surveyed his family. His daughter looked bored as she dreamed of being out dancing with her friends down St Lo, the dance hall; Robin avidly watching the television, whilst Richard sat quietly thinking heaven knows what. He turned to the fire and picking up the poker knocked away the ashes and spent coals into the iron trough beneath. He disliked the visits from Mrs Mackenzie as much as his family did but at the same time reluctantly recognised that without them, and the goods she brought, it would have been a very frugal Christmas. Having settled the fire to his satisfaction he sat back down and watched the television, drawing, as the seconds went by, with less urgency on his cigarette.

* * *

"Goodbye," called Mrs Luckhurst finally, then listened intently as Mrs Mackenzie's son opened the gate for his mother with a flourish, saying, "After you mater." His words almost lost in a gust of wind as Mrs Mackenzie sailed past. Turning to wave a last goodbye, copied half-heartedly by her son, Mrs Mackenzie got into the car and started the engine. After waiting for her son to get in, and shut the door, she drove off.

Mrs Luckhurst watched the car disappear down the road taking with it, it seemed, the affluence and security possessed by the better-off which, very briefly, she had been able to share, if only vicariously. Mrs Mackenzie's son's words echoed in her mind as she stood there long after the car had gone, 'After you mater.' The words had followed each other as if they were the most natural thing to say. Probably, she thought, through much usage. Quietly she closed the front door and stood in the hall, thinking, then abruptly switched off the light and walked into the back room. Richard began watching the television with the others whilst their dad still drew on his cigarette, starting to feel a bit more relaxed.

Shutting the door behind her Mrs Luckhurst surveyed this blissful scene for a moment. With all the windows closed the heat from the fire was beginning to have a soporific effect on the room's occupants. "Pay attention everyone." Richard, Robin and Marilyn jerked upright at the note of command in their mother's voice. Their father lowered the newspaper he had started to pick up but retained a hold on it. When she was sure that she had everyone's attention she resumed, directing herself particularly at Richard and Robin, "From now on I wish to be known as 'Mater', not mum or mother, but 'Mater', especially when we are outside." She looked down at Richard and Robin, aware of their barely comprehending faces and thought she had better drive the point home. "Do you understand?"

Richard and Robin looked at each other for a moment. They had understood what their mother had said but not the reasoning behind it so it didn't make any sense to them. The safe answer was to agree with whatever their mother said regardless of whether it made any sense or not. "Yes," replied Richard, followed quickly by Robin and Marilyn.

The expression on their mothers face told them that this was not entirely correct – something was missing. Richard thought hurriedly for a moment desperately seeking the right answer. His thoughts flashing here and there in his head, searching for the proper thing to say as his mother said, "Yes what?"

Robin looked at his brother, his face a mixture of puzzlement and alarm. He had, as usual, not been listening properly to what his mother had said. He never did when Richard was around since he relied on him to act as spokesman in any given situation and tell him later, if it was worthwhile, what their mother was going on about. He was worried now in case his mother asked him directly what had been said. His eyes mirrored his dilemma as he tried to attract his brother's attention but Richard seemed lost in his own thoughts.

"Well!" said his mother, making him jump, "I'm waiting."

Richard looked up; he had the answer, at least he thought he did. "Yes, Mater," he replied. Robin felt his body relax. He hadn't realised how tense he had become.

Their mother smiled back warmly and turned to Robin, "Now you." Without prompting Robin replied easily as if he had said it for years, "Yes Mater." Their mother smiled at them, as a farmer would gaze at his prime pigs. "There, that was easy – now make sure you don't forget it, will you?" She waited.

Feeling lightheaded, it took a few seconds for it to dawn on Richard that this was a question. When he realised this he hurriedly said, "No, Mater," which was echoed by Robin and Marilyn. Happy, feeling that she was a step nearer, if only a very small one, to her dream of obtaining acceptance within that upper middle-class community, which surrounded the church and to which Richard, because of his singing, was unwittingly already accepted as an equal, she left the room.

Richard breathed an audible sigh of relief to the obvious amusement of his dad. "What does Mater mean Dad?" Richard asked. His father put down his paper and looked at him for a moment, and then at Robin before replying, "It's what upper class kids call their mother. It's Latin and they call their father 'Pater', OK?"

Richard looked at Robin, grinned and then looked back at his father, "Yes, Pater," he replied, his mischievous eyes full of false innocence.

"Anything you say, Pater," continued Robin, joining in. The scowl they received from their father before he returned to his paper made them burst into laughter. He at least was happy to be known as Dad.

Chapter 10: **Christmas shopping**

"Hurry up and finish your breakfast, then get down to the butcher's and pick up that chicken," said Richard's mother as she walked passed him. This demand was accompanied by a stinging clout round the head from his mother, which caused Richard to jar the spoon that was in his mouth, up against his teeth and then to skid off onto his gums. Removing the spoon carefully from his mouth, taking care not touch the now damaged gum, he mumbled a reply.

"Yes Mater." At the sound his mother returned to the kitchen, "Where's Robin?" Richard looked at his brother's empty seat for a second before replying. "He's in the garden tidying up like you said."

His mother turned away with a 'humph' but not before dragging a long nail through the butter on the table and conveying the large globule to her mouth. With a further "Hurry up, don't be all day," she returned to the back room licking her fingernail clean.

Sighing silently, Richard resumed eating his porridge, which as usual included some of Robin's. Having finished the porridge and drunk his tea he took his bowl and mug and placed them in the sink. First sprinkling the dirty dishes with Surf washing powder he took the kettle from the top of the stove and poured hot water into the sink, then mixed some cold water from the tap to take the edge off the hot. Rolling up his sleeves Richard plunged his hands into the water in the sink and began to wash up – swishing the water from side to side for a while in order to dissolve the detergent.

"Stop playing with the water and go and get that blasted chicken." His mother's shrill voice cut through the air to make him jump.

"I'm just doing the washing up," he explained.

"Don't you dare answer me back," replied his mother angrily.

Richard remained silent, aware of the rightness of his position but still he hurried with washing the crockery and spoons until he came to the porridge pot. Richard reached for it gingerly. It had been half filled with cold water by his father after serving the porridge that morning. Richard hated it when the porridge peeled away from the side of the pot in one piece, like a snake sloughing its skin. Scraping the remaining lumps of porridge from the pot he washed it as best he could with his fingers having to scrape again and again, with his short bitten fingernails, the stubborn lumps of porridge, which seemed glued to the side and bottom of the pot. Finally he was able to rinse the pot out and put it on the draining board at the side of the sink. Pulling the plug out of the sink the water was unable to drain away since it was, as usual clogged by lumps of porridge. Richard patiently cleared the plughole with his fingers, pushing the slimy mass of porridge through the holes in the grid. Having done that successfully; he took a rag from beside the taps on the chipped and stained sink and having rinsed it out, wiped the kitchen table. After rinsing out the rag again he dried his hands quickly on the worn towel, and then hung it on the rail on the back of the larder door.

Going to the hall he took his navy blue raincoat off a peg, put it on and belted it. Returning to the kitchen he took one of the wickerwork baskets made by his father out of the larder, closed the door and walked the few steps to the back room where his mother sat still licking her finger and reading the newspaper. He stood there for a while but getting no response he asked, "Are there any other messages?" His mother continued to read for a moment then looked him up and down and then at the sideboard. Richard walked quickly over to the sideboard and picked up the list and read through it before putting it in his raincoat pocket. Then picking up the money that lay there he carefully put it in his trouser pocket. He turned to go but was stopped by his mother's sudden command.

"Don't forget to ask the butcher for the nice boiling chicken I asked him to put by and tell him Mrs Mackenzie has left some money in my name to pay for it."

"Yes, Mater," replied Richard, and then walked to the larder to get another bag since he knew from the number of articles on the list he would not get them all into the basket he was carrying. Having got the bag, he opened the kitchen door but was stopped again by his mother calling out.

"And get some sausages as well, pork for a change. Might as well enjoy ourselves as it's Christmas and not costing us anything."

Richard mumbled an affirmative, stepping quickly into the porch and letting out a sigh of relief. He breathed in the cold air eagerly trying to rid his lungs of the smell and taste of paraffin from the heater in the kitchen. He would not have minded if it had been possible to open a window in the house during winter but it never was, except in their bedroom. After pausing to watch his breath dissipate into the air he manoeuvred his bicycle out of the porch and leaned it against the wall. Taking his gauntlets out of his raincoat pockets he put them on and walked to the side of the porch. Easing his head around the corner of the porch he saw his brother, Robin huddled up on a small wooden bench their father had made for him and his brother to sit on. Richard watched Robin, who was oblivious to his being there, for a moment, and then said very quietly, mimicking his mother's voice, "Robin!"

His brother jumped up and appeared about to launch into an explanation of why he wasn't tidying up when he realised it was Richard standing there smiling at him. Robin raised his fist and brandished it at Richard's nose. "You, you..." he said but dropped his hand and slumped down once again on the bench. Putting his hands back in his pockets, he looked up at Richard. "It's freezing out here; do you think I can go in now?"

Richard looked at his brother. His nose and ears were bright red and he was shivering a little. He looked about the garden, which seemed fairly tidy to him. "Have you finished tidying up?" he asked.

Robin came back from staring at his shoes and gave his brother a scornful look. "Of course I have." Have you ever seen this place look as tidy?"

Richard too looked around. "Well, I think it's tidy but will she?" Robin didn't waste his breath replying, since his mother was never satisfied with anything they did, and just shrugged his shoulders before hunching his neck deeper, if that was possible, into his coat.

Richard stood for a moment looking at his brother, wanting to stay and talk but knowing that he had better hurry and get the shopping. "I've gotta go," he said at last and turned away. "If it gets too cold I'd chance it and go in. It's so cold out here I don't think she'll come out here and check what you've done."

Robin looked up at this suggestion and thought about it for a moment. "That's right," he said, standing up suddenly. "I'll wait a few more minutes, which will make it about half an hour, then go in. Thanks Ricky," and slapped his brother on the back.

Richard grinned back, then walked to his bicycle and wheeled it out onto the road and set off for the shops at St. Peter's roundabout. There was a cold wind blowing, which made his ears burn and knees and nose cold. He was glad of the protection of the gauntlets on his hands but even his fingers, by the time he reached the shops, felt chilled. Arriving at the butchers he leant his bicycle against the wall, took off his gauntlets, put them in the saddlebag and walked into the shop.

Inwardly, he breathed a sigh of relief when he saw that there was only one old lady there who had just finished being served. Richard looked at the rows of chickens and a few turkeys hanging from the rails in the shop window and then at the old lady now receiving her change from the butcher. Unconsciously he moved his feet backwards and forwards in the sawdust, willing any passers-by who stopped to look in the window to keep moving. He hated going to the butchers at Christmas when some money had been left on their behalf by Mrs Mackenzie, representing the local WVS. Especially when it came to paying and he had to explain to the assistant butcher that it was already paid for. Usually, as now, it was the owner but sometimes when he got the assistant, who not knowing anything about the matter would go and ask, subsequently broadcasting the arrangement to the whole shop. At such times Richard thought he would probably die from embarrassment but he usually survived only to have to live it all again another time.

"Yes son, what can I do for you?" said the butcher.

Richard looked around suddenly. He had been so intent on what he was thinking that he hadn't realised the butcher had been waiting for him. Taking a deep breath he said, "Please Mr Overton, my mum said I am to pick up a chicken for Christmas." He paused for a moment, not wishing to add anything.

The butcher leaned forward, his eyes twinkling. "Right young Luckhurst; let's see what I can do for you." He walked away into the back, saying to no-one in particular, "I believe it's already paid for."

Just as the butcher was about to disappear into the back room Richard remembered the sausages he was supposed to get and cried out to Mr Overton, "And a pound of beef sausages please." Mr Overton stopped momentarily and touched his straw boater with his right index finger to indicate he had heard as he continued on his way.

Richard relaxed, leaned on his the counter and resumed making patterns in the sawdust with his feet and daydreamed – his favourite hobby since his real life at home was so bad. School was finished until after Christmas but he might see Emma as she could not go home for Christmas since her parents were abroad. He thought back to their meeting last Sunday when she had given him a Christmas present. He had given her some perfume, which he had bought with money he had earned singing at weddings. Not that she needed it, of course, but that was what Barry had suggested as something all girls wanted. As Richard's sister was always getting perfume from her boyfriends Richard had readily agreed. Emma had asked Richard to give her a penny before she handed over his present, in order, she said, not to cut their friendship. He then knew that it must be something sharp – possibly a penknife, it certainly looked like it from the size and shape of the packet – but he was not going to open it until Christmas day, although at times the temptation was almost too great to do so.

The feeling that he was being watched finally impinged on his awareness, making him look up. Barry stood leaning against the shop door frame with his hands in his pockets.

"You were miles away then," he said, standing up straight and strolling into the shop, kicking the sawdust before him. Richard was prevented from replying by Mr Overton returning from the back of the shop with a white feathered chicken and a packet.

Holding on to the chicken he gave the packet to Richard. "Here you are, young man, one pound of beef sausages." Richard took the packet and put it into the bottom of one of his baskets whilst the butcher wrapped up the chicken. Mr Overton then handed that over the counter, saying, "Here you are son, one nice boiling chicken as ordered by your mother."

Seeing the size of the chicken, Richard put down the wickerwork basket and took hold of the chicken with both hands. It was heavy. Straining with the effort he turned to put it into the basket. As it was too narrow this would have been difficult but Barry, seeing what was needed, held the sides of the basket apart.

"Thanks," said Richard as he dropped the chicken in the basket where, as Barry released the sides, it lodged tight. For a second he wondered if they would ever be able to get the chicken out again but decided not to worry about that now.

"Strewth," said Barry counting his fingers to make sure they were all there. Richard grinned at the look on his friends face after his narrow escape from being maimed by a dead chicken.

Meanwhile Mr Overton had taken a card out of a box next to the till and wrote on it with a stub of pencil he kept behind his right ear, licking the point of it before writing. Looking up, he said to Richard, "Tell your mum that leaves £2.15s.6d, all right?"

Richard nodded and smiled. "Thank you very much," and, as he would not be coming back until after Christmas, added "Merry Christmas."

Mr Overton smiled back and, tipping his straw boater forward, replied, "Merry Christmas to you too, Richard," then turned to serve another customer who had come into the shop.

Barry walked with Richard to his bicycle and helped as, with an effort they heaved the handles of the basket onto, and along, the bicycle's handlebars. Taking out the shopping list and a pencil, Richard crossed off the chicken and sausages then put both items back in his pocket.

"Where are you going now?" asked Barry as Richard taking the bicycle from the wall, got on and prepared to move off.

"To the greengrocers, Lawfords," Richard replied.

Barry looked up at the sky. It was very dark and looked as if it might just snow for Christmas. "How about coming down the beach?"

"In this weather!?" replied Richard. "It'll be freezing with the wind, anyway after shopping I've some jobs to do when I get home."

Barry knew when not to press the point, aware that probably Richard was confined to the house after being out late carol singing. "I suppose you're right. I've got to go home too, really." He stopped for a moment as if deep in thought, so Richard waited. Raising his head Barry continued, "I forgot to ask, did you give Emma her present on Sunday?"

Richard smiled. "Yes, I did," pausing for a moment's reflection. "I did as you suggested and bought some perfume. I hope she likes it." His face suddenly filled with concern.

Barry smiled at the look on his friend's face and punched him, none too gently, on the arm, "Of course she will, don't worry."

A gust of wind blew suddenly sending a shiver through them both. "I had better get going," said Richard, "see you." Barry nodded as Richard, leaning hard on the pedals cycled off, turning back to wave at Barry, who did likewise.

Cycling part way around the roundabout Richard turned into Church Street and made his way to Lawfords the greengrocers, which was in St Peter's High Street. He knew Mr Lawford well as his son went to the same school as Richard. Arriving at the shop he cycled across the road where he could lean his bicycle against a flint wall. Leaving the basket containing the chicken and sausages on the bicycle he took the other basket and re-crossed the road.

Richard stood outside the shop for a moment, looking at the display. He always marvelled at the variety of colours on show, more vivid at Christmas than at any other time. Bright oranges, orange red Cox's and green Granny Smith apples, yellow and green bananas, pomegranates, cabbages, potatoes, sprouts, nuts and as it was Christmas, exotic wares such as figs and dates from distant lands that Richard could only dream about. He especially liked the dates, which he only tasted at Christmas, and made him think of the Holy Land. As the shop didn't have a window, only a shutter that rolled up and down, the smell of all these wares threatened to overwhelm his senses.

Suddenly Mr Lawford rushed out of the shop, almost running into Richard but at the last second neatly side-stepping him. Pausing only to scoop handfuls of chestnuts into a brown paper bag, he rushed back into the shop with only a brief nod of his head, acknowledging Richard's presence. Richard smiled. Mr Lawford was always rushing about: one of those people who never seemed to be able to relax. Following him into the shop Richard took his place in the queue and looked about him whilst Mr Lawford rushed to and fro; serving first one customer then the next, until at last it was Richard's turn to be served.

As usual Mr Lawford held out his hand and Richard placed in it the shopping list and the money he had taken from the sideboard at home. Although Mr Lawford had smiled at him he seemed, in some way to be distracted. This did not however slow him down in any way and he continued to rush to and fro filling Richard's basket with the items on the list, crossing them off as he did so. At last he was finished and going to the small wooden register he leant on it totalling up the various items. Richard watched him as he did so and was surprised to see him write on the back of the list. Having finished writing, Mr Lawford pulled open the draw of the cash box, placed in the money Richard had given him and took out the change. Turning to Richard he gave him the change in one hand and then carefully folded up the shopping list, which he pressed firmly into Richard's other hand. Leaning forward he whispered, "Be sure to give that to you mother or father, promise?"

Richard looked him straight in the eye. "Of course, Mr Lawford," and put the note in his trouser pocket. Mr Lawford smiled and suddenly seemed much less agitated. "Thank you. See you in church."

Nodding, Richard picked up the basket and with a backward wave walked out of the shop. Pausing at the edge of the kerb he quickly crossed the road and in one motion swung the now heavy basket onto the vacant handlebar of his bicycle. Pulling his bicycle away from the wall he wheeled it into the road and cycled off. As the heavy baskets made it difficult to steer his bicycle properly, he stopped for a moment and put some of the fruit and vegetables into his saddlebag, then set off again, although it was still not easy to cycle. First back up the High Street, back along Church Street, turning left into Northdown Road.

He had cycled passed 'Tucker's' the local newsagent when a thought struck him. Looking round to see that the road was clear, he cycled in a semi-circle, very carefully since it was difficult controlling the bicycle with two heavy baskets, and went back along Northdown Road until he arrived at the newsagents.

A few spots of rain accompanied by one or two snowflakes attracted his attention as his leaned his bicycle against the picket fence covering up the wired boards advertising different newspapers. Looking up he saw black clouds emerging from the tops of the trees at the back of the houses across the road. A gust of wind blew some rain mixed with snow across his cheek and Richard knew that he had better hurry if he was not going to get caught in a storm. Turning up the collar of his raincoat he walked to the door of the shop. Pushing the handle down Richard opened the door, causing a bell to tinkle, then a second time as he closed the door behind him.

Walking up to the counter he waited, surveying the sweets and chocolate bars set out before him as he did so. Along the wall shelves were large jars of loose sweets, including his favourites, pineapple chunks, cough candy twists and mint imperials. Arranged in front of him on the counter were also several small boxes containing aniseed balls, black jacks, fruit salad, and bull's eye gobstoppers. Richard resisted the urge to pick one up and after a few moments a curtain at the side of the shop was pulled aide and Richard recognised Mr Tucker as he emerged from his back room. He was a small grey-haired man with a waxed moustache the long pointed ends of which stuck out rigidly from his face. He had a military bearing, which was at odds with the brightly coloured bow ties he always wore. He looked at Richard and smiled, then marched around to his counter.

"Hallo, Richard, what can I do for you?"

Richard smiled back. "May I have half an ounce of Old Holborn, please?" and then added as an afterthought, "It's for my father."

Mr Tucker's smile broadened at this additional information and he chuckled to himself as he reached down under the counter, took the tobacco from the shelf and handed it to Richard, "There you are that will be 1/6d."

Richard reached into the pocket where he kept his own money and took out half a crown, which he gave to Mr Tucker, who put it in the till and gave him one shilling change. "Thank you very much," said Richard, taking the tobacco and putting it in his raincoat pocket, "Bye," and turned to walk out of the shop followed by Mr Tucker's eyes.

"See you in church," said Mr Tucker as Richard reached and placed his hand on the door handle. Turning his head sideways Richard nodded and smiled then with a quick wave was outside the door and shutting it behind him.

The rain, mixed with flurries of snow, was falling faster now. Walking quickly to his bicycle he wiped his damp saddle with the sleeve of his raincoat, got on and cycled off, precariously at first then easier as his speed increased. As he cycled Richard realised that he had better hurry if he was not to get too wet. The wind blew more fiercely now, so much so that he had to stand on his pedals to get along the small rise leading to the hump back bridge, which went over the railway line. He then freewheeled down the other side, his eyes slitted against the wind, rain and snow that battered his face until it stung. Reaching the bottom of the hill he cycled hard to maintain his momentum as he cycled up Northdown Hill to his house. Although going slower and slower as the hill got steeper, Richard refused to give up cycling. Maintaining his tortuously slow pace yard by yard, he edged up the hill until in triumph he was finally level with the house. Checking first to see the road was clear, he cycled across the road, through the open gate where, thankfully, he got off his bicycle and walked quickly along the path down the side of the house where, sheltered by the wall the wind, rain and snow suddenly stopped, leaving his ears ringing in the sudden vacuum of the elements.

* * *

Richard's father sat on a chair in the kitchen idly reading a newspaper, frequently gazing out of the Kitchen window for a sign of Richard. Spots of rain spattered the glass and a few snowflakes landed at random to cling for a second before melting and running down the window pane. Mr Luckhurst returned to his newspaper only to look up suddenly as, from the corner of his eye, he saw Richard go passed. He heard the porch door open and, from the noises which followed, knew Richard was lifting his bicycle into the porch, taking the baskets off his handlebars and then putting them down outside the kitchen door. Mr Luckhurst had started to lever himself off his seat to open the door when it opened. There was Richard bending down to pick up the bags, which he then deposited on the kitchen floor, stepping in after them. Mr Luckhurst noticed his son's face was aglow from the ride in the wind, rain and snow. His hair too sparkled with half melted snowflakes, which glittered and flashed in the light as he turned. But most of all was the welcoming smile on his son's face as he greeted him.

"Hullo Dad."

Mr Luckhurst smiled in return, and then asked concernedly, "Get everything?" Richard smiled.

"Yes, Dad," he looked around, his face becoming solemn for a moment. "Is Mum about?" he enquired.

His father shook his head. "No, she's upstairs having a nap, says she feels tired."

Richard grinned, "Good." Then putting his hand into his pocket took out the tobacco he had bought and gave it to his father. "Here, Dad, an early Christmas present for you."

Mr Luckhurst took the tobacco gratefully and turned it over in his large hands. He hadn't had a smoke since last night and it was making him edgy but there was nothing he could do about it. He looked up at his son with a conspiratorial smile on his face. It lasted only a second before Richard bent over and began removing the shopping from the bags, which he placed on the kitchen table. Mr Luckhurst put out a hand onto his son's shoulder, making Richard stop what he was doing and look up. Mr Luckhurst swallowed; the love he felt for his son, arising out of this unexpected gift, threatening to engulf him. "Thanks Ricky."

Richard smiled back and got on with his work, saying, "That's alright Dad, forget it."

Mr Luckhurst could not. This was not the first time Richard had brought him tobacco and helped him out in other ways. Watching his son, who he knew was more badly treated by his wife then any of the others compelled him to speak further. He blurted out, "Ricky." The stopped as Richard looked up, and wondered how he could go on, not sure of what he really wanted to say or how to express it.

Richard noticed his father's hesitation, so asked, "Yes Dad?"

His father gestured helplessly with his empty hands. "How is it," he began, then stopped and started again. "How is it that that all the trials and tribulations of life seem to bounce off you like, like," he looked around looking for the right word, "like hail bouncing off a window pane, eh?"

Richard stopped what he was doing and looked at his father. Whilst not fully understanding what had been said he was not surprised by his father's words. He knew, from other conversations he had had with this father that in his Navy days, especially during the war, he had written poetry, which had been broadcast on the radio in Russia, when he was on the Russian convoys. "I don't know, Dad," he replied and shrugged helplessly. "Perhaps I take after you". Further conversation was prevented by the sound of heavy footsteps on the floorboards upstairs followed by the noise of someone stomping downstairs. Richard looked at the tobacco still in his father's hand. "Better put that away before she comes down."

Richard's father sighed loudly and put it into his pocket, reluctant for this moment to end, then placing his hand on Richard's shoulder and giving it a squeeze he resumed reading the newspaper as his wife burst into the kitchen.

"So you're back then!" his mother stated needlessly, glaring at him and looking at the bags of fruit and vegetables on the table. "Where's the change?" she demanded, holding out her hand. Richard reached into this trouser pocket and took out the change, which he handed to his mother, who checked it suspiciously. Unable to find anything amiss, she looked at Richard who was now holding out the shopping list. "What's that?" she asked, sitting down on a chair, taking an orange out of a bag and starting to peel it.

Richard held the note nearer, explaining, "It's the shopping list," he faded under his mother's withering look but having promised Mr Lawford, he persevered. "Mr Lawford wrote something on it and made me promise that I give it to you." He continued to hold it out until his mother indicated with a flick of her head that he should give it to his father, which he did.

Taking the carefully folded note, his father unfolded it then holding it at arm's length, because he was longsighted, read it to himself. Looking up at his wife he cleared his throat and then read the note out loud. "My brother-in-law has just died. Pray for me." He looked puzzled. "What does that mean?" then placed the note in his wife's outstretched hand, who then read it for herself. Richard stood waiting, wondering what was going on, until his mother spoke.

"It's simple, the shop he works at is called 'Tyrell's, his brother-in-law's name, now if he is dead presumably he hope to get the shop."

Richard's father nodded, understanding, before adding, "And if he doesn't he'll be out of a job – like me," he added under his breath.

Richard's mother carried on eating the orange, her eyes far away, and after a moment, his father picked up the paper and resumed reading. Several seconds elapsed whilst Richard, at his place by the door, could stand the waiting no longer and blurted out, "Are we going to pray for him then?"

Both his parents looked at him for a moment before his mother picked up the note and after reading it again crumpled it up and threw it into a corner where some rubbish lay waiting to be taken out to the dustbin. "No," she finally said, "why should we, I don't believe in it and besides he done nothing for us." Looking at Richard she pointed to the bag holding the chicken and sausages. "Get that shopping put away and then go and tell your lazy brother that I want him down here, at once!"

Richard did as he was told. Unloading the chicken and putting it on the stone shelf in the larder with the sausages next to it. Leaving the kitchen he took off his wet coat and hung it on a hook in the hall and went upstairs. His brother was not in their bedroom so Richard tried the bathroom door. It was bolted and he could hear the rustle as the pages of a comic were being turned over. Knocking on the door, he said, "Oi, you-know-who wants you downstairs, so hurry up." There was silence so Richard knocked again, not wishing his brother to get into trouble for not being told he was wanted. "Do you hear me Robin – what shall I tell her?"

There was a further period of silence, which ended suddenly by the sound of his brother letting off a big fart. Richard smiled to himself; his brother had heard him alright. "Well don't say I didn't tell you," he added, walking away from the bathroom door into the bedroom, being followed by the sound of another fart, where he sat down on the side of his bunk.

Chewing a finger nail he thought about Mr Lawford, the note and what his mother had said. He liked Mr Lawford and didn't want him to lose his shop. Standing up suddenly, having made his mind up, Richard walked to the door and listened for a few seconds. Robin was still in the bathroom and his parents could be heard talking in the kitchen. Pushing the door to, but not closing it completely, Richard knelt down on the floor. Putting his hands together he tried to think of how he should pray but not knowing what to say, just spoke his thoughts out loud.

"Dear God, I'm sorry to hear about Mr Lawford's brother-in-law but I hope that everything goes all right and hope that Mr Lawford doesn't lose his job. I hope that it will be possible for him to own the shop now because he is a nice man, I like him and so do lots of people and he deserves to keep the shop."

Richard stopped and thought about what he had said for a few moments, wondering if there was anything else that he ought to add. Not being able to think about anything more, he added, "Through Jesus Christ our Lord, Amen." Then, as he usually did, so quietly only he knew he said it, punctuated the prayer with another "Amen."

Feeling better at having tried to do something for Mr Lawford, he stood up and walked to the window and watched the rain and snow leaping about the sky before falling to earth. Robin entered the room and walked up to his brother, throwing the comic he had been reading onto the bed as he did so.

"What does she want now?" he asked, gazing out of the window for a moment then throwing himself flat on the bed. Richard turned to his brother. "I don't know, do I, but you had better get down there."

Robin was about to argue, that he wasn't going to be ordered about, but the words died on his lips as their mother cried out. "Richard, get down here at once." Both of them froze at the sound as she added, "And you too, Robin!"

The summons having been delivered, the kitchen door slammed shut, the noise echoing back and forth. Without another word Robin bounded off the bed, shot across the landing and started down the stairs, almost before Richard had turned around properly from looking out of the window. Sighing to himself Richard followed after his brother wondering what on earth could be wrong now. Walking down the stairs he saw Robin at the bottom waiting for him to come down, his courage having deserted him at the last moment. He wasn't prepared to enter the kitchen alone. Robin smiling, and with a mock bow; regally waved his brother to the door that he had kindly opened for him. Richard walked through, followed quickly by Robin who shut the door behind him.

Their mother sat on a chair in the kitchen and glared at them as they entered. After staring hard at Richard she pointed at the parcel on the kitchen table. "What's that?" she demanded.

Richard looked at the parcel, which he recognised as containing the sausages from the butcher. Perplexed, he replied, "Sausages?"

His mother continued to stare at him. "Open it," she commanded. Richard did so and found himself looking at a pound of sausages. He looked up at his mother. "It's a pound of sausages like you said to get." The wild glimmer in his mother's eyes sent shrill warnings through his mind and he could sense his brother, who had also noticed the look, move uneasily behind him.

Their mother stood up and, placing two hands on the table, leaned forward. In a voice so quiet that Richard had to strain to hear she said, "I asked you to get pork sausages, not beef."

Richard's heart sank; he had automatically ordered beef sausages since that was what they always ate. Now recalling to mind what his mother had said before he went shopping, he realised he had made a mistake. Richard's mother, taking the silence for insolence, slapped him hard across the face and demanded, "Well?!"

His head ringing from the blow, Richard started to move his hand up to feel his cheek but as his mother raised her hand, as if to strike him again, he dropped it and answered quickly, "I'm sorry, I forgot."

This seemed to mollify his mother who sat down heavily in the chair, repeating the words to herself. "You're sorry, you forgot! Well I'm going to make sure you are sorry. You don't listen to what I say, do you!" She shouted at Richard.

"Yes," he replied quickly, thinking it the right answer at the time but a further slap from his mother, as quick as a snake strike, disabused him of this. "No" he said, just as hurriedly, which prevented further punishment.

His mother looked behind him. "Robin, go and fetch the cricket bat." Richard moved as Robin brushed passed him on his way to the porch as his mother turned her unfeeling eyes on him saying, "Get your trousers down and bend over that chair."

Richard's heart began to beat a little faster and erratically. He had been beaten with a cricket bat before so knew what to expect, but hated having to take his trousers and underpants down. He looked at his mother who stared back unflinchingly. Swallowing, he said, "Please don't hit me, I'll take the sausages back and change them."

His mother's attitude towards him seemed to soften a little. "I know you'll take them back but before you do, you'll be punished." She paused for a moment. "Do you know what for?"

Richard nodded, hopefully, thinking that an immediate reply would somehow lessen his impending punishment, "For getting the wrong sort of sausages."

"No!" screamed his mother at him, "it's because you never listen to a word I say, you're too busy daydreaming; now bend over that chair."

Richard did so, just as Robin entered the room with the cricket bat. Snatching the bat out of his hands she hefted it for a moment then swung it round to land with a solid dull thump on Richard's buttocks. Richard stifled a gasp as at first one blow then another followed without any pause. He didn't bother to count the blows as he knew from experience his mother would finish when she had had enough and not when he pleaded her to stop. His only consolation was that his mother in her eagerness to mete out the punishment had forgotten to make him remove his trousers. Tears had forced their way between his tightly closed eyelids when his mother finally stopped and leaning over, pulled him upright. Noticing the tears she slapped him round the face.

"Stop crying or I'll give you something to cry about; now go and change those sausages."

Richard rubbed his eyes dry as he walked passed Robin to the hall, picked up his wet coat and put it on. Returning to the kitchen he re-wrapped the sausages and went out to the porch and put them in his saddlebag.

"And don't be all day about it either", said his mother as he started to get his bicycle out of the porch.

Richard nodded, not recognising that a reply was required. "Do you hear me?" came the insistent voice of his mother.

"Yes, Mater," called Richard hurriedly, and then taking his bicycle he stepped out into the rain. Any trace of tears remaining on his cheeks was soon driven away by the rain and snow, which spattered his face. Pulling his coat belt tighter round his waist Richard walked out to the road and cycled off down the hill to the roundabout. Roll on Christmas, then we can all get back to school and away from our mother, he thought before he disappeared into the miasma that was the December storm.

Chapter 11: **Season of Goodwill**

Christmas morning finally arrived. For Richard Christmas was never a time of real rejoicing and he was usually glad when it was over. Someone always managed to do something that their mother thought was wrong, which soon made the false gaiety she injected into the occasion disperse quicker than water down the plughole. He also knew, and accepted, that there would be no costly presents for his brother, sister or himself. He didn't mind that too much, but used to hate the post-Christmas comparisons among his friends when they would tell each other what they had received. He was glad that his friends now understood that he didn't get anything special for Christmas and didn't bother to ask him anymore. He lay in his bed relishing these few moments of peace and quiet before the day started.

But thinking about it some more Richard decided that he had looked forward to Christmas this year. He was excited not just because of the solo he would sing this morning, before the choir processed around the church, which was regarded as one of the most important in the church's year. But that he would finally open Emma's present, which lay secure inside his mattress, having been pushed there through a tear in the cover as possibly the only place where his mother would never think to look. He was thinking about whether to look at Emma's present and started to feel under the mattress when he stopped as, without any warning, Robin dropped down from the top bunk and looked at him in the dark.

"Are you coming down, Ricky?"

Richard nodded, "In a minute, put the light on, will you." Also nodding, Robin said,

"Right, see you downstairs." Grabbing his trousers as he hurried out of the bedroom, Robin flicked on the light with a nonchalant brush of his hand down the wall.

Richard sat with his eyes closed for a second until he thought they had become accustomed to the glare, and then opened them slowly. He still had to squint but he was determined to keep his eyes open. He turned to the wall and with his hand lifted the sheet and felt for the hole in his thin mattress where he had secreted Emma's present. It had moved inward from where he had placed it and was now in quite deep. Regardless of the further damage he would cause, he pushed his hand into the mattress, ignoring the faint tearing sound as the cover gave way some more. At last his fingers closed around the small package and he pulled it out just as his father, unnoticed by him, stuck his head around the door.

"Merry Christmas, Ricky!"

Richard started and jerked round guiltily. "Merry Christmas, Dad. What time is it?"

Richard's father looked wryly at the loudly ticking clock held in his left hand. "Half past six." He grimaced. "Better than last year, eh?"

Richard smiled. "Yes, Dad," remembering their father complaining about their being up at five thirty.

"Coming down?" enquired his father. Richard nodded.

"In a minute, I'll get dressed first." His father shivered artificially.

"Right, I'd better get the fire going or we'll all freeze down there." Richard smiled at his father as he left the room and waited until his footsteps had receded a little before he opened his hands.

He looked at the carefully wrapped present for a moment, and then painstakingly opened it. Inside was a small narrow cardboard box and written on the top 'To Richard love Emma,' with a kiss added. Richard stared at it for a few moments then lifted the lid off. Inside was an object wrapped in tissue paper. He knew immediately that it was a knife. Gingerly, as if it was fragile and would break, he lifted it out and unfolded the tissue paper. He picked up the knife, the handle of which was a pale almost translucent blue, whilst each end of the knife was silver. Richard had never seen such a knife before. It was beautiful. It also looked very expensive. He was suddenly glad he had spent so much on Emma's present and hoped that she would like it as much as he did his.

Holding the knife carefully in his left hand he inserted his thumbnail into the indentation in the blade and opened the blade into the halfway position. Having examined it for a moment he pulled it open with his fingers until it locked with a satisfying click. He looked at the brightly polished blade, which reflected the light from the bulb hanging from the ceiling. He frowned, seeing part of one of his fingerprints on the blade and wiped it off gently with his nightshirt until the blade was pristine again. Very cautiously he ran a finger along the blade and thought it felt very sharp: he would have to be careful. Although tempted to try cutting a piece of paper with it he resisted since he had heard somewhere that it blunted the blade. The knife felt good, as with the handle nestled in his hand he turned it round and round, then moved it back and forth one hand to the next, marvelling both at the perfection of the workmanship and that someone should like him enough to give him such a present.

Richard would have done this for quite a while, except he heard a noise from his parent's bedroom. Hurriedly he closed up the knife, enfolded it with the tissue paper, replaced it in the box, then re-wrapping the present, kissed it before secreting it back in the mattress. As quietly as he could he dressed hurriedly in order to get downstairs before his mother. There could be no excuse, unless he was dying he thought, for not getting downstairs as quickly as his brother on Christmas morning; his mother would think it very odd his remaining upstairs at such a time and might start asking awkward questions.

As if for the first time he now heard his brother's excited talking, then the deeper bearlike growl of his father's voice answering questions and giving advice. Tiptoeing to the door in his socks, Richard crept, catlike, across the landing and descended the stairs, avoiding the two steps which creaked. As he went down his heart grew even lighter, buoyed up by the present he had received and those still to come and, as it was Christmas, no porridge for breakfast but cake. It was a tradition he and Robin, welcomed. As he safely reached the bottom of the stairs he was suddenly overwhelmed with sadness that it couldn't be like Christmas everyday of the year.

* * *

Richard looked again at the words of the solo he was about to sing: the first verse of the hymn, 'Once in Royal David's City'. He would sing the first verse unaccompanied in the old vestry behind the organ, after which the choir were to process round the church. He could hardly believe that he had been practising this for the last month. Now it was suddenly Christmas day. Around him the other choristers, boys and men, shuffled to and fro. Occasionally someone would clear their throat nervously although he couldn't think what they were nervous about, he was the one who should be nervous; the church was packed as usual. Christmas and Easter were the only times when you could guarantee a full congregation.

Someone rattled a tin in his ear and he turned to see Barry offering him a Nigroid. Richard shook his head and smiled; he wouldn't have time to suck it before he would have to sing. If he chewed it up a piece might slip down, and stick in his throat and make him want to cough at a crucial moment. Barry understood and put the tin away in his cassock pocket. Unable to speak out loud because of the nearness of the congregation, Barry gave Richard a thumbs up sign. Richard nodded and smiled in return. In the quiet which followed Richard heard the clock strike the four quarters, followed by the hour. Eleven o'clock. The organ music rolled to a conclusion and shortly after Mr Owen appeared at the door. Nodding to everyone present he beckoned Richard forward from the others and then pulled from his waistcoat pocket a tuning fork. Striking it gently on his knuckle he then placed the base on the wood panelling and let its muted note dissipate into the air. Everyone was silent as Mr Owen hummed the note and then looked at Richard. Having practised this for weeks Richard knew the right note by heart. He had been dreaming of and also dreading, this moment for weeks and now it was here.

Richard nodded to Mr Owen who, slipping the tuning fork back into his pocket, raised his hands in order to conduct Richard through his solo. Taking two deep breaths Richard watched Mr Owen's hands as they waved back and forth, giving him the time, which he took up with his right foot and at the command, a nod of the head, launched into the first verse.

The first line rang out clearly and beautifully; instantly quieting the faint murmur that had been emanating from the congregation. As one they strained to listen as the notes of the carol rang out across the church. In the old vestry Richard realised by the end of the first line that he was half a beat behind. Leading straight into the second line of the carol he watched Mr Owen's face getting darker and darker as his hands waved back and forth with greater emphasis, willing Richard to retrieve the lost half-a-beat. Struggling through the second and then the third lines Richard tried to get in touch with Mr Owen's conducting, which was out of step with his own foot tapping by a whole beat and was now beginning to confuse him. Richard decided to ignore Mr Owen and rely on his own metronome in his head and feet. Into the fourth line he leapt with a deep breath and an outward assuredness he did not really feel. Mr Owen too had decided to let Richard get on with it because with an exasperated sigh he gave up conducting and leaning his arm on a bookcase, he rested his chin in the palm of his hand. He glared at Richard for a moment with a combination of disgust and resignation before realising, with a start that he had better get ready to play the organ for the second verse.

Watching Mr Owen rush off, some of the anxiety seemed to leave Richard. His earlier nervousness and tension dissipated as he sang the remaining two lines perfectly. He had caught up with the lost beat, which he doubted if anyone else had noticed; he had not sung sharp or flat and was happy with what he had sung. It was true that Mr Owen had not been pleased but did it really matter where the fault lay for his performance? With this final thought Richard came to the end of his solo and rested whilst the whole choir began to sing the second verse.

Looking round at his friends, Richard noticed that they too had been worried since, now that he had finished successfully, the relief was evident on their faces. He caught the eye of Mr Parker who winked at him, as if to say it was all right. Richard smiled his thanks back and then got ready with Barry to lead the choir out round the church at the start of the third verse. He enjoyed processing round the church, singing. Part of the pleasure was hearing the congregation sing. It seemed to Richard that they always sang a bit more assertively when the choir went passed.

As Barry and he set off, Richard went over in his mind the events of the morning, especially opening Emma's present. His only regret being that Emma wasn't with him to share the happiness she had given. His thoughts were interrupted as they passed a particularly shrill-sounding woman. Richard smiled when Barry made a face as, almost unseen by the congregation; they turned around passed the west door of the church and began the long walk up the nave to the choir stalls in the chancel. As he walked Richard felt the weight of the knife in his trouser pocket on his leg but rather than inconvenience him it made, if anything, his step a little lighter. Just before the morning service he had shown the knife to Barry who had agreed that it was fantastic, giving it envious glances whilst he handled it and felt the sharpness of the blade. As he had watched Richard was torn between either keeping it just as it was, or using it. After a lot of heart searching he had decided to use it but at the same time make sure it would not get rusty like his last knife. Having resolved this problem, which had been nagging at the back of his mind since he saw the knife, he concentrated on his singing and looking forward to his Christmas dinner. Putting his whole being into the last line of the verse he was at that moment singing, '*And He shareth in our gladness.*'

* * *

Even as he walked into the kitchen, out of the wind and rain, Richard knew something was wrong. Robin was nowhere to be seen, nor was Marilyn. Leaving his sou'wester on a stool in the kitchen he took off his wet coat very aware of his mother's eyes on him. The oven was switched on and the air was filled with the smell of the chicken boiling on a hotplate. Outside the rain spattered against the partially steamed up windows, belying the warmth inside

Richard was about to take his coat into the hall when his mother's voice stopped him in his tracks.

"Get in here at once."

Turning, he walked into the back room clutching his wet coat. His father sat watching television whilst his mother just looked at him standing with her back to the fire with her skirt hitched up to feel the warmth better from the coals. Only the muted sounds from the television broke the silence as Richard waited for his mother to speak again. Unconsciously his eyes strove to see what was happening on the television but each time he realised he was doing so he dragged them back again to rest at a point in front of his mother.

After a few minutes silence his mother abruptly let go her skirt and strode passed Richard, pushing him to one side, to the sideboard. Picking up an envelope she waved it in the air, saying, "Well, what is the meaning of this?"

Richard crumpled inwardly at the sight of the envelope, which from having read it so often; he recognised as that containing the letter from Emma. He had left it under his pillow originally but thinking is safer, had put it in a Penguin paperback book on his small bookshelf. He had thought it wouldn't be found there as his mother never read books.

"Well," his mother demanded, looking at him fiercely. Richard didn't know what to say. His mother had obviously read the letter and knew what it contained.

Steeling himself, he replied, "It's a letter."

His mother continued to look at him, her features demanding more but when it was obvious nothing else was forthcoming, she stepped closer and slapped him hard across the side of the face, making him stagger. "I know it's a letter, do you take me for a fool? Eh?" She hit Richard again with the back of her hand on the other side of his face, which made his eyes water. "Who's this Emma Wesley, then, eh?"

Richard stood silent but the lifted hand threatening another blow was sufficient to break his fragile resolve. "She's a girl," he blurted out but when this seemed insufficient to ward off the impending blow he quickly added, "Just a girl I met," he paused for a second. He couldn't say he met her at church otherwise his mother would soon put two and two together and know she came from Landen Hall. His mother would then probably complain to the girl's school and that would be the end of any further meetings with Emma. Also Emma might get blamed in some way. The thought of her suffering on his behalf was unthinkable. "Down the beach," he finally finished.

His mother looked at him triumphantly. "Just a girl, eh?" she said, walking passed Richard to the fireplace. Richard nodded. "Who you met down the beach, eh?" Richard nodded again. "Well," said his mother maliciously, "in that case it won't matter if I burn it then." With that she dropped the letter into the fire where, after a moment's hesitation, it blackened, caught fire and turned rapidly to ash.

Involuntarily Richard had stepped forward when the letter had been released. This had not gone unnoticed by his mother, who now watched Richard as he stood rooted to the spot. His father, seemingly unaware, or not wishing to get involved in what was going on; continued to watch television whilst Richard didn't know what he should do, whether to go, stay, sit or continue to stand. The silence stretched on whilst his mother resumed her stance by the fire. Hitching up her skirt at the back and swaying backwards and forwards.

After a few minutes she stopped. "You lied, didn't you? You never met that girl down the beach?"

Richard remained mute: with the destruction of the letter a little bit of him, like the letter a few moments before, seemed to have turned to ashes inside. If it came to a choice now of betraying Emma who he knew he loved, and being beaten, he would take the beating. He had been beaten before for no real reason, so what was another. Whatever he said he was going to be punished, since his mother had said time and again girl friends were forbidden him, so why bother to say anything? Having made his mind up Richard felt calmer but it did not last long. A momentary stab of fear flashed though him as he realised the penknife was still in his pocket. It now felt overlarge and he was surprised that his mother hadn't already noticed it. If he lost that as well he did not know what he would do. Richard firmed his resolve. What he felt for Emma was something special; about which he was unwilling to compromise or share with anyone. It would always be his to cling to, no matter what happened.

"I asked you a question," demanded his mother, "and I'll thank you for an answer."

Richard looked straight ahead. In trying to sort out his thoughts on what to do he had forgotten what the original question was or if, despite his new resolve, he ought to attempt to answer it. Should he say 'yes' or 'no' at least he had a fifty-fifty chance of getting the right answer and putting his mother off the scent. Unable to make up his mind he remained silent, hoping that the question would be repeated.

"Well," said his mother, "I'm waiting."

Richard knew that time was running short; it was clear that the question was not going to be repeated.

What should he do? His mind was in turmoil, 'yes' and 'no' going round endlessly in his head as he vainly struggled to remember the question. So intent was he in trying to think of the correct answer that he failed to notice his mother who, thinking that he was merely being insolent, had decided to wait no longer.

Releasing the hold on her skirt and with her lips pressed tightly together, she reached out and picked up the broom leaning against the wall beside the fireplace; holding it in her hands so that the brush end was nearest to her body. Taking careful aim she swung it in a vicious arc so that the end of the handle hit Richard full on the mouth with a hard cracking noise. Not seeing it coming, the blow knocked Richard off his feet. Staggering backwards he fell over the pouffe and hit the ground hard with his elbow.

"Get up!" cried his mother as Richard cautiously felt his numb lips, which had been split by the impact of the handle on his teeth. Gingerly, with his tongue, he pushed out what felt like a piece of grit but was, he realised as it fell into his hand, a chip off one of his teeth. Holding the piece of tooth tightly in his hand – he knew not why since it probably could not be stuck on again – he tried to get to his feet. Being dazed from the blow he was finding this difficult. He was distracted by a large drop of blood that fell from his open mouth and landed on the yellow plastic of the pouffe on which he was leaning in an effort to stand up.

"Get up" get up!" cried his mother again, then rained a series of blows on his head, shoulders and back with the broom handle, when he did not respond as quickly as she thought he should have done. Richard's father, who up until now had been preoccupied by the television, turned and seeing Richard defenceless on the floor, called out.

That's enough, Mum – you've punished him enough, he won't do it again, will you?" he asked Richard, who feebly shook his head.

Richard's mother stopped. Breathless, she leaned on the broom for support and gave Richard a kick. "No he won't or else he'll get double next time." She breathed heavily for a moment and then poked Richard with the broom handle. "Get up to your room this instant."

Richard, his head and body still reeling from the blows they had sustained, felt unable to stand. Knowing he better get moving to avoid further punishment he crawled slowly from the room with one hand cupped under his mouth trying not to drop blood on the lino, which would only cause him more trouble. Out in the hall he reached up and closed the door, and then using the door handle as a lever, lurched to his feet. Spurred on by his mother's shrill voice in the back room in case she called him back, he slowly and painfully climbed the stairs. Points of light danced in front of his eyes and he paused for a moment in an attempt to clear his head. He thought he was going to be sick but fought the impulse down before resuming the climb. As he came round the corner of the stairs he saw Robin sitting on the top step.

Richard stopped and looked closely at his young brother. His cheeks were tear-streaked, the left side of his face was red, as if from a blow or several blows, and his nose had been bleeding. Robin stood, then came down the few remaining steps and taking hold of Richard's arm, helped him up to the landing and into the bathroom.

Robin sat on the side of the bath while Richard looked into the small shaving mirror. A piece of tooth had been knocked off one of his front teeth so that it now resembled a fang rather than a tooth. He held out the bloody hand containing the piece of tooth to his brother.

"Look what she did with the broom handle."

Robin could only shrug in reply and Richard looked at himself in the mirror, as unbidden, tears flooded his eyes. What would Emma think when she saw his broken tooth – would she think him ugly? Taking a last look at the piece of tooth he threw it into the toilet, pulled the chain then washed his hands and face. The cut on his lip wouldn't stop bleeding, even when he held it under the running water from the cold tap. Giving up, he dried his face and hands, looking at his brother, his head still throbbing from the blows it had received and his back beginning to ache and stiffen. Trying to ease the strain by flexing his back, but only succeeding in making it feel worse, he sat on the toilet seat and looked at his brother.

"What happened to you?" he asked.

Robin stared at the floor and mumbled, "Nothing."

Richard sat and prepared to wait, cautiously feeling his front tooth with his tongue, which was now very rough and jagged and also felt slightly loose. As the touch made him shiver and feel nauseous he withdrew his tongue. It would be better if I left it alone, he thought.

"It was your stupid letter," said Robin in an aggrieved tone. "She found it when she was poking around in our room and asked me what it was and when I said 'I don't know' she hit me." He paused for a moment, collecting his thoughts. His eyes opened wide as he continued. "She went mad. You know she doesn't like us to have girlfriends or even talk to girls, well she thought I was lying, trying to protect you, and that's how I got this bleeding nose, because of you. It's not fair."

Richard got up and went over to sit next to his brother on the bath and put his arm round him, although he tried, half-heartedly, to pull away, and gave him a hug. "I'm sorry, Robin, I didn't mean to get you into trouble." He then gave his brother another hug.

Somewhat mollified, Robin got up and washed his face to get rid of the blood, then taking the towel from Richard, spoke. "I wouldn't have minded but I honestly didn't know anything about it."

Richard stayed silent. This explained the savageness of the punishment. It had obviously been going round and round in his mother's head all morning whilst he had been at church. He hadn't said anything to his little brother in order to protect him, because he knew how his mother would react if she had found out. Now that she had, it seemed pointless keeping silent about it any longer. Standing up, he took the towel from Robin and draped it over the side of the bath. Beckoning to Robin he said, "Come into the bedroom and I'll tell you all about it."

Keeping his voice in a whisper, Richard told Robin all about his meeting Emma and what she looked like. It only occurred to him when Robin mentioned it that he didn't have a photograph of her. But as they didn't have a camera, nor did anyone else he knew, the thought hadn't crossed his mind before. He put it at the back of his mind; he would ask Emma next time he saw her, or perhaps get hold of a camera somehow and take a picture himself. Yes, he decided, that was the thing to do. He continued telling Robin about Emma and reverently took out his new penknife and, with a certain amount of reluctance, gave it to Robin who handled it with great care, as if it were fragile, like glass. His mouth open with amazement at what Richard had been up to these last few weeks. Robin had just handed the knife back to Richard when their mother called up the stairs, making them jump.

"Robin, get down here at once for your dinner."

Robin shot upright. "Come on, let's go."

But Richard knew his mother better than his young brother. Sadly he shook his head. "No, she didn't mention me."

Robin stopped at the door. He couldn't believe that she would be so mean, not on Christmas day, surely. He returned to Richard's bunk and taking his arm, pulled him off the bed. "Come on, let's go."

Richard resisted for only a moment then with a resigned shrug; replied "OK, but you'll soon see."

They walked to the stairs together with Richard slightly behind his brother. As they rounded the corner of the stairs the saw their mother standing in the hall, her arms akimbo on her hips, her fists clenched. Raising her arm she pointed at Robin.

"Him, not you."

Richard stayed where he was as Robin continued down the stairs, edged around his mother to escape to the front room where they ate on special occasions, to join his dad and sister. Richard stood on the stairs as his mother turned to go, then raising her head, spoke.

"You get back to your room until I tell you it's time to eat; if at all."

"Yes, Mater," replied Richard. With a heavy heart and step he returned to his room and lay down on his bunk, his broken tooth aching anew whilst he waited for his Christmas dinner.

* * *

Richard peered out through the window of the front room, where he had been told to stay. He was not being allowed to join the others in the warmth of the back room. On the outside, the window was streaked with rain, which fell relentlessly from the dark sky, whilst inside condensation, broken only by rivulets of moisture that he had caused by wiping a circle on the window, wended their way first wearily and then with gaining momentum to rest eventually on the window sill. A car swished by, a black blur against the leaden sky. Richard looked back into the room. Around him lay the debris from the Christmas lunch he had been unable to enjoy: torn crackers, pieces of food, the remnants of the chicken, once plump and pleasing, now the thin white bones making it seem somehow obscene in its unwilling nakedness; an empty bottle of cider and two of 'Bing'.

Turning away from looking at the table Richard gently fingered his swollen lip. His now broken front tooth still aching from the blow it had received from the broom handle. As his gaze returned to the window he noticed that, unwatched by him, a car had drawn up outside the house, its shape indistinct and wavering as sheet after sheet of rain lashed against the window pane. Someone has stopped to light a cigarette, Richard thought to himself. He looked back at the mess on the table, which he now had to clear up as a punishment, whilst the rest of the family watched television in the back room.

The sound of a car door slamming made him look back out of the window in time to see someone open the front gate and start to run down the path. It was a girl. For, at first, some unknown reason, Richard leapt to his feet and rushed to the front door. There it dawned on him that it might be a friend of Emma's or, worse, Emma herself. A thrill of horror went through him. Turning the lock he pulled the door open just as the girl arrived at the doorstep where she paused for a moment sheltered by the small porch, to catch her breath. The girl was wearing a navy blue duffle coat on which drops of rain sparkled. The hood was up but bits of her blonde hair were plastered to her forehead. Her cheeks were red. Richard vaguely recognised her and suddenly remembered that she was one of the vicar's daughters. Still slightly breathless from running up the path she spoke.

"Are you Richard Luckhurst?"

Richard stared; things were happening too quickly for him to take it in properly. He nodded in reply then managed finally to speak. "Yes."

The girl looked at his face intently for a moment, noticing the bruised and cut lip and then suddenly thrust out her hand, which Richard, for the first time, saw contained a parcel wrapped in Christmas paper. "Merry Christmas" she said. "It's for you."

Richard looked at the girl again, who name he had now remembered was Amanda. Richard took hold of the parcel that seemed hard to his touch. "For me?" he enquired.

The girl smiled at his surprised and pleased expression. "Yes: Merry Christmas." With that she turned and ran back up the path, pausing once to wave before disappearing into the car, which immediately drove off, leaving Richard clutching the parcel in one hand and waving goodbye with the other to only the rain.

He stood for a moment watching sheets of rain being blown across the field opposite to fall into the front garden and lash against the house wall. It had all seemed so dreamlike. Only the wet parcel in his hand gave substance to reality. Hoping to prolong the moment, he continued to watch and then regretfully he closed the door and returned to the front room.

Richard put the parcel on the table and read the words written on the paper. '*For Richard, Merry Christmas*'. Richard unpicked the sellotape which bound the end of the parcel, careful not to tear the paper. Having done so he looked in and saw the words 'Cambridge Bible. Authorised Version'. A bible – he didn't have a bible. He held the paper so that the bible slid out into his hand. It was protected by a green cardboard cover, like a pouch, with the words 'Cambridge Bibles', lions and pictures of bibles printed all over it. Very gently Richard pulled the bible out of the protective cardboard case, and then stopped. Looking at his hands he was relieved to find them clean but nevertheless wiped them on his shirt for good measure. The bible was maroon with the words 'Holy Bible' stamped in gold on the front. On the spine this was repeated with the word 'Apocrypha', whatever that meant and further down, 'Illustrated'. Richard felt the words with his finger. He knew what Holy Bible and Illustrated meant, but what was the 'Apocrypha'. He shrugged. If it was important he would find out. He opened the bible and turned over the first page.

He could see that someone had written on the page after since the ink had come through. He quickly turned it over and read the following:

Richard Luckhurst
Head Chorister unto the Parish Church
of
St Peter in Thanet

Christmas 1958   *P R Chaderit*
                         Vicar

"Be strong in the Lord and in the power
of His might. Put on the whole armour
of God.

Ephesians 6:10.11"

Richard read it through several times, his eyes misting over as he remembered the conversation he had with the Vicar some weeks back. The Vicar had said that he should read what they had been discussing in his bible and referred him to the right section. Richard had replied automatically, without any forethought or ulterior motive that he didn't have one. The Vicar had paused and looked at him for a moment and, when given the same answer to the question, "Was there one in the house at all", he had told Richard to read it from the church's bible that rested on the brass eagle. Richard had done so and thought no more about it. Now he had his own bible. Richard opened the bible and looked up the reference written by the Vicar and read it through again several times along with the verses that came before and after them. Then, closing the bible he put it reverently back into its cardboard case.

Richard sat down on the armchair and gazed out of the window. The rain was still lashing the windows but he no longer felt so damp and chilled as he had a few minutes before. After a while he stood and, picking up the bible with the wrapping paper, walked out of the room to show the present to his family. Even his mother could not object to his having a bible as a Christmas present. Could she?

Chapter 12: Emma and Evening Prayer

As he leant against a tree in the Garden of Remembrance, Richard reflected on how he had been dreading his meeting with Emma all morning. Although he had been happy to agree to do so, when he met one of her friends after Evensong, but now that the time had come he was not so sure. Only a week had gone by since the nightmare of Christmas day. He had hoped that by the time he met Emma the bruises on his mouth and face would have healed a bit more and not look too bad. He had, much to his surprise, been able to get out fairly easily, having asked Barry to call round for him on the pretext of going to help him with Barry's new rowing boat, after which he said he would stay at Barry's for tea.

He had in fact gone and looked at the new boat that Barry's dad had bought him for Christmas; as he was bound to be asked about it. It was just what Barry had asked for and he took pride in showing it off to Richard. It was about ten and a half feet long and some four feet wide at the stern. Up at the bow was a small locker for storage. It had two seats, one in the middle and one at the stern, a set of oars, rowlocks and two paddles for emergency use in case one or other of the oars was lost.

The inside was painted white with a red outside and the bottom was tarred. Richard was keen to examine the boat and like Barry looked forward to the spring or summer when it could be taken out to sea and they could go fishing. The only drawback was that it was made of solid wood and seemed very heavy to lift. He and Barry had tried it and confirmed the view that it would probably take at least four of them to lift it off the ground and put it into the water. Reluctantly, Richard took his leave of his friend and with another quick word of thanks for helping him get out of the house, and a hasty goodbye, went off to meet Emma: at the Garden of Remembrance in the churchyard.

A cold wind blew around the edges of the tree against which he was sheltering. Heavy dark clouds began to collect and then hung menacingly overhead before reluctantly drifting away without shedding their watery burdens. The clock on the church tower chimed a quarter passed four making Richard look up and then along the path in the direction that he thought Emma would come. It had been agreed that they would meet here. Perhaps she wouldn't be able to come after all, he thought to himself as the minutes dragged by. Nervously he felt his lip, on which the bruising was now a bluish purple colour, and then with his tongue he felt the rough edge of his chipped tooth. It felt enormous although he knew it felt worse than it looked when he viewed it in the mirror.

Pressing his lips tight together as if hiding the bruise would make it disappear, he resumed watching the clouds drift passed the church tower, making it look as if the tower was moving and not the clouds. Voices made him dive behind the tree in case it was someone who he recognised or would recognise him, even though it was beginning to get dark now. Two old ladies appeared from around the corner of the south wall of the church arm in arm; they were oblivious to Richard's form clinging to, and mostly obscured by, the large oak tree. Richard watched them pass by. The drone of the one woman who was speaking taking longer to fade than did the figures, which were soon obscured by the evergreen trees and bushes.

An indefinable sensation on his ankle made him shake his foot slightly. It disappeared only to return even more insistent than before. He looked down to see Marmaduke sniffing his socks. The puzzled expression on Richard's face gave way first to comprehension and then joy as he saw Emma standing a few feet away, smiling at him. He had been so absorbed in watching the two old ladies that he had not noticed her approach. Richard bent down to pat Marmaduke on the head, and then straightened to look at Emma standing there in her school uniform. Now that the waiting was over he didn't know what to do. He suddenly felt nervous and shy as if he were meeting her again for the first time. He called her name and then stepped forward and suddenly was giving her a hug, whilst Marmaduke ran around them in circles barking.

Emma kissed him, pulled back for a moment, her eyes looking into his, and then roaming round his face: pausing to look at the partly healed bruises on his lips. Emma let go of him, a worried and questioning look appearing on her face. "Richard, what has happened to you face?"

Richard turned away, knelt down and patted Marmaduke. He was torn between lying and telling the truth. Emma came and crouched down beside him. "Richard?" she asked.

Richard, relieved that Emma had not been put off by what he considered to be a major disfigurement, decided just to tell the truth, not that many people would believe or understand it. "My mother hit me with a broom handle." He paused, not knowing whether to tell the rest. That he had been punished because his mother had found Emma's letter. Or rather that he had refused to tell her who Emma was, which really led to the viciousness of the punishment.

Emma raised her hand and very lightly brushed the tips of her fingers across Richard's lips as if to draw away the bruising. "Why is your mother always hitting you? You must be very bad all the time, but you're not when you're with me," Emma smiled as she said this and Richard smiled in return, but stopped immediately when Emma cried out.

"Oh, your poor tooth!"

Keeping his mouth shut, lips pressed tightly together, Richard shrugged and waited, stroking Marmaduke until Emma took his hand in hers and led him to a nearby bench.

They sat there side by side, holding hands but saying nothing. Richard felt at ease for the first time since Christmas. His fears, that Emma might not like him still because of his injuries, had disappeared. He laughed inwardly as he recollected the hours he had spent agonising over this moment. The countless times he had looked into a mirror and endlessly touching his tooth as if doing so would somehow make it grow back again. Although, now that it was getting dark the cold was becoming more intense, Richard sat there bathed in warmth as he thanked Emma for his present, which made her bashful, then it was his turn as she thanked him for his. He was happy just to listen to her tell him about her Christmas at school with the other girls whose parents worked abroad and all the things they did to pass the time. Then they just sat there happy both to sit in silence and then talking; it didn't matter which as long as they were together.

After a while Marmaduke, who had been sitting patiently in the cold by their feet, began to whimper. Richard stopped talking and looked guiltily down at Marmaduke, who looked up, his eyes pleading to be on the move. With his free hand Richard reached down and patted him, in doing so accidentally touching the dog's nose: it was freezing.

"I think Marmaduke has had enough exercise for one day." Emma let go of his hand, reached down and picked Marmaduke up and gave him a hug, talking to him softly.

Richard stood up. He didn't want to keep Emma out too long in case she was stopped from taking Marmaduke out for walks in future. If she took him back to the school half-frozen she might not be allowed out with Marmaduke again. On the other hand he wanted to prolong this meeting, even though, hopefully, he would be seeing her again very soon. Emma must have been of the same mind as, clipping on Marmaduke's lead, she put him back on the ground. Then taking Richard's hand they walked out of the Garden of Remembrance and along the path leading to the High Street. On reaching the south door of the church, Richard stopped. He had something else to do tonight, which he did not wish to put off any longer. Emma stopped as well and looked at him questioningly, whilst Marmaduke plonked himself down and yawned, hoping they wouldn't be too long now that they were at last going home.

"I have to go in here," said Richard. "I have to see the vicar." Emma smiled and nodded her instant understanding, which made Richard's heart go out to her. Impulsively he reached up and brushed a piece of hair, blown by the wind, out of her eyes. "I'll see you Sunday?" he finally plucked up the courage to ask.

Emma smiled even wider. "Yes, of course. I had better get back," she added as Marmaduke, finally taking matters into his own 'hands', had stood up and was attempting to pull Emma away. Emma reached up and kissed Richard lightly on the cheek and then hurried off, stopping only when she reached the end of the drive to wave at Richard before crossing the road and running off down the High Street. Richard waited until he could no longer see her properly then with a sigh of longing and relief, stepped into the church porch.

* * *

Richard walked through the open south door of the church. It was time for Evensong, which was due to start at 5.00 PM. He had never been to a weekly Evensong before and didn't know whether there would be anyone else there but he hoped not. Or even if there was it would not prevent him doing what he had come there to do.

He looked about him. The church seemed deserted and somehow empty. All the lights were off except those in the side chapel near the door. Taking a prayer book from the bookcase by the side of the door Richard went and sat in a pew near the front. He opened the prayer book to 'The Order for Evening Prayer' and then knelt down and said a quick prayer. Having done so, he sat back up again and waited and wondered. On the sheet by the door listing the order of services at the time of Evensong there had been written the single word 'Said'. Presumably, thought Richard, there would be no singing tonight. He was stopped in his day-dreaming by the sound of footsteps on the path outside. Holding his breath, so as to hear better, he waited for the steps to enter the church. Though he thought they hesitated for a moment, they continued on down the path to the High Street.

Richard breathed out slowly and looked around him. The old stone Roman style arches, familiar friends, protected him on one side from the darkness of the church, which seemed to lurk like some tangible living force. The faint yellow lights overhead did little to dispel the gloom, whilst a draught from the door made the thick velvet curtains, which hung from a brass railing behind him, to move suddenly which caused him to start. Even though he afterwards told himself not to be silly, since of all the places he knew he had nothing to fear in a church. The only bright light was that surrounding the altar, making the gold in the embroidered green altar cloth sparkle.

In the tower the clock struck the hour, the last note hanging in the air like dust on a windless day. Footsteps sounded in the passage from the vestry then the large oak door opened, closed, and the footsteps resumed. Closer and closer they came until they passed Richard and he saw for the first time that it was the vicar and not the curate who would take this service. He breathed a sigh of relief. The vicar reached the altar and then turned around. If the vicar had noticed Richard he made no sign but merely opened his prayer book and began to read out loud the sentences of scripture.

Richard picked up his prayer book and followed the passages as they were read out, then joined in the service as it progressed from the general Confession, the Psalm, Creed and responses, prayers and collects until the final blessing. After which there was a period of silence during which he, and no doubt the vicar, said a silent personal prayer. As he prayed Richard reflected on how, as it was being read, he had begun to regard that Evensong service as his own. Admittedly it didn't have the sense of ceremony of a sung Evensong, although the absence of singing had originally felt wrong, it had somehow seemed exactly right by the end of the service. The said Evensong was altogether more intimate and profound because of its simplicity.

Richard eased his knees off the hassock, resumed his seat in the pew and waited, happy to just sit whilst the vicar continued to pray. Then he too raised his head to gaze for a moment on the silver cross and then abruptly stood up to face Richard. Beaming a smile at him, he walked the few paces to where Richard was and then sat down in the pew in front, turning round to face him. Smiling back, Richard made as if to get up but was waved down by the vicar.

"Good evening, sir," said Richard.

The vicar replied, "Good evening, Richard, how are you?" Though he smiled, his restless eyes flickered over Richard's face, taking in the now partly healed bruising and Richard's chipped front tooth as he spoke.

"I'm fine, thank you sir." The vicar waited since it was clear that there was more to come. Richard looked down for a moment collecting his thoughts, since it was important to get this right. Raising his head he began at first hesitatingly, then in a rush in case he should forget something, "I, I just wanted to say thank you very much for the Bible. It's, it's the most beautiful present I've ever had and I'll keep it and read it always."

The vicar smiled at Richard's description of the Bible as beautiful, a view he shared, and also at Richard's earnestness. He loved this boy, as a son he had never had, who despite all that he had heard about his home life, still managed to refrain from being either bitter or cynical. "Thank you, Richard." He paused. "I'm glad you liked it." The vicar went on to ask Richard about his family and friends, soon putting him at his ease.

Richard, for his part had always liked the vicar from his very first day when he had joined the choir as a probationer when he was eight years old. The smallest cassock they had available when he had arrived for his first Matins had been five or six inches too long. Mrs Nuckell, whose craggy features and name, belied her true nature and who looked after the chorister's clothes, said that she would take it up to make it the right length for next Sunday but could do nothing before the service. The vicar entering the vestry at that point had resolved the dilemma immediately. He took off his leather belt, which was around the waist of his cassock, and lifting up Richard's cassock to the required height, placed the leather belt around Richard twice since his waist was so small, and let the extra cassock length hang over the belt. Saying, "Once you have your surplice on no-one would see what has been done, and you will not look any different from the other choristers." Richard had been much relieved at the time, as he had been on the verge of tears at the thought of not being able to sing.

Even though he enjoyed speaking to the Vicar, on the rare occasions when he was able, after chatting happily for about fifteen minutes Richard felt he ought to be going, otherwise his mother might become suspicious about where he had been. Taking his leave of the vicar, who said he had another appointment, Richard with a final thank you for the bible left the church.

Closing the south door quietly behind him he stepped out onto the path just as a few spots of rain hit the ground in his path. Richard hurried round to where he had placed his bicycle in the forecourt to the vestry. The rain was falling harder now and with it came a strong squally wind, driving the rain into his face. Reaching his bicycle he hurriedly took his cape and sou'wester out of his saddlebag and put them on. Then wiping the few spots of rain off his saddle he got on his bicycle and hurried off home, hoping he would do so before the full force of the storm was on him. He was not worried especially about getting wet or even his mother now. Emma still loved him, in spite of what he regarded as a major disfigurement, and his talk with the vicar had, as usual, eased his mind. Bowing his head before the oncoming storm, but in no way submissively, he cycled home.

* * *

Leaving his bicycle in the porch Richard turned to shut the porch door, having to lean heavily on the door against the wind, which drove raindrops hard against the glass. Having shut the door he put the hook in the eye to keep it closed. The wind howled around the ill-fitting door frame but still managed to keep out the worst of the weather.

Through the glass panes Richard saw blurrily the trees in the green being blown here and there by the wind. A sudden gust, bringing with it a multitude of rain drops which hurled themselves viciously against the glass and made him draw back in alarm. Taking off his cape and sou'wester he shook the rain off them and then hung them on his bicycle to dry. Unbuttoning his coat he unlaced his shoes and opening the back door stepped into the kitchen.

Heads in the back room turned as he entered and stepped out of his wet shoes leaving them behind in the porch.

"Hallo, I'm back."

A few grunts were the only response as he hurried through the kitchen to the hall and hung up his coat. Having done that he returned to the back room directly via the hall door. Opening the door the heat from the fire and the occupants hit him like a wall after the cold damp outside. His cheeks already glowing from the wind and rain looked like the coals in the fire and with his body trying to adapt to the sudden change in temperature he felt momentarily weak.

His mother and father sat on the armchairs whilst his sister sat on the two-seater settee. Robin lay on the floor in front of the fire and appeared to be dozing, his eyes blearily regarding the television. Richard sat down on the pouffe and move closer to the fire.

"Move your fat head," said his sister, "I can't see a thing now."

Richard looked round. If he was going to get near the fire for warmth he would have to get onto the floor in order not to block the others' view. "Sorry," he replied as he slid off the pouffe onto the floor, leaning on it for support. His sister grumbled about his selfishness but was ignored by everyone else. "Move up a bit," Richard said to Robin, who regarded him vaguely from the floor for a moment, the direct heat at this level having a considerable soporific effect, before reluctantly moving.

Richard waited until everyone had settled down before his next spoke, wondering whether or not it was the right moment, then decided whether it was or not he had better speak out since the outing was next week. "Is it alright if I go to the choir outing next Saturday, to the pantomime?" he asked no-one in particular, but everyone knew it was directed at his mother.

She turned and looked at him as his father asked, "What panto is it this year?" Richard twisted his head around so that he could see his father properly.

"Robinson Crusoe." He looked around again as his mother moved and stretched, then replied to his question.

"Yes, alright." Richard sighed inwardly, pleased that he had been allowed to go since it was the only outing the choristers had in winter. Afterwards they got on a coach and went to the Railway Hotel in Broadstairs, opposite the Railway Station, to have a feed of sausages, baked beans and chips, a delicious combination. Just thinking about it made his mouth water. Richard was suddenly alert as his mother made a further comment in case it was important; he didn't want to be accused of not paying attention.

"The good thing about a pantomime is that it's the only time when sex doesn't rear its ugly head." Having made that esoteric remark she resumed her somnolent attitude.

Richard looked questioningly at his father in response to his mother's statement, one she made every year at this time, but he only raised his eyebrows quickly before he too resumed watching the television. Richard pondered his mother's words whilst he pretended interest in the screen. Although he admitted to himself that he knew little about sex, what he did know did not seem to be ugly. After thinking about it for a few minute he decided that his mother's statement was a riddle that he could not unravel – yet. He decided to forget it. There were lots of things she said he either did not understand or even, with his limited knowledge about the subject in question, make sense. He often wondered if his mother knew what she was talking about. However, he had found out long ago never to question what his mother said: even if it was complete nonsense. She was always right and no-one dared say otherwise. Richard turned his attention back to the television, but at the back of his mind he was thinking about the visit to the pantomime and then meeting Emma on the Sunday. Perhaps next year would be a happy one for him and everyone else.

PART FOUR: LENT

Chapter 13: Happy Families

Struggling with a very heavy shopping basket Richard staggered out of Vye and Son, next door to the Vestry, and got onto his bicycle, heaving the basket onto his handlebars as he did so. He looked around as he caught his breath. Yesterday's snow had almost vanished with only a few scattered lumps of ice here and there in sheltered spots and on roofs that didn't see the sun. He was about to cycle off when a woman who had got out of a car parked behind his bicycle stopped and looked searchingly at him for a moment.

"Hallo," she said continuing to stare. Richard looked back; the woman's face was vaguely familiar but he wasn't sure why: perhaps she came to St Peter's on Sunday.

"Hullo," he replied and would have cycled off but the woman stood staring still. Richard smiled hesitatingly and uncomfortably not wishing to appear rude by cycling off but wanting to go home with the shopping, knowing that he did not have any spare time to talk or socialise and well aware that he would get into trouble if the shopping ever took longer than his mother thought it should: not that she did any shopping herself.

The woman smiled back. "Aren't you the boy who came to our house last Christmas with some friends to sing carols?"

Richard looked at the woman strangely for a moment and then he realised. The big house and the pound note. "Yes, I am," replied Richard, giving his broadest smile. The woman smiled back just as widely.

"I thought so. Well, I'm afraid I didn't get the chance to thank you properly that night but you all sang beautifully, beautifully." She looked away for a moment wistfully as if attempting to make up her mind about something and having decided, turned back and continued in a rush, "I'm afraid my father died shortly after Christmas but he often remarked how wonderful it was to hear you all singing those carols. It made him very happy." She stopped, having said it all.

Richard squirmed uncomfortably on the saddle. He didn't know what he should say in response to this bad news and so just said the first thing that came into his head. "I'm sorry to hear about your father. I'm glad he liked the carols," he paused, not knowing what else to say, then added, pointing to the church, "we all sing in the church choir."

The woman seemed to have recovered her composure and smiled mysteriously at Richard's words. Patting him on the head she said, "I know." Then raising her hand in a farewell gesture she entered the grocer's shop. Richard shrugged his shoulders, thinking to himself that he hadn't seen the old man for a while. Leaning on his pedals he cycled off down Church Street. Although it was Lent, unconsciously at first and then more positively, he hummed and sang a carol to himself.

* * *

Richard came downstairs and then paused in the hallway. Having done the shopping he had been upstairs to change prior to setting off to the vestry for a singing lesson. He had had these increasingly since becoming head chorister and he could now sight read music. It also gave Mr Owen the opportunity to give Richard some extra practise for the solos he had to perform. Richard looked forward to this additional requirement to attend church, especially because of the peace and quiet of the vestry on a Saturday morning. Usually it was just Mr Owen and himself but now and again the vicar or the curate would be there. Either catching up on paperwork or just passing through, in which case they always stopped to pass the time of day with Mr Owen who would sit by the piano, nodding his head and chewing his gum whilst his fingers would be beating a tattoo on his trousers, betraying the fact that all he really wanted to do was to get on with his music.

Richard smiled at the recollection but this dissipated when he also recalled the questioning from his mother whenever he returned from these 'private' singing lessons. She was relentless in her questioning of what exactly happened from the moment he set foot in the vestry until he returned home; and throughout such interrogation would be repeated the same question – "He didn't do anything?" To which Richard replied "No." Then he would look puzzled, since at the outset he was, and asked innocently, "Do what?" It was only after this had happened a few times that he mentioned it to Barry who had rolled about laughing before explaining the reason for this questioning. After that Richard found the questioning even more obnoxious.

His mother's voice, raised in anger, made him listen to what was being said in the kitchen. Though unable to make out exactly what she was saying from behind the closed door it was clear from the tone of his mother's voice that she was in a bad mood, again; Robin often said her bad mood was permanent. For a moment he was undecided whether to go back upstairs or brave the danger and go outside via the front door. He looked momentarily at the door. Although he and Robin were not supposed to use it they did so occasionally when it was the lesser of two evils.

Walking quietly to the front door, Richard turned the small brass handle of the lock, which had the sign of the three legs of the Isle of Man stamped on it. Having done this he pulled, but the door moved only very slightly. Looking quickly at the bolts, to check that they were free, Richard realised why the door would not pull open easily. He remembered last weekend when he had helped his father to put in a thin copper strip as a draught excluder. It kept the draughts out alright, especially the cold north-east wind, which blew across the fields but his father was now the only one strong enough to open the door from the inside. Richard and Robin could only manage it from the outside when they put their combined weight against the door.

Sighing to himself, Richard gently released the handle and then walked back across the hall and entered the back room. The volume of his mother's voice had increased as he entered. It was clear that she was very annoyed about something, again, but what? Richard walked to the window, and looked out at his brother who was throwing their father's jack knife into the ground. He watched his brother for a moment, his figure distorted by the sheet of plastic put up every winter to keep the draughts out.

He made his mind up. He had to leave for church soon so must go outside. He walked quickly to the door to the kitchen and noticed that his father was standing in a corner as he usually did, with his arms folded against his chest. His mother sat across the room, her arms resting on the table, her face set in a frown. Richard reached up and turned the round Bakelite handle of the door to the porch, partially opening it, but was stopped from going any further by his mother's voice. "Richard!" It was a definite command for him to stop and he did so, his hand remained resting on the large round brown handle. He looked around, dropping his hand. His mother's face did not have its usual look of fury on it that it normally had when he was in trouble.

"Yes, Mater?" he replied and waited.

His mother looked up at his father and then said, "Your father has got something he wants to tell you."

Turning to his Dad Richard smiled encouragingly; he was not in trouble after all, it seemed. "Yes, Dad?" he asked. His father's eyes averted Richard's gaze and he looked away uncomfortably for a moment. Clearing his throat he started to say something, then stopped.

"Tell him!" commanded Richard's mother.

Richard looked around in alarm at the barely restrained anger in his mother's voice but found that it was directed solely at his father. Confused, Richard looked at his Dad who seemed still unable to face him as he started talking. Clearing his throat again he began.

"Well, er you know that last night I was talking to you about the war and that?" Richard nodded; it had been one of those few times when his usually taciturn father had been willing to open up and talk about the war. He had really enjoyed listening to his father relate what had happened in the Navy and, when he had really got going, how the war started and why it took so long to end. It was like being there yourself rather than having to listen to a teacher relate it mechanically from a book.

His father continued after a further lengthy pause, twisting his fingers round and round. "Well, I just want to say, forget about everything I said because I don't know nothing about history an' that and never will." Richard looked up, astonished at his father's words but his father refused to look him in the eye, only adding quietly, "I know nothing about nothing."

Richard looked across at his mother and saw the malicious gleam of triumph in her eyes and the smile on her face.

"Right, remember that, Richard, now go outside and play."

Richard nodded his head and was about to go outside when he turned. The smile had not faded from his mother's face, and she had that look usually reserved for when she was beating someone. Richard took a deep breath. "I've..." he faltered under his mother's impatient stare but continued doggedly, "I've got a singing lesson in fifteen minutes." He paused again but getting no response, felt further explanation was necessary, and added, "I've got to practise a solo for Sunday evening."

His mother had furrowed her brow at the mention of singing lessons and now seemed to consider the matter. Finally pursing her lips she nodded her head, slowly. "All right, but don't be late back for dinner."

Richard nodded, "No, Mater." Then quickly in case she should suddenly change her mind, as she frequently did, he opened the door and hurried out to the porch.

Walking out of the porch to the back garden he sat on the small wooden bench their father had made. Behind the other side of the porch, obscured from his view, he could hear the sound of Robin throwing the knife into the ground – practising for playing stretch at school. He thought about what his father had just said. It didn't make sense. Of course he knew a lot about history, he knows a lot more than I do. He was prevented from pursuing this line of thought by something, which flickered in the corner of his eye and thudded to the ground near his foot. It was his father's jack knife. Richard looked round to see Robin's grinning face leaning round the corner of the porch. Worried about what had just happened in the kitchen he did not respond and his serious manner caused Robin to lose his smile.

Leaning forward, Richard pulled the knife out of the ground and looked at it, whilst Robin joined him on the bench. Richard threw the knife into the ground a couple of times and then gave it back to Robin, who folded it and put it in his pocket.

"What's the matter?" he asked Richard, who shrugged in reply. Robin settled back to wait until his brother was prepared to talk, happy in their silent companionship. Whatever was bothering his big brother would eventually come out. He settled more firmly on the bench, leaning back against the flaking paint on the wall and closed his eyes. Sheltered from the wind at the front of the house the gentle sun was blood red through his eyelids and gave him a feeling of security and calm: something that was rare here.

"I've just had a funny talk with Dad," said Richard suddenly. Robin opened an eye to indicate he was listening, then closed it again as Richard continued, "You know last night Dad was telling me about the war and his time in the navy?" Robin murmured assent.

"Well, this morning Mum made him tell me that he knew nothing about the war and history." He stopped and raised his hands helplessly. "How can that be? He fought in it didn't he?" Robin opened his eyes.

"Of course he did" then in confirmation added, "We've seen his medals, haven't we?"

Richard nodded in agreement. He had forgotten the five medals their Dad had been awarded from the war. Four brass stars and a round silver medal. "In that case, why should Mum make him say that he knows nothing about the War?"

Robin closed his eyes again; he had long given up trying to understand his mother. "Gawd knows – I reckon she's barmy."

Richard smiled at this summation of their mother and decided to forget about it since it was also beyond his understanding. It didn't make sense. No wonder his Dad was usually so quiet if every time he opened his mouth he had to go round and tell people he did not know what he was talking about. It would have been funny, he thought, if it hadn't been so sad. Now their father would probably be more taciturn than ever for a while. That's what usually happened after he had been in the doghouse. In that respect he was no better off than Richard or his brother and sister, only it didn't happen so often. Usually, however, it was much more violent. Richard still shuddered when he recollected one occasion when his mother, after throwing all the crockery at their father, had chased him out of the house with a knife but not before she had pushed his head through the glass partition of the front door.

It had been the usual sort of argument, as they had been explaining to a neighbour's son when he had asked what all the noise was about; especially the sound of smashing crockery. The next thing they heard was the sound of broken glass as their father's cut and bleeding face had suddenly appeared through the window in the top half of the front door, smashing it. Both Robin and himself had been aghast at the sight as, waiting there for a second or two – presumably, Richard later thought, to make sure he could withdraw his head without cutting his throat – he had just as quickly pulled his head back. The front door had then been thrown open and their father has rushed out across the garden and down the road. They did not see him again for some days after that but it took a long time for the cuts on his face to heal properly.

The other thing that stuck in Richard's mind for that day was that it was the last time they ever had rabbit stew for dinner. He especially remembered it because, as all the crockery had been broken by his mother in the argument, their mother just put the aluminium pot on the table and left Robin and himself to help themselves. Marilyn was away at the time with their grandmother in Scotland. After eating all the rabbit stew, which had been meant for four, Robin and Richard finally staggered away from the table. It was just as well they had eaten so much, since it was the only meal they were to get that day and the next.

Richard smiled ruefully at the remembrance of that day. The only good thing about those fights was that they usually resulted in a period of relative calm and tranquillity. A normalness of family life – except of course that one or other of their parents would be missing for a while and once Robin and he had to go and stay in a children's home.

Turning to look at his young brother, who had now gone very quiet, Richard could hear the slow rhythmic breathing of someone who was sound asleep. He was of two minds whether to poke him in the ribs, or not, but decided against it. He had never known anyone like his brother when it came to trying to get him out of bed in the morning. He also had the ability of being able to fall asleep almost anywhere. Richard stood up slowly and, although aware that his brother could neither hear nor see him, waved farewell, adding quietly, so as not to wake him, "See you later Rob." Wheeling his bicycle down the side path of the house he set off for his singing lesson.

* * *

Richard usually enjoyed the 'private' singing lessons he had on the Saturday mornings when Mr Owen was free. But last night after choir practice, he had eaten too many apples. He had also had some this morning. Perhaps it was because they were too cold coming from David's uncle's oast house, where the farms apples were stored for the winter, or perhaps some of them were off. Whatever it was the occasional jolt of pain in his stomach was bad enough to cause him to suddenly falter in his singing. He gritted his teeth as he lah'd the few bars of a solo he was to sing tomorrow, then sang them again in a different key. At the end of which he faltered again as a twinge of pain lanced through his abdomen.

Mr Owen stopped playing and looked round at his head chorister who was, he thought, definitely off today. Chewing his gum he eyed Richard for a moment and watched as Richard gently massaged his stomach, his eyes concentrating on his actions. "What's wrong?" he enquired after a few seconds had elapsed.

Richard focussed his eyes on Mr Owen and dropped his hands to his sides. "I've got a stomach ache, sir," he volunteered, wincing as another stab of pain shot through him, making him draw in his stomach muscles in an attempt to lessen the pain.

Mr Owen frowned. It was an important solo tomorrow; the Bishop was coming to give a sermon. With a note of concern in his voice both for Richard and tomorrow's service, he asked, "What have you been eating, Richard, to give you a stomach ache? What's your mother been giving you to eat, eh?"

Grimacing Richard said, "Nothing, sir," he paused and decided to tell the truth. "But last night I ate quite a few apples brought to choir practise.

Mr Owen smiled and nodded, understanding flickering across his features. "Ah ha!" he exclaimed adding "Quite a few probably, well don't worry it'll pass." He began to play the piano again for a few seconds, and then turned his head back to face Richard with a mischievous look. "Right, then. Let's put some words to the music." He paused for effect as Richard looked at him enquiringly. "Sing 'Oh those apples', all right?"

Richard looked at him for a moment, wondering whether Mr Owen meant it or was pulling his leg. Mr Owen played the notes once then waited and turned round to Richard and raised his eyebrows encouragingly. Seeing he meant it, Richard shrugged mentally then, taking a deep breath, sang "Oh those apples."

"Again" commanded Mr Owen. Richard sang the phrase again and again: drawing out the "Oh" before running down the scales to sing the rest. Although at first it was amusing to sing these words to the music, after practising it for a while he found it easier to sing the proper words. It was, after all, a good singing exercise and not just a joke. The only fear he now had was that when he came to sing his solo in church tomorrow he might sing 'Oh those apples' instead of the words he was supposed to sing.

As another shaft of pain reached a peak of intensity, Richard tensed his stomach muscles then relaxed as the pain slowly faded away. He also had a desperate urge to fart but couldn't possibly do so here. He would just have to wait a bit longer. Surreptitiously he looked up at the church clock on the tower. He had been singing now on and off for three quarters of an hour. Although normally welcoming these lessons, in his present state, a combination of a wracking stomach ache and enough excess gas that made him think he would explode if he did not let it out soon, it had become a misery. He looked again at the church clock, which had grudgingly moved another minute nearer the hour. Roll on this afternoon, he thought, when he would meet Barry and Herbert down the beach at Joss Bay to explore the tunnels. Then tomorrow he would sing this solo at Evensong and would be meeting Emma afterwards. Pushing these thoughts to the back of his mind he concentrated on singing the solo to both his and Mr Owen's satisfaction.

Chapter 14: **The Tunnels**

Richard turned his handlebars to the left as he cycled around the corner into Elmwood Avenue from Reading Street. He stopped pedalling and freewheeled down the hill. The wind which blew up from Joss Bay and the sea was channelled by the hedgerows and trees that grew on either side of the road, making it seem fiercer than it really was. The few leaves left on the trees rattled ominously as a cloud obscured the sun for a moment and one or two blew about his face and hair.

He applied his brakes gently and stopped where the trees, which surrounded the buildings at Elmwood Farm, gave way on his right to an open field speckled with chalk; the smell of the rotting cauliflower leaves and stalks left behind after harvesting suddenly very strong in his nostrils. Up on the headland was the North Foreland Lighthouse whose mournful foghorn he frequently heard from his bedroom. It was not sounding now. On his left the golf course, with its greens and fairways, gently undulated down to the cliff edge, which sat as if a guardian of the land overlooking the rough sea.

Richard released his hold on the brakes and, since he did not pedal, precariously maintained his balance until the bicycle picked up sufficient speed to enable him to balance. He gazed out to sea as he gathered greater speed noting that the tide was out and that there was a heavy surf crashing onto the rocks of the wave cut platform. He grimaced as he saw that by being delayed by his mother he had missed the low tide. He looked down at the pungering iron tied to the crossbar of his bicycle. Even though they had not intended to go pungering he had brought his iron along just in case. Richard smiled grimly to himself as he recalled some of the larger crabs that he had pulled from the crevices in the rocks. Especially, he thought, that giant crab he had let go last November.

The bicycle was travelling quite fast down the hill now and, as there was no traffic, Richard swayed the bicycle from one side of the road to the other. The faster he travelled the noisier the wind roared in his ears. Giving himself up to the speed he pedalled faster and faster down the hill until he was going so fast that it was useless to attempt to pedal anymore. With his eyelids slitted against the force of the wind he looked forward to where the road ended at a cross-road with Joss Gap Road and North Foreland Hill before it plunged down a short concrete slope to the sandy beach.

Hardly noticing the jolts as the wheels banged over bumps and ruts in his path, Richard gripped the handlebars even more determinedly. Gradually the hill turned into a slope and then levelled off. As his speed diminished Richard resumed cycling, the calves of his legs aching from the pumping up and down motion as he tried to maintain his speed. He looked quickly left and right as he got close to the crossroads; as he did do tears were forced from his eyes by the wind. Since no cars were coming from either direction he shot across the road, which ran along the cliff top and down the concrete slope to the beach.

Grabbing hold of the brakes as the beach rushed towards him; Richard started to skid and would have stopped safely had his front wheel not hit a large lump of flint partially buried in the sand, which jolted him so hard that he let go of his handle bars and was thrown off his cycle, somersaulting through the air to land with a thump on his back in the sand. He lay there with a big grin on his face, gasping for breath, looking up at the bright blue February sky. A few white fluffy clouds floated hurriedly across his vision whilst dimly, as if far away, he heard his cycle crash into the tea hut, which was immediately followed by a muffled yell of surprise.

He continued to look up at the sky; the thrill of the mad rush down the hill had not yet left Richard. At the sound of someone moving his bicycle he lifted his head as Barry, dropping the bike, walked towards him. In one hand he held a lump of chalk, in the other a penknife; his clothes were streaked with chalk and his face had an angry hue. "Hullo, Barry," said Richard brightly, "sorry I'm late," he paused for a moment scrutinising his friend's face, "what are you doing?"

Barry scowled for a moment then sat down on the sand with a thump. "You stupid sod." He stopped for a second or two, at a loss for words whilst Richard continued to grin at him. Barry pointed at the tea hut, with the piece of chalk in his hand, and then continued, "I'm sitting quietly, waiting for you and Bert and I'm trying to cut this fossil from this piece of chalk and then you come along and all hell breaks loose and I've practically cut the bleedin' thing in half."

Richard's grin began to fade. "I'm sorry," he replied, reaching for the lump of chalk. "Let's have a look." Barry stared at him for a moment but at a further gesture from Richard looked quickly at the piece of chalk and grudgingly handed it over. Sighing loudly he stood up then walked off towards the sea.

Richard studied the fossilised sea urchin for a moment, noticing the vicious gash right across the fossil, presumably caused by Barry jerking away when his bicycle crashed into the tea hut. He stood up, brushing the sand from the back of his shorts but stopping when he noticed that he was marking them with chalk. He looked up and called to Barry, sorry that he had ruined his friend's fossil. "It's not a very good one anyway," he paused and Barry looked up from washing his hands and penknife in a pool left by the retreating tide. "Do you still want it?" At a negative shake of the head from Barry, Richard gave it a final glance before he tossed it aside and after checking that his bicycle was all right, ran along the sand towards Barry; the dry sand squeaking underfoot.

Arriving at the pool slightly breathless Richard knelt down and quickly washed the chalk off his hands. Standing up he looked around and watched the waves running onto the flat rock covered with seaweed and mussels. At last Barry finished washing his hands and stood up. Carefully wiping his penknife blade dry on his trousers he inspected it for wet spots, gave it a final wipe, snapped it shut and put it in his pocket. Shaking his hands to remove some of the moisture he wiped them dry on the back of his shorts before putting them in his pockets. "Shall we go to the tunnels now?" he asked.

Richard turned and looked at him oddly. "We'll have to wait for Bert to turn up first, won't we?"

Barry looked at his watch. They had promised to show Herbert the tunnels in the cliffs left over from the war, since he had never seen them, but he was late as usual. He crouched down and dropped a pebble in the pool then abruptly stood up again. "Come on, let's go," he looked about. "It'll be dark in a couple of hours."

As Barry started to walk off towards the cliffs Richard shook his head. "No, let's wait a bit longer, five minutes."

Shaking his head, Barry turned around walking backwards, waving a torch in his hand. "No, I'll see you up there. I want to do something," and with that he turned and walked up to the cliff-face towards the large holes cut into the cliff.

Richard watched Barry go, and then turned round to look at the sea. He would have preferred to have gone with Barry, but having promised Herbert that they would meet him here he felt compelled to wait a little longer at least. He sat down and looked at a seagull standing on a rock now submerged by the sea so it looked as if the seagull was standing on the water. Richard daydreamed until an insistent noise brought him suddenly out of his reverie.

For the third time Herbert, who had been standing behind him said, "Hallo, Ricky." Richard stood up quickly, slightly startled, and wished he hadn't as his knee joints ached from being kept in the same position for such a long time.

"Hallo, Bert, where have you been – you're late."

Herbert grimaced, wondered what explanation to give and as he knew Richard wouldn't laugh, decided to tell the truth. "I got a bit dirty when I was out this morning in my granddad's allotment, so I had to have a bath." He shrugged helplessly.

Richard bit his lip to stop himself from smiling. "Never mind, you're here now so let's go."

They moved off together as Herbert asked, "Where's Barry, is he not coming?"

Richard nodded his head. "He's already here but decided to scout on ahead." Herbert nodded his understanding and for a while they walked on in silence along the damp sand, occasionally skirting large boulders of wave weathered chalk or huge clumps of rotting seaweed abandoned by the tide.

Herbert finally gave voice to a worry that had been going round in his head ever since he had agreed to come on this trip. He eyed Richard speculatively for a moment, wondering if it was at all wise to voice his fears. Knowing that Richard was the most understanding of his friends he decided to speak out as they reached the dry sand and followed along it away from Joss Bay into Kingsgate Bay. They walked into one of the many smaller nameless bays, which the sea had cut into the cliff face in that part of the coast in-between the main bays. His words punctuated by the squeaking noise of their soles of their shoes on the dry sand Herbert began, hesitatingly at first, then faster, just in case Richard was not as sympathetic as he had imagined.

"Ricky, it won't be too dark in there, will it? It's not that I'm scared of the dark or anything, it's that I just don't like it if it's too dark – it won't be will it?" Richard kept a straight face and clapped Herbert on the shoulder to reassure him.

"Don't worry; it is a bit dark but Barry has got a torch, I've got some matches and there's light for the tunnels coming in from the holes cut horizontally into the cliff."

Herbert smiled inwardly; he knew he must be a bit silly to worry about such things. "Thanks, Ricky," he muttered then with a lighter heart and firmer step he walked beside Richard, who stopped occasionally to examine recent rock falls for any fossils to replace the one he had unwittingly caused Barry to almost cut in half. They moved from one small bay on to the next until Richard pointed at a small cave part way up the cliff which seemed partially blocked by a rock fall.

"Here we are Bert." Then raising his hand he pointed to the holes cut into the cliff above the cave. As black, thought Herbert when he looked, as the empty eye sockets on pirate's skull and crossbones flag. "Look there, and there and there," said Richard, looking down to make sure that Herbert was watching before continuing, "That's where the gun emplacements were during the war and look out posts in case there was an invasion." Richard looked about him then out to sea, wondering what it must have been like in wartime, crouched up there in the cliff day after day. Eyes straining, nerves on edge, wondering if at any minute an invasion force would appear on the horizon: his heart raced a little at the thought. Thumping Herbert on the back, he walked towards the small cave. "Come on Bert, let's go."

Taking one last look at the eye-like caves in the cliff-face that seemed to be watching him, Herbert followed hesitatingly, wishing again that he hadn't agreed to come on this trip and wondering how he could get out of it without saying he was scared. But knowing, deep in his heart, it was far too late for such thoughts.

Reaching the small cave Richard, as was his habit, after examining the freshly broken chalk for fossils moved around the recent fall and into the cave proper. Taking only a few steps he paused, waiting for Herbert to catch up and for his eyes to become accustomed to the gloom. Contrasted with the sun shining on the white cliffs outside it had originally looked as black as night. He closed his eyes, as he knew this helped, and waited until he heard Herbert enter the cave and stumble up to him. He turned away from the entrance before opening his eyes again, not wishing to affect his vision by looking at the light coming in from outside. He sniffed, taking in the cold air, and smell of the sea shore, a mixture of damp sand and rotting seaweed left by a particularly high tide that had managed to penetrate the cave.

"It's a bit dark in here," said Herbert, unable to stop himself from looking round at the entrance all the time for reassurance, as if afraid that someone would close an imaginary door, which would leave them shut up in the darkness forever. Entombed like the slaves and priests buried with a pharaoh he had seen in a film at the cinema.

Before replying Richard looked around; noting the angular shaped walls and ceiling resulting from the odd-shaped chunks of chalk which had dropped off in the past; some of which now lay partially buried by broken chalk. "It's not too bad," he replied, his eyes now accustomed to the gloom, "Come on, let's go." Richard moved forward and started to climb a steep hill of compressed fallen chalk which, from where Herbert remained standing, seemed to lead right up to the roof of the cave.

"It's a dead end," he replied causing Richard to pause.

"No it's not, come up and see." Richard resumed climbing easily up the mound.

Although originally made of loose chalk tunnelled out of the cliff the mound had over the years solidified into one large mass. Richard reached the top and, as it was only about three feet from the roof, remained crouched down waiting for Herbert to climb up. As he was waiting he looked down the other side. A shallow slope for about nine feet was stopped abruptly by a brick wall; part of which had been broken down to allow them to have access. He turned as, puffing loudly, Herbert reached the top. He was not very athletic and even the smallest amount of exertion left him winded. Richard waited until Herbert seemed to have caught his breath then asked,

"OK Bert? The rest of it is not so difficult." Herbert looked down as Richard, crouching at first then standing when he was able, scrambled down to the wall. Leaning against it he stuck his head round the opening and called out Barry's name. Rather than echo as he thought it would, it seemed to be swallowed up by the darkness. He tried again, stepping inside the tunnel, this time a bit louder. Again the sound was absorbed by the angular walls. He looked round at Herbert. "He can't hear us."

Herbert was not at all surprised. He was beginning to wonder if he was going to get out of this adventure alive. He looked longingly at the light coming through the cave entrance, wondering whatever madness had possessed him to come on this trip. Although he knew he had done so, to enhance his standing with his friends, all of whom, with the exception of Richard, thought him a bit soft. He looked back again at the light. Would it be worth being branded a coward just to get out of here alive? Richard broke into his thoughts. "Come on Bert, let's go in.

Smothering his fear before it did the same to him, Herbert crept reluctantly down the slope to stand beside Richard. Without the comfort of the light from the entrance the darkness seemed more oppressive and the damp cold more piercing. He shivered. Richard looked worriedly at Herbert. "Are you alright, Bert?"

Herbert smiled, his teeth looking unnaturally white in the gloom. A feeble "Yes" was all he could muster.

Richard became all businesslike. "Right, well we go through here and we can turn either left or right. If we go left it leads out to the big hole you can see in the cliff in Joss Bay. I'm not sure if Barry is down that way but do you want to do that, or shall we go right which takes us out to Kingsgate Bay, which takes a bit longer?"

Herbert jerked involuntarily as he realised he was being asked a question. His mind had been wandering as he looked into the tunnel, thinking about bats, ghosts and any other ephemeral creatures that might be lurking down here. He didn't fancy the long journey to Kingsgate Bay – or the short one for that matter – but at least it would be the lesser of the two. "Yes, all right," he said, trying to inject a note of lightness into his voice, "Let's try Joss Bay."

Nodding Richard ducked into the tunnel, going left, and disappeared. Swallowing, Herbert took a deep breath, as if he was going under water, and followed Richard into the opening. What little light there had been in the cave was gone completely. Rather than darkness, which he was used to, there was a complete absence of light. He moved his left foot forward once then, reluctantly letting go of the edge of the hole, moved his right foot forward. After a few more steps Herbert stopped and held out his hand in front of his eyes but he couldn't see a thing. It was so dark he wondered if he had unwittingly or unknowingly closed his eyes or gone blind. He checked by poking a finger in his eye. He jerked back on contact. They were open. Rather than reassure him, this scared him even more. Panic began to build up within him. He fought to keep it down but the dark and, save for his own breathing, silence, now partially offset by the roaring in his mind, made him for the first time in his life feel totally alone. He cried out, louder than he had intended. "Ricky, where are you?"

"I'm here," said a voice about a foot away from his face, making him jump. "What are you shouting for?"

Herbert giggled in his nervousness then suppressed it. He reached out and touched Richard's arm. "I thought you had gone on ahead and left me", he trailed off as Richard, ignoring his answer, continued briskly.

"Never mind. I won't light any matches on this side since they hurt the eyes and there are a lot of light holes and side tunnels to the cliff face along this tunnel. OK?"

Herbert nodded, his last hope that they would light their way with some matches died. He nodded his agreement again before realising that Richard couldn't see him. "OK Ricky."

"Right," replied Richard. "All you have to do is keep your hand on the side of the tunnel." He reached out and felt for Herbert's hand, took hold of it and placed it on the chalk. Startled at first, Herbert suddenly realised how the people he had seen on television felt when they had been suddenly grabbed by the 'Invisible Man'.

He paid attention to Richard as he continued, "and the ground is smooth so you won't trip over anything."

Richard moved off, still talking so it was only because his voice had started to fade that Herbert realised he was being left alone. With a start he began walking, slowly at first, and then with greater confidence as he realised the ground was smooth, the tunnel high enough for him not to have to stoop and the sticky, clammy feel of the smooth chalk wall felt comforting after a while. His movements became less and less jerky as he progressed and he was feeling quite confident and no longer afraid about being enclosed in the tunnel when his eyes, much to his surprise, picked out the unrecognisable shape of something that appeared to be walking towards him. He stopped suddenly as almost, he felt, did his heart, until he realised it was Richard who had also stopped and turned round to face him. Herbert hurried forward, almost breaking into a run to join Richard in the half-light. Richard pointed up through the vertical slot to a grating, which let in the light.

"See?" he asked. Herbert nodded. After the darkness this grey white light seemed like a spotlight by comparison. Richard moved off. "Over here, Bert."

Turning round Herbert followed Richard to a small branch tunnel, which narrowed as they entered it and stopped where it had an opening onto the cliff face about eighteen inches in diameter. Richard pointed, indicating that Herbert should look through. Herbert stuck his head through the hole and was amazed, both at how high up he was, but more that his head was sticking out of the cliff face. Down on the beach he could see people walking about. He doubted if they could see him and felt secretly pleased with himself. As if he had climbed a great mountain. With the wind on his face but his body enclosed by the chalk, he felt happy and secure for the first time since they had entered the cave.

Waiting patiently for Herbert to let him see out from the hole in the cliff Richard walked back to the main tunnel and called out Barry's name a few times, but got no response. Finally he walked back to Herbert and pulled him away from the hole. "Come on, Bert, let's get going and find Barry."

Reluctantly Herbert followed Richard as without looking back he disappeared into the tunnel. With a last look back at the light streaming through the hole, Herbert followed, slowly at first then more hurriedly. Afraid lest his new found courage evaporated too soon and in case he got separated from Richard. After about fifty yards, when the only sound he had heard was that of his own laboured breathing, he again saw the shadowy outline of Richard as he approached another hole cut into the cliff, this time much larger than the first.

Pausing, Richard waited for Herbert to catch up. "There's not much to see here Bert, and anyway I want to get to the end in case Barry is there." Herbert was about to protest since he was beginning to enjoy the adventure but noting the look on Richard's face, decided not to. Richard nodded, glad that Herbert had not objected. He was a bit concerned by not having heard anything from Barry since they had agreed they would go along this shorter tunnel first before the longer one. "Keep to the left hand side of the tunnel from now on, there's a lot of large storage caverns cut into the cliff on the right hand side where you might get lost, all right?"

Herbert nodded automatically before the full import of what Richard had been saying sunk in.

"Oh, by the way," continued Richard, "it's fairly long this bit, about a hundred yards." With that Richard, with his left hand resting lightly on the left hand wall of the tunnel, disappeared from view.

His mind in turmoil, Herbert watched him go. He felt '*stuck between the devil and the deep blue sea*', though he had no clear idea of what that really meant. He didn't like the idea of going on and getting lost in the caverns, which in his mind had taken on the proportions of a cathedral; neither did he wish to go back alone, with all that meant, particularly the loss of face with his friends. He couldn't really stay here either. "Oh, well," he said aloud to himself, and stepped into the tunnel, keeping close to the left hand side. The ground here was just as flat and smooth at the other tunnel had been and gradually he walked faster and with greater confidence the further he went without mishap. 'If only it wasn't so quiet' he thought, followed immediately by 'I wish Ricky hadn't rushed off like that'. Herbert continued on his mind full of conflicting thoughts.

After about fifty yards he sensed a change in the tunnel, something he couldn't quite define, as sense of emptiness. With his fingertips resting lightly on the left hand wall he waved his arm about but couldn't feel the other wall. He wondered if he would dare move to the right and then did so almost without thinking about it – two paces. He still could not feel anything. 'The Caverns!' The thought flashed through his mind and with it the image of himself wandering aimlessly around them until he starved to death. With a vigour he hardly knew he possessed he threw himself back where he thought the left hand wall was. It was closer than his estimate since he suddenly banged up against it, winding himself in the process. The distance he had yet to travel along the tunnel heightened by the darkness made the vague feeling of claustrophobia, which had been lurking at the back of his mind, rise to the surface. It threatened to overwhelm him. With a sudden sob, not caring if he was heard or not and his eyes screwed tightly shut to somehow lessen the impact of the darkness, he ran along the tunnel to catch up with Richard as soon as he could. His left hand dragging along the wall, hard, served both to assure him that he was travelling in the right direction and the pain distracted his mind from the feeling of being entombed.

* * *

Up ahead, moving almost as quickly, Richard at last made out the light indicating the end of the tunnel. Although still a long way off it brought a sense of relief. Richard walked a little faster. He could hear Herbert running behind him and, for a moment, wondered at his friend's foolhardiness; in that he was doing something during his first visit when it had taken Barry and himself a number of visits and careful investigation of the tunnel, before they had had the courage to run blindly along the tunnels without any fear of injuring themselves or plunging over an abyss.

Richard covered the last fifty yards or so at a run, and then slowed down to a walk to stop at the last horizontal point before the floor sloped down to the end of the tunnel at the cliff face. There, hanging over the edge, his fingers gripped on the only sizeable small outcrop of chalk on the smooth surface, was Barry. His face resting on the chalk, but he raised it at the sound of Richard's approach.

Barry smiled weakly. "About bleedin' time," and then more worriedly, "I can't get back."

Nodding, Richard looked down at the floor. The distance from where he stood to the bottom edge of the hole was about eight feet sloping down at an angle of about thirty degrees. The hole in the cliff face was itself about seven feet in diameter, which allowed in the wind and the rain. As a result the sloping chalk floor of the tunnel was treacherous and slippery, covered with a grey white oil-like slime. Because of this none of the boys had actually gone to the edge of the hole in the cliff face. Barry must have thought it was possible by climbing along the side wall. Richard's mind was in turmoil. If Barry was unable to hold on there was a thirty or forty foot drop to the ground made up of chalk boulders and flint. Behind him he could hear Herbert, now thumping along the tunnel as if the furies were after him. "Hold on a minute Barry."

He ran a few steps back down the tunnel and standing in the middle with his arms outstretched, shouted, "Bert, slow down." Just as his friend appeared out of the gloom with what, Richard thought when he opened them, was a wild gleam in his eyes. Herbert slowed but not enough to stop himself crashing into Richard. "Are you all right?" asked Richard, a puzzled expression on his face as Herbert gasped for breath.

Herbert nodded; relieved to be in human company and the light again, not sure at that particular moment what was more important. Keeping hold of Herbert's arm Richard let him to the last level part of the tunnel.

He pointed at Barry, "Don't go beyond this point Bert, the grounds slippery and you might go down and over the edge like Barry." Unconsciously Herbert, his eyes wide with horror, went backwards two steps, then embarrassed, moved forward one as Barry raised his head.

"Hallo Bert, didn't think you were going to turn up."

I had to have a bath," he blurted out as all he could think to say. To his surprise Barry didn't laugh as he thought he would but merely nodded his head.

Richard undid his trouser belt and slipped it through the loops round the top of his shorts. "Give us your belt Bert." Herbert looked at him for a moment then, realisation dawning in his eyes, he unhooked the belt and gave it to Richard who took it and joined it with his. They were both of the same type, made of elasticated material with an 'S' shaped hook patterned as if it was a snake, and an 'eye' at the other end. Standing as close as he could to the slope, Richard knelt down and threw out the improvised 'rope'. "Here, catch," he said as he threw one end, keeping tight hold of the other.

Barry watched it fall then reluctantly, and very carefully, released one hand from its tenuous hold on the small nub of chalk, which had stopped his slide down to the flinty sand, and stretched out. He couldn't reach it. Quickly, lest he lose the slight grip he had on the outcrop of chalk he put his hand back again. Richard looked; it was probably useless to try again, there was just too much ground to cover. He sat down on the chalk, and then stretched out with his legs resting on the horizontal floor and his body lying on the slope, uncaring about the mess he was making of his clothes from the slime of chalk that covered the sloping surface.

Taking hold of the belt again he threw it at Barry, retaining a tight hold on his end. It landed quite close. "Go on, grab hold," said Richard.

Barry did so with one hand, still keeping tight hold on the small chalk lump with the other. Backing away to a safe spot, Richard pulled on the belts. They stretched longer then he thought they would, and had almost reached the limit of their elasticity when the belts suddenly unhooked themselves. Richard fell back onto Herbert, whilst Barry quickly let go of the belt he was holding and resumed his hold on the chalk outcrop. The belt, watched by Barry, hesitated for a moment, and then slithered over the edge. Barry concerned with maintaining his hold did not even try to save it.

"My belt!" wailed Herbert, and would have attempted to retrieve it had not Richard held him back.

"Don't worry about it, we'll get it back later," said Richard, who turned back to Barry. "Are you sure you can't climb back up?" Barry shook his head, his knees and shins were sore, his arms were tired and he was beginning to lose the sense of feeling in his fingers. He shook his head again.

"No, I've tried that but it's too bleedin' slippery and I'm scared I'll just go over the edge." Richard looked at the floor and knelt down again, a half-formulated idea lurked at the back of his mind. Perhaps they could cut hand-holds for Barry to use to pull himself up, but they'd need a knife.

"Has anyone got a penknife?" he asked. "I've left mine at home."

"I have," replied Barry. Very slowly he reached down to his blazer pocket, took out his knife and with the minimum of effort threw it at Richard, before resuming his hold on the chalk. Richard grabbed the knife as it landed on the ground and before it slipped down the slope. Opening the blade, he began to cut a hole in the ground where the level surface started to slope downwards. The chalk was soft and he had dug one hole and started another when Herbert spoke.

"I, I saw a film once." He was interrupted by Barry.

"Not now Bert, for Gawd's sake." He was not in the mood for one of Herbert's long, usually complex and boring stories.

Herbert persisted. "No. It was a war film and these soldiers wanted to get one of their mates out of a hole and they didn't have a rope so a soldier hung over the edge, whilst another held his feet and the one in the hole climbed out over him. It was easy." He ended.

Stopping his digging into the chalk for a moment Richard let Herbert's idea crystallise in his head. "That's it!" He looked at Barry and gauged the distance from the holes he had been digging to Barry, then resumed digging feverishly, talking as he did so. "I'll dig these holes a bit more so I can stick my toecaps in them, then you hold onto my ankles, Bert," he looked up and waited until Herbert nodded before continuing, "then you," he looked at Barry, 'can climb over me, right?"

Get on with it, please," said Barry. Richard finished digging; the holes looked deep enough. Moving forward he jammed the toecaps of his shoes into the two hollows he had dug out. "Get hold of my ankles, Bert." Herbert sat down hard and grabbed hold of Richard's ankles as tight as he possibly could.

"Right, Ricky," he said, glad to be of use, not realising that he had already been by his suggestion. Richard smiled at Herbert's eagerness but, with the knife grasped in his hand, concentrated on stretching out slowly so as not to lose his foothold in the holes by any sudden movements. Fully stretched out, Richard's hands were only a few inches from Barry. Taking a firm grip on the knife he raised it in the air and brought it down hard into the chalk where it jammed tight. Happier now that he had a secondary form of support, he looked at Barry, saying hurriedly, "Quick, climb over me."

Needing no further urging, Barry let go of the spur of chalk with one hand and gripped Richard's wrist, then did the same with the other. Pulling himself up over the edge of the hole, grunting and straining with the effort, made worse by aching muscles, he scrambled up and over Richard to safety.

Only during the initial pull had Richard felt uneasy when the toecaps of his shoes threatened to pop out of the holes he had dug in the chalk. Suddenly they had seemed too shallow. With Herbert still holding on to his ankles Richard waggled the knife to and fro to release it, and then pulled it free. Looking back for a second he said, "Hold on tight Bert," then slowly pushed himself upwards to first kneel then lean backwards as Bert got hold of him and pulled him to safety. Both he and Herbert exhaled noisily. "Phew!"

Richard looked at Barry who, although shaken, was rapidly regaining some of his usual aplomb. Handing back his knife Richard asked him. "You OK?"

Barry grimaced, "Yes, thanks Ricky, thanks Bert. Thought I was a goner for a moment." He looked down at the slope he had fallen onto when he had tried to get down to the edge of the hole in the cliff. He suddenly spat on the slope. "Bleedin' chalk," he said his voice a mixture of anger and exasperation.

Richard meanwhile tried to brush some of the whiteness out of his clothes. It would have been difficult enough to do so with dry chalk dust but with the chalk slime from the slope it was near nigh impossible. With his best friend being out of danger the full import of his mother's reaction to his state of his clothes was beginning to dawn on him.

Suddenly noticing Richard's face, which was looking more and more like the chalk floor by the moment, Barry placed a hand on Richard's shoulder. "Don't worry Ricky, come home with me. My Mum's got a new washing machine and a dryer. It'll soon get that stuff off. I've had enough excitement for one day. Let's go home." Richard, his immediate problem solved, nodded his agreement.

"And I've got to get my belt back before the tide comes in," said Herbert. He made as if to step forward to the cliff edge but abruptly stopped himself in time. Barry placed an arm on Richard's and Herbert's shoulders and pushed them back into the tunnel. "Come on heroes, let's go home."

They retreated back through the tunnel; itself unmindful of the minor drama that had unfolded there. As their footsteps, dulled by the soft chalk surface of the floor, slowly faded into silence, leaving only the sound of the waves breaking on the flat rock, Barry's voice floated out of the tunnel as if it were the darkness speaking, "Bleedin' slope."

Chapter 15: **The Hurricane after the storm**

Cautiously coming out of the vestry Richard looked up at the sky. The sudden storm that had been raging a few minutes ago was now moving across the fields. From the Blacksmith's in Church Street came a clanging noise, this was unusual for a Sunday. He walked to his bicycle, the saddle of which was covered with fallen rain. Taking a handkerchief out of his pocket he methodically began to wipe it dry. With a laugh, Barry rushed out of the vestry, slapped Richard hard on the back, crying, "I told you there was nothing to worry about, see you tonight."

Richard nodded as Barry grabbed his bicycle and, not concerned about it being wet, jumped on and cycled off down Church Street. Richard continued to wipe his wet saddle until he thought it dry enough to sit on. After squeezing the water out of the sodden handkerchief he dropped it into his saddlebag to take out and wash and dry it when he got home.

Getting on his bicycle Richard carefully cycled out of the vestry yard then slowly down Church Street, watching Barry disappear into the distance. The saddle still felt a bit damp but as there was nothing else he could do he decided to ignore it. He passed the piggery and heard the pigs grunting contentedly in their sties, no doubt as glad as he was that the storm was over. As he continued down Church Street the hammering from the blacksmith continued apace, then gradually faded as he cycled into and then along Northdown Road.

One or two raindrops fell on his new jacket. He paused for a moment to look up at the sky to see if it would be necessary to seek shelter – perhaps in the nearby newsagents. He must not get his new jacket wet. He wished now that he had worn his old raincoat but had been too keen to show off his new jacket and, for once, look smart like his friends. Richard continued to scan the sky. No more rain fell. They must have been a few tardy drops from the storm clouds that, having soaked the area, were now drifting over the fields on their way to do the same in Margate. Richard carried on, thinking that whilst he might be a bit late for Sunday dinner at least his new jacket was alright. He cycled on over the railway bridge where he stopped for a moment to see if a train was passing. Since there was not he hurried on past the bus depot then up the hill to his house.

Although the sun was shining through the clouds the paths and house were very wet, evidence that the storm had only just passed over. Richard jumped off his bicycle and walked up the garden path humming to himself a hymn sung at Matins. He noticed his young brother, Robin, peering through the steamed up window of the front room and waved to him. Oddly, Robin looked round quickly and then gave a thumbs-down sign, which filled Richard with a sense of foreboding. Not being able to think of anything he had done wrong recently – even in his mother's eyes – he shrugged and continued to the back porch where he left his bicycle.

Untying his shoes he opened the door and stepped into the kitchen, closing the door quietly behind him.

His father was sitting in an armchair in the back room reading a newspaper. He looked up as Richard entered and shook his head from side to side and then went back to his paper. Richard's mother was leaning over the stove, pushing a fork into a pot of potatoes and as Richard was about to go into the back room she spoke. "Do you think we're made of money then?"

If he had doubts before, the threatening tone of his mother's voice warned Richard that something was wrong. He still could not think what it was but replied warily, "No?" and began to edge into the back room. His mother's voice brought him to a sudden halt.

"Stand still when I'm talking to you!"

Richard stopped as his mother turned round from the stove. He knew from the look in her eye, furrowed forehead and the way her mouth twitched uncontrollably that he was in trouble, deep trouble. He watched warily as she drained the potatoes into the sink and started to put them out onto plates on the kitchen table.

"We scrimp and save to buy you nice clothes and what thanks do we get," she paused, "eh, come on, tell me, what?"

Richard knew that since the only thing he possessed, which had been bought new was his jacket, it must be that. He looked up and started to speak but his mother got there before him.

"First time you wear it you bring it home soaking wet. Just shows what you think of your jacket, not to mention what you think of us."

Richard was nonplussed, apart from one or two spots his jacket was bone dry. "The jacket isn't wet."

Richard took it off. "Look," he said, holding it out. "It's dry." His mother turned away refusing to believe. Richard realised that with his arriving just after the storm had passed over it must seem that he had travelled through it. He tried again. "Honestly, my jacket isn't wet, look," and he turned to his father appealing for help.

His mother fixed him again with her voice. "Do you know how much that jacket cost? Do you understand what it means to us, the sacrifices we have to make just so you can look smart in church with your posh friends?"

Inwardly Richard gave up, knowing he was lost. His mother had made up her mind that the jacket was wet, even though it wasn't, and he was going to suffer for it. He resolved to take his punishment, even though he had not done anything wrong. He mumbled, "Yes."

His mother turned away, saying sorrowfully, "No, I don't think you do." She carried on dishing out the food then suddenly shouted, "Get out of my sight."

Richard walked quickly into the back room whilst his mother continued talking to herself, every now and then her voice reaching a crescendo, which jarred on his nerves, making him jump with fear. He held out his jacket to his father, who felt it, acknowledging it was dry but he just shrugged and hurriedly looked down at his paper as his wife cried out.

"Robin, Marilyn, come and get your dinner, and you," she added to her husband who slowly and deliberately got up out of the armchair. Ever since his illness he had had great difficulty getting out of upholstered chairs and usually preferred sitting on a straight backed chair. But these were all in the kitchen to be used at dinner-time. He walked into the kitchen followed by Richard. Robin and Marilyn had entered by the other door and were already sitting down eating quickly and quietly. They looked anxiously at Richard as he entered the kitchen. His mother looked up as he started to walk to his place at the table. "What do you want?" she spat.

Richard looked at the meal waiting at his place, and then cleared his throat and pointing nervously said in a very faint voice, "You said come to dinner."

His mother watched him squirm uncomfortably for a while and then in an equally quiet voice, replied "Dinner, you want some dinner do you?" Richard too scared to talk by the venom in her voice, could only nod dumbly. "Right," said his mother, "here it is." And with a maniacal gleam in her eye picked up the plate and threw it at Richard.

Robin looked aghast, his mouth open, as, too shocked to move, a chipped edge of the plate caught Richard a glancing blow on his left cheek before hitting the wall and dropping to the floor where it broke and scattered randomly across the lino. A mixture of blood and gravy welled up out of the cut and dripped down Richard's cheek as pieces of food dropped off his clothes, whilst others slid slowly down the wall behind him leaving behind the brown trails of the gravy.

His mother wasn't finished with him yet. Getting out of her chair she rushed up to Richard and grabbing him by the hair pushed his face into the food sliding down the wall, yelling "Eat, go on, eat, you wanted to eat, so eat." She banged his head against the wall a few times and then picked up a piece of meat and forced it into

Richard's mouth still yelling, "Go on, eat, I'll teach you not to take care of your new clothes, go on, eat."

Richard made a few half-hearted attempts to chew whilst his mother, after punctuating her shouting by banging his head a few more times on the wall, threw him to the floor and returned to her chair. Even though she had meted out the punishment her fervour was in no way diminished.

"Get up to your room this instant," she hissed.

Richard started to push himself to his feet. The half-eaten piece of meat in his mouth threatened to choke him. His father seeing he was somewhat dazed went to help him up, muttering.

"I'll give him a hand, Mum." His wife looked up from her plate.

"You leave him alone!" She stared for a moment. "And get on with your dinner." She turned to Robin. "And you." Robin returned to his plate with renewed vigour, whilst Richard was ignored as he stumbled out of the kitchen through the back room and made his way upstairs.

Safe for the moment, he paused on the stairs to wipe some gravy out of his eyes then carried on up the stairs and walked into the bathroom. After looking at himself in the mirror for a few seconds he took the half chewed meat out of his mouth and flushed it down the toilet, then washed his face. He stopped suddenly for a moment when he realised that his new jacket was still lying on the settee downstairs. He shrugged, having been punished for a non-existent offence; what were a few wrinkles? Anyway the love he had first felt for the jacket when it had been bought for him, and again when he had put it on this morning, was rapidly turning to hatred for the trouble it had unwittingly caused him. He mused on this for a while then smiled ruefully to himself. 'You can't hate inanimate objects,' and then dried his face and put the towel back on the side of the bath. Noticing there was blood on it from the gash on his cheek he hurriedly rinsed the towel under the cold tap. After wringing it out, as best he could, he draped it over the edge of the bath to dry.

Walking out of the bathroom, Richard was careful not to make any noise as he went across the narrow landing into the bedroom and lay down on his bunk, which creaked under his weight. In the kitchen he could hear his mother's voice, seemingly endlessly and tirelessly, going on and on about himself and his 'wet' jacket with occasionally the deeper murmurings of the voice of his father. He turned his face to the window sill where he kept the few books that he had. Picking up the Oxford Psalter, which he had bought with the money he had earned from singing at weddings, he turned to Psalm 42. This was one of his favourite Psalms and he easily recalled to mind a suitable chant. He sang very softly to himself and when he came to the third verse,

'My tears have been my meat day and night:
while they daily say unto me, Where is now thy God?'

Richard stopped, and, whilst he had not cried when he had been beaten, a few tears now began to roll down his cheeks. He wiped these hurriedly away with his fingers and returned the Psalter to the window-sill and thought for a moment. It was not fair. It did not matter what he tried to do to please his mother, or just keep out of the way of her capricious nature, he always ended up doing the 'wrong' thing and getting punished as a consequence of it. He gazed out of the window and watched a flock of crows flying over the house to the fields opposite the front of the house. A pall of smoke from the rubbish dump next to the railway line drifted overhead and cast a gloom over the sky; where there was now no trace of the earlier storm, which had caused him so much trouble.

It had gone quiet in the kitchen; apart from the occasional chink of crockery. After a few moments the door from the kitchen opened and closed, followed by the sound of footsteps on the stairs. Richard tensed, then relaxed as he realised they belonged to Robin. Robin reached the top of the stair and walked into the bedroom holding in front of him a cheese sandwich. He offered it to Richard, saying quietly.

"Here, this is for you."

Richard threw his legs over the side of the bunk and sat up, taking the sandwich and making room for Robin who sat down beside him. Richard took a bite and then looked inside. "There's no butter on the bread."

"I know," said Robin, "I couldn't get any without her knowing so I left it. Richard shrugged. "Doesn't matter," then he took another bite. He nodded. "Not bad."

"How are you feeling?" asked Robin, "your face is a right mess." Richard's head was by now beginning to ache but he smiled. "It's OK, I've had worse."

Robin got off the bed and walked to the window. "It's been bad today; Dad got it this morning and you have at dinnertime, perhaps I'll get it in the neck tonight." He stopped talking and studied Richard's face intently for a while and went on, "Well, you won't be able to go to church looking like that tonight," and added, almost as an afterthought, "she won't let you." He stopped for a second and then went on. "If people only knew what it was really like in here," he paused, at a loss for words then shrugged helplessly, sighed and looked up at the Sunderland flying boat hanging from the ceiling.

Richard looked up in alarm. That he would be stopped from going to church hadn't occurred to him. He stood up holding the half eaten sandwich in his left hand. Walking over to the wardrobe, in which there was a mirror, he peered in, watched by Robin who stood with his arms crossed and his back to the window. Richard realised for the first time the full extent of his injuries. Where the side of his face had been repeatedly banged against the wall was now a livid mass of bruising. He turned to Robin, his eyes starting to well with tears. "But I've got to go tonight, I'm singing a solo and afterwards I'm seeing Emma!"

Robin shook his head from side to side. Deep down Richard knew that his brother was right. The knowledge of this was more painful to bear than the pain from his beating. After all the practising he had done yesterday morning and in the previous weeks it was heartbreaking. But more than that, he would be letting the choir down. This was unthinkable. "It's no good, I'll just have to go downstairs and ask if I can go to church tonight. I can't not go."

Robin looked at his brother, both aware of what it meant to him but knowing he was asking for a miracle. "Are you mad? With the mood she's in you'll just get another belting then you won't be able to go out of the house for at least another week."

Richard continued to stare at the mirror. He knew from experience that Robin wasn't just exaggerating to make a point. Their sister had once been so badly beaten that she had had to stay away from school. Then there was the time when their mother had thrown a fork at their sister and she had had to go to hospital. Richard, forgetting his own pain, shivered at the remembrance of it all. He had been standing by the door to the kitchen, his mother had been sitting down shouting at his sister when, without any sort of warning she had picked up the nearest available object, which happened to be a fork, and threw it hard at Marilyn. Richard had watched it, mesmerised, as it spun through the air to land in his sister's stomach. Piercing the clothes and the skin it had sunk into the flesh and then just hung there for a moment or two until it finally slid slowly out to fall on the floor with a loud clang. Their father had taken her to hospital as the wound wouldn't stop bleeding. But Marilyn had been made to promise, by their father to say, if she was asked by the doctor, that another kid had done it and not their mother, otherwise as their mother had threatened, Marilyn would be put in a home.

Shaking himself to get rid of the memory as, unwillingly his mind had made him relive the incident. He looked dejectedly up at his brother. There was nothing he could do about it, so why worry? Perhaps he ought not to bother going back to sing in the choir at all, why fight it any longer, it was just all too hard? Then in the next second he dismissed such fanciful thoughts. He loved singing in the choir and would do almost anything to ensure that he could go to church. If he couldn't tonight, another chorister could sing the solo, not as well as himself he felt, but still, perhaps it wasn't the end of the world. He resolved not to think about it anymore, and sat back on his bunk to finish the sandwich Robin had brought him: eating slowly to help his aching jaw and face muscles.

"I could go and tell Barry I suppose," said Robin thinking out loud, "but then I don't think I'll be allowed out either."

Richard shook his head. "No, it's not worth it. It doesn't matter." Although he knew in his heart it did to him.

They lapsed into silence again but it did not last long. The door between the hall and the kitchen opened and their mother's voice rang out, so loud and clear that Robin jumped, thinking for just a split second that somehow she was in the room with them. "Robin, get down here and wash up." She paused for breath before adding, "Now!"

Robin moved fast. Not bothering to say goodbye he rushed out of the room as the kitchen door slammed shut again. Richard smiled at the speed of his brother's departure. He was not surprised as he knew his mother would be slowly counting to herself and if Robin didn't get down by the count of ten he would get a slap for every count after ten. He followed the sound of his brother thumping down the stairs and as the door was opened and shut, "Five," said Richard out loud. The suddenly appearing knot of tension in his stomach was now able to dissipate as quickly as it had started.

Having finished his sandwich Richard went and had another look at his face in the mirror then returned to lie on his bunk. He hummed a few bars of the solo he was going to sing tonight, or rather, he thought to himself, he probably would not be singing, then turned over facing the wall and closed his eyes. It had been a long tiresome day. Nothing had gone right and he had still not got over yesterday's excitement in the tunnels. The only good thing had been that his mother had not found out about it. Barry's mother had washed and dried his clothes and given them all something to eat. Herbert had been treated as a hero, thanks to his idea to rescue Barry, and had been too tongue-tied with embarrassment to say anything to Barry's mother: alternatively blushing and beaming as first Richard and then Barry had extolled his virtues. As he recounted in his mind the events of yesterday, Richard dozed and finally fell asleep.

* * *

Waking suddenly from his fitful sleep Richard had remained upstairs wondering what time it was. As it was getting dark it must be near five o'clock. He went to wash his face and clean his teeth to rid himself of that staleness he had acquired from sleeping in the afternoon. Returning to the bedroom he read for a while and put the light on when it became too dark to read by the light from the window. He read some more until the stomach cramps he suffered made it difficult to concentrate. Being used to a large meal on Sunday – the only time they actually got enough to eat – and having eaten only a small sandwich, his stomach was having difficulty in adjusting to this change from its normal routine. What made it worse was that he could hear the sounds of the rest of the family having their tea.

Richard put his book down and gazed out of the window. He had not bothered to draw the curtains closed. The moon demanded his attention. It was bright, very bright. He had always regarded the moon as a particular friend of his, accepting that many others probably felt the same. The words of the poem *Macavity's a Mystery Cat* came unbidden into his mind. He loved that poem. It had been a task set for homework one afternoon to be recited individually in class the next day. Although he had made a – what he thought – was a valiant attempt to learn it he had eventually given up and watched Robin Hood on television instead, going to bed prepared to face the wrath of his English teacher the next day.

He wasn't quite sure what had woken him in the middle of the night. It was probably the cold air blowing through the window that always, unaccountably, made him sweat. He had got out of bed to move the window in a notch when he had been struck by the brilliance of the moon. He had often seen it bright before but that time, night had literally been turned into day. After gazing out of the window watching a cat prowl around the back garden, he had picked up a book to see if he could read in the moonlight. It had been the poetry book he had brought up with him in a final attempt to learn a few lines of the poem before he fell asleep, but tiredness had overtaken him before he had made much progress. Now he opened the book at the right page and read through the first few lines. He could see them perfectly. As he did not feel tired he settled down by the window and, to his surprise, very quickly learned the whole poem off by heart. The next day he wondered whether if he had dreamed the whole episode but he could still remember the poem and was able to recite it faultlessly when called upon to do so in class that day.

The bang of a door closing brought him back to the present. His body tensing until he realised it was the footsteps of his brother. He remained where he was, just in case. It was not until Robin showed his cheery face round the side of the door that he relaxed.

"We've finished tea," he said, "and I've been told to tell you to come down and get yours."

Standing up slowly Richard frowned. "What sort of mood is she in?" he asked cautiously.

Robin snorted and then shrugged his shoulders. "Not too bad, I suppose, but then we're not in her bad books," he joked. "Provided you don't fart when you're eating I suppose it'll be OK."

Richard smiled briefly at his brother's attempt to cheer him up and punched him lightly on the shoulder. He then walked slowly down the stairs to have his belated tea alone in the cold kitchen.

* * *

Having finished his cheese sandwich and drunk his cup of watered milk Richard sat at his place picking up breadcrumbs with a previously licked finger. There was nothing more for him to eat and he only sat there since he did not want to go into the back room and watch television with the others. The only reason for not doing so, he finally admitted to himself, was that he was scared. The beating he had received at Sunday dinner was still too fresh in his mind and just a sudden noise from the other room made him flinch in case it was a prelude to his mother coming into the kitchen and either giving him a gratuitous swipe around the head in passing, as she had often done in the past to himself and the others, or start all over again about the same thing as if he had not already been punished.

Richard looked down at his plate again; it had been polished clean by his moistened fingers. The lino-covered table top had also been picked bare. Sighing only to himself, he knew he could not delay much longer; if he did his mother might think he was either sulking or being awkward, in which case he would warrant more punishment just to stop him being wilful. As quietly as he possibly could, Richard stood up and, taking his plate and cup to the sink, washed them thoroughly in 'Surf', several times, before he was satisfied that they were perfect for his mother's scrutiny, then put them on the draining board to dry. Having dried his hands he looked around the kitchen. There was nothing else to be put away or washed. He had better go into the back room and join the others. He shivered, both from the cold and the anticipation, then taking a deep breath he walked into the back room.

His arrival, though not unnoticed, went unheralded. From bitter experience his brother and sister knew it was best to ignore whoever was currently in their mother's bad books. Richard knew this and was merely glad that everyone was so engrossed in the television that he was able to sit on the hardback chair against the wall. He looked back at the clock in the kitchen. By now he should be on his way to church but knowing he would not be allowed to go, especially looking as he did, he had not bothered to ask his mother. He had whispered to his father, when he had given him his sandwich, whether he would be allowed to go to church but he had merely shaken his head sadly from side to side. When Richard had persisted he had shaken his head more vigorously and mouthed, "Don't ask."

With only half a mind Richard pretended to be absorbed in watching television. It was, he felt, an activity that did not require much effort. It was easy to look as if you were involved to the same degree as the others. He felt odd sitting here at this time when he was usually in church. He heard faintly the church bells ring out as usual, only this time they sounded strangely muted as if they knew he would not be joining them that evening.

Richard shook himself mentally; there was no point in going on like this. He would not be going to church tonight and that was it. Although he had to fight down an urge to stop from rushing out of the house, because of his need to go and sing, something else also restrained him. He had kept it at the back of his mind ever since he had looked at his face in the mirror – what on earth would Emma think when she saw his bruises? Although their meetings had been few and for him, painfully brief, they had become more and more important. Now he had not just his love of church music to offset the daily doses of terror which his mother imposed on them. In the last few months he had felt Emma and himself draw closer together. They had no secrets from each other and Richard had told her why he was more often than not bruised from a beating he had received from his mother. Like Richard, Emma had, more or less, come to accept the amount of violence involved in his home life but she did not properly understand it. Richard admitted to himself that he did not understand it either: mostly why any of his brother's and sister's actions usually resulted in quite vicious punishment.

As far as he could tell none of his friends' mothers' behaved as his did. Admittedly they were punished if they had done something wrong but they weren't beaten either as hard or a frequently as Richard was. Neither did they get punished just for being there: for existing.

Lightly running his fingers over his taut, bruised skin brought home to Richard that his injuries were bad and might take some time to get better. His mother moved suddenly in her seat making him hastily withdraw his fingers from his face in case she felt he was in some oblique way criticising her – as had happened previously. In a way he was glad he would not be going to church. It tore his heart to see the way Emma flinched, as if experiencing the blow herself, whenever she saw yet another bruise on his face or a split lip. Richard cleared his mind of these and other thoughts and began to watch the television again. It would be switched off once this programmed ended, until the evening's entertainment resumed. Their mother usually went and had a bath then, which allowed them all a brief respite when they could be themselves, not needing to be constantly on their guard for fear of inadvertently saying or doing something which might displease her. It did not take much, and the difficulty was that almost anything could or would make her go absolutely mad with anger. Even things known in the past to be innocuous might suddenly send her into a rage. Roll on the next few minutes, mused Richard, when, if only for a short time, we can pretend we are a normal family and act without fear of the capricious and irrational consequences.

* * *

The coal in the fire moved, dislodging the covering of grey brown dust and revealing the vermilion interior, hesitated then fell languorously to the floor, landing unnoticed by Richard's foot. "Ricky!" his father called out, making him jump then look round quickly aware of the urgency in his father's voice. He father, from his seat, pointed at Richard's foot. "Coal" he said. Richard looked down at the coal burning into the linoleum. Quickly, almost faster than his father's eye could follow the movement, he licked his fingers then reached down, picked up the coal and threw it into the ash can below the grate of the fire. As he had done this a small spark fell from the fire to the ground to be immediately stamped on by Richard, extinguishing forever its light.

Richard resumed reading with occasional glimpses at the television whilst his father, with a deep sigh, heaved himself with difficulty out of his seat. Staggering with stiffness, and easing his back, he moved over to the fire, leaning on Richard as he went passed, who gave way slowly like a spring taking up pressure then moving up again as his father's hand, and weight, left his shoulder. Taking the worn and bent poker, which was laying on the top of the range, Richard's father stuck it between the vertical grill, which housed the fire, loosening the coals and getting rid of the ash now threatening to stifle the fire. Having done that to his satisfaction he put down the poke and picked up the iron bucket and emptied some fresh coke onto the fire. Putting the bucket down he picked up the poker again and firmed the now crackling and spitting coke down, then lifted the cover over the fire to increase the draft and make it catch alight more easily. Satisfied that it had been done properly, he poked the coals again through the grill then raked the poker back and forth a few times with, Richard who was watching felt, one for luck to remove the dust. Having finished and finally laid the poker down he went back to his seat the way he had come, leaning on the responsive spring that was Richard, before letting himself fall back into the welcome embrace of the old settee.

He looked across at Richard reading and watching television, his auburn hair glinting from the glow of the fire: engrossed in his book almost to the exclusion of everything else around him. Richard's father admired his son's ability to focus his concentration.

"You all right, Ricky?" he asked nonchalantly.

"Yes, Dad," came the automatic response.

Richard's father smiled to himself. It never failed when his son was reading. He was on automatic pilot again. Happy in the shared silence he picked up his paper and resumed reading. Robin came into the room from upstairs and flopped down on the floor next to Richard and looked up at the television. The room settled down again, only the sound of turning pages breaking the silence, but did not interrupt the companionable solitude, but rather served to enhance it.

Two sharp raps on the front door sounded as if far off. Although he had heard the noise, Richard dismissed it as just that; almost immediately before the echo in his mind had faded. A few seconds elapsed before the sound recurred. This time he jerked up as he recognised it for what it was: the front door knocker being banged. Putting aside his book he got to his feet and walked to the door to the hall as his father remarked, "Who could that be at this time, on a Sunday?"

No-one bothered to reply as Richard reached the door and had partially opened it when he and the others in the room heard the front door being pulled open by their mother, who had been in the front room, followed by the sound of their mother speaking, giving the alarm. Her voice full of artificial pleasure and much too loud with a hint of nervousness.

"It's the Vicar!"

Rushing back from the door to the hall Richard plunged back into the room and, with his father's and Robin's assistance, scurried around tidying up in the few seconds they knew they had before the vicar came into the room. Richard heard the sound of the front door closing and his mother saying what a pleasant surprise, as he picked up comics and newspapers and hid them away, whilst his brother and father helped put away other odds and ends whilst plumping up cushions.

Richard and the others stopped, as suddenly as they had begun, and straightened up as the vicar bustled into the room trying to look stern but with a smile lurking beneath his cherubic features. He stood by the edge of the settee and surveyed them all as their mother followed him into the room. He looked round at the settee and began to sit on the high side arm saying, his voice and features belying his words, "I'm very angry with you all."

He got no further since having reached that point he put his full weight on the arm of the settee which, being so old and the mechanism inside that held it up being broken, collapsed suddenly under his weight, pitching him to the floor.

Richard stood there for a moment aghast before rushing forward and helping the Vicar up onto the settee proper.

"Are you alright, sir?" he asked as the Vicar, obviously shaken, by his unexpected tumble eased himself slowly and cautiously down onto a lumpy cushion, looking suspiciously at the end piece, which had just collapsed under his weight. He leaned away from it as Richard put it upright again in case it should 'attack' him further by falling on him this time.

"Yes, thank you, Richard," replied the vicar taking out a handkerchief and after removing his spectacles, wiped off the sheen of sweat, which had suddenly appeared on his face. "Now where was I?"

Richard's mother spoke up, her voice fulsome in its concern and attempted gentile charm, "Would you like a cup of tea, Vicar?" The vicar looked round, thankful for the interruption allowing him to collect his thoughts and presence.

"Yes, please," he replied, then jerked sideways violently as the side of the settee suddenly fell down again to the floor.

Everyone looked at it for a moment then spontaneously burst out laughing. The vicar was forced to join in with the rest of them. For a few minutes everyone was helpless with laughter save, Richard noticed, their mother who, mortified at being horribly embarrassed in front of the vicar by the worn furniture, had walked tight-lipped into the kitchen.

Gradually the laughter subsided but both Richard and Robin had to bite the inside of their lips to stop breaking out into laughter afresh. During the respite the vicar took the opportunity not only to look around and familiarise himself with the room but also to look, as surreptitiously as he could, at Richard's face. He had been surprised and disappointed that Richard had not come to evensong that evening, especially since the anthem in which he was to have sung a solo had had to be cancelled. On asking Barry Mitchell if he knew where Richard was he had been told of Richard's worry after Matins about waiting for the rain to stop before attempting to go home since he did not want to get his jacket wet or his mother would kill him. The Vicar had been about to dismiss this as natural schoolboy exaggeration when he recalled Richard's face at Christmastime, the broken tooth and swollen lip. At that alarm bells began to ring in his head. He had consequently decided, whilst mulling it over through evensong, to come straight round to Richard's house when the service had finished.

"Well now," he said, looking round at the expectant faces surrounding him, trying to avoid Richard's bruised face, "how are you all?" He beamed at Mr Luckhurst who fidgeted under the unwinking gaze before replying self-consciously.

"Oh we're fine, vicar; aren't we boys?" He asked his sons for support. He didn't go to church and was just a bit over-awed by this little man behind whose childlike features lurked a mind like quicksilver.

Robin and Richard nodded their agreement. Although not normally reticent with the vicar Richard was unwilling to say anything, which later might be misconstrued negatively by his mother.

"Why, Richard," said the vicar suddenly, his voice full of surprise as is he had just noticed the bruising, "what on earth has happened to your face?"

Now it was Richard's turn to feel uncomfortable. He could not possibly tell a lie to the vicar, it would be unforgivable. On the other hand he could hardly tell the truth, either in part of full, because of the repercussions not just for himself but for his brother and sister.

His father cleared his throat nervously and loudly. The vicar turned to him, his face full of innocence awaiting enlightenment. "He…" began Richard's father, but stopped when he realised he had nothing to say but could only open his hands, palms upwards, helplessly.

"It was banged against a wall," blurted out Richard suddenly, hoping that a half truth was better than lying. A short silence ensued, only for a few seconds, but just enough for the vicar to appreciate that all was not as simple as it sounded.

"He's been fighting again," came his mother's voice through the open door to the kitchen. Mr Luckhurst's sudden release of breath was not lost on the vicar as she continued, walking into the room as she did so. "I've told him 'til I'm sick to death of telling him, but will he listen? Oh no." She shook her head and wrung her hands in a 'what am I to do' gesture.

The vicar threw a questioning glance in Richard's direction, catching his eye, but Richard could not meet it and looked away. This confirmed the vicar's view of what he already thought had probably happened. Richard was not the sort of boy to go and fight with other boys just for the sake of it. Unlike some, he knew Richard did not make a habit of fighting. It was clear to the vicar that Richard's mother was probably not telling the whole truth and the others, at least Richard and Robin and possibly the father, had no choice but to keep quiet, through fear of the consequences. He shook his head from side to side; there was nothing he could do to help Richard this time but perhaps he might be able to prevent a recurrence. He tutted before speaking, injecting a serious note into his voice.

"This won't do Richard. You really cannot go around fighting all the time. Especially by the look of your face it's not something you exactly excel at, eh?" He looked down at Richard who raised his head and shook it from side to side. "And besides," continued the vicar, "you were sorely missed at evensong tonight." Richard looked up at this. Although he had been resigned to missing evensong his absence had nagged at his insides like a live animal tearing at his flesh. "Well! Now will you promise me not to do any more fighting?"

Richard's mother re-entered the room from the kitchen at this point with a cup of tea, which she gave to the vicar, who sipped at it without enthusiasm whilst he waited for Richard's reply.

"Yes, sir," replied Richard. It was the best he could do in the circumstances but he still felt more than a bit of a fraud. He had, for just a split second, toyed with the idea of blurting out the truth, pointing at his mother and accusing her of his present predicament. However, his father, probably aware that he was thinking such thoughts, had narrowed his eyes and minutely shaken his head as a warning to him. Richard, knowing it was pointless, had dismissed the partially formed thought. He would only be regarded as being overwrought and would definitely get another hiding when the vicar left.

"Good." The vicar nodded and smiled, adding emphatically, "Very good," then pointedly looked at Richard's mother, about whom he had heard some odd reports, "Well, that's settled then, he won't have bruises like that again, will he, Mrs Luckhurst?"

Although Richard's mother was more than slightly taken aback by this more than pertinent question directed at her. She recovered quickly. "No, he won't vicar." She paused for thought. "A promise is a promise and I'll see that he keeps it," she hesitated only momentarily before adding, "he won't have bruises on his face again."

Beaming the vicar and turned to Richard and winked. "Good, well that's settled then," and resumed drinking his tea. Richard wondered if it was. The implied threat in his mother's last words had sent a chill down his spine. Knowing his mother it probably meant that he would have bruises everywhere else on his body save his face.

The vicar finished his tea with gusto. He had done what he had set out to do and thought it better if he left. "Well, I must be off. I only dropped in as I was passing." He stood up, as did everyone else and shook hands with Richard's father. He made for the door.

"I'll see you out, vicar," said Richard's mother, as with a wave of his hand, a hasty general goodbye and a "See you on Sunday, Richard," he left the room followed by Richard's mother.

Everyone sat down and listened as their mother effusively bade farewell to the vicar and then shut the door. Silence ensued, heightened by the fact that the sound on the television, which had been turned down at the vicar's arrival, had not been turned up again. All three waited expectantly as Mrs Luckhurst returned to the back room, her footsteps sounding unnaturally loud on the linoleum. As Richard had expected, her face was white with anger, as if she knew that the vicar's visit had not been just by chance but did not know where to lay the blame. She surveyed the room, whilst her husband exhaled noisily and then she pointed at Robin and Richard with her finger. "You and you, get up to bed."

Richard stood up straight away but Robin opened his mouth to argue since it was nowhere near what he considered to be his bedtime. However, on looking again at his mother's face he decided not to. Meanwhile, Richard, all the muscles in his body tensed, walked slowly passed his mother and, as expected, was speeded on his way by a hard slap on the back of his head.

Forewarned, Robin nimbly avoided most of the blow aimed at him and followed quickly behind Richard, joining him in the hall. The door slammed shut behind them and, as if at a signal, their mother's strident voice, muffled only slightly by the door, rang out. Robin, facing the door, slowly stuck out his tongue and stood there for a moment, grinning all over his face, finally turning to join Richard and walk with him slowly up the stairs.

PART FIVE: EASTER

Chapter 16: **Hot cross bun day**

Having cycled along Church Street, Richard slowed as he approached the short alleyway that led up to the Smithy and paused for a moment. The doors and windows were shut. There was no sound from the forge or smoke from the chimney. A gust of wind bringing with it the smell of baking hot cross buns impelled him to move on to the baker's shop a few yards up the road. Arriving at the shop he leaned his bicycle upright on the kerb and taking a carrier bag from his saddlebag, joined the queue, the end of which was out on the pavement, and leaned against the flint wall.

It was early morning on Good Friday, the day when they were allowed to have hot cross buns for breakfast rather than porridge. Richard had got up before everyone else this morning to do this errand. Robin had eyed him blearily as he had dressed, thankful that he was spared having to go shopping on this cold morning and could stay in the warmth of his bed until Richard returned and then he had to get up for breakfast. Going downstairs, Richard had put on his coat, and then taken the money left on the kitchen table the night before, pausing only to brush a fly away from the sugar bowl.

Edging forward with the queue, Richard patted his trouser pocket to make sure that the money was still there. The smell of hot cross buns was, if anything, much stronger now, although Richard wondered how that could be. With one foot on the step he could see into the shop and saw that Mrs White was serving, as was her daughter as usual, but Mr White was also there with his apron covered with flour dust. Apart from a few loaves, dotted here and there on the shelves behind the counter the place was given over to hot cross buns. Moving gradually still further into the shop with the queue Richard was swamped by the smell. It was so overpowering that he began to doubt is he would ever be able to smell anything else in his life.

The queue seemed to move more quickly now that he was inside the shop and soon it was his turn to be served. At the enquiring look and smile from Mrs White, he gave his order. "Ten hot cross buns, please."

The customer who was being served in front of him by Mr White turned round and stared in surprise at the size of the order, but Mr White who knew him just smiled.

"Hello, Richard, is the family all right?" Richard stood a little straighter, Mr White always addressed him as if he were and adult.

"Yes, thank you Mr White. How are you?"

Mr White smiled at this response. "Fine, thank you," and then took from his wife three large paper bags filled with freshly baked hot cross buns and put them into the carrier bag proffered by Richard, one bag on top of the other. Richard handed over the money and felt the warmth of the buns through the bag, whilst waiting for his change; then left with a cheery goodbye ringing in his ears.

Getting on his bicycle, Richard hung the carrier bag over his left handlebar. Checking to see that the road was clear he set off cycling back the way he had come. Although only a few minutes had passed since he had arrived at the bakers the sun seemed a little higher and warmer now. Richard cycled slowly, there was a freshness about the cool wind, which blew about his face and hands that made everything cleaner.

Richard paused for a moment at the hump-back bridge, looking along the railway line to Margate and then down to Broadstairs. The wind blew fiercer here, channelled by the cutting along which the railway line ran, but it could not dispel the inevitable fact of the coming of spring. Opening his mouth wide Richard breathed in the air deeply and, because of the strength of the wind, effortlessly. Revived, he pushed away from the dusty old brick wall and cycled off down the small hill that was the tail end of Northdown Road and up Northdown Hill to his house.

Leaning his bicycle against the wall he wiped his shoes on the mat in the porch and stepped into the kitchen. Around the table sat Robin and Marilyn, whilst their father busied himself with making the tea. Richard noticed the gleam in his brother's eyes as he hefted the bag onto a stool and took out the top paper bag of hot cross buns. He reached into the carrier bag for the second bag and found it a lot smaller that it was when Mr White had put it into the carrier bag. The third was smaller still. His father seeing the look on his face, came over and took the third bag from Richard and laid it on the table. Tearing the paper bag open he eyed the contents, watched eagerly by his sons. The hot cross buns had been flattened by the weight of the others on top.

"That's the trouble with buns freshly baked, they're too soft," he remarked.

Robin leaned across the table and picked one up, eyed it doubtfully for a moment and then commented, "Look more like hot cross pancakes."

Everyone laughed at this save Richard, who sat down on the stool and glowered. As the laughter continued, between mouthfuls of hot cross buns, he said, "Well next year you can go and get them yourself."

Robin just grinned and carried on eating, then having finished one, picked up another. "Hm, lovely. I like Hot Cross Bun day," he said as he bit into his second bun.

"Not so fast," said their father to Robin, handing out mugs of tea, which he had poured. "You'll make yourself sick."

Richard looking up from his comic added. "It's not called hot cross bun day, and you know it. Today is Good Friday."

"No it isn't" said Robin.

"Yes it is," replied Richard as menacingly as he could manage. Robin stopped arguing, which Richard regarded with some relief, as the conversation was about to degenerate into a pantomime routine.

Robin looked innocently up at the ceiling, as if seeking inspiration and then down at Richard. "It must be hot cross bun day since this is the only day that we get to eat hot cross buns."

"No it isn't," said Richard.

Robin look at him as he said "Well, perhaps Ricky you can explain why today is called Good Friday." He paused here and put his finger to the side of his head and twiddled it around as if to say Richard was barmy, making the Marilyn laugh. "Then we can decide which of us is right." He sat back in his chair just waiting for Richard to speak.

"That's not fair," said Richard, looking round to his father for support but he had, unnoticed, left the kitchen.

"Why isn't it?" asked Robin gleefully.

"Because....." started Richard, but unable to think of a suitable thing to say merely added lamely, "Because it isn't." Silence ensued whilst Richard carried on eating, watched by Marilyn and Robin.

"Well, go on then," prompted Robin, none too gently.

"Come on, Ricky," said Marilyn.

Richard reluctantly lifted his head. "All right then, but no interruptions." The serious tone of his voice warned against argument and his siblings nodded; Robin rather mischievously. With a deep sigh Richard began the story of the Crucifixion. Stopping every now and then to ask questions of his listeners to ensure they knew were able to follow what he was saying. As the tale unfolded Richard found that both he and the others became quite involved in it. Especially when he finished with the Roman Centurion saying, "Truly this man was the Son of God." He finished at that point; adding that the reason today was called Good Friday because it led to Jesus' resurrection and his victory over death and sin at Easter. He sat back and looked smugly at Robin, who did not seem at all abashed.

Robin raised his hand. "I have a question. If all you've said is true...."

"It is," interrupted Richard quickly.

"Then why is it still called 'Good Friday' – shouldn't it be called 'Bad Friday', or 'terrible Friday' after all the horrible things that happened on the actual day?"

Richard sighed loudly. He had not made the point clear enough to Robin. "Yes it's true that terrible things happened on Good Friday but the goodness of the day is not about what happened at the crucifixion but the good things that happened as a consequence of the bad thing."

"Fair enough" said Robin righteously but then added "but as far as I'm concerned it will always be 'Hot Cross Bun day'. Right Marilyn?" Robin lounged nonchalantly on the table, his attitude reflecting his expectation of success.

Marilyn, who had long ago lost interest in the whole argument looked up from her magazine, turned from Robin to Richard and said, "Yes."

Richard merely shook his head from side to side, ignoring Robin who stuck out his tongue who then spoke to Marilyn. "And of course, on Sunday," said Robin, "It's Easter Egg Day, when the Easter Bunny brings...." He got no further as Richard exploded at this blasphemy.

"No, it isn't, it's Easter Sunday. The day Jesus rose from the dead after his crucifixion on the cross." He paused for a moment before continuing noticing Robin's grin. "I give up!"

Robin assumed an air of concerned interest, whilst Marilyn went back to reading her magazine. "I suppose it says that this Sunday is Easter Sunday in that Bible of yours." Richard nodded his head, falling neatly into the trap set for him as Robin continued, "Well you show me where it says in the Bible that the day after tomorrow is Easter Sunday then we'll believe you. Marilyn?" She nodded without raising her head from the magazine as Robin turned to Richard, awaiting an answer.

Sighing in disgust, Richard looked away and then back again at Robin who was obviously enjoying this battle of wits with his elder brother.

"You know as well as I do that Sunday isn't called Easter Sunday in the Bible and that isn't what I was agreeing to when I said that Sunday was the day celebrating the day that Jesus rose from the dead." He stopped when he saw that Robin was laughing; only partly obscured behind a hot cross bun held in his hand in front of his face. He nodded to himself; he was being led on by his brother.

"Bah," he said disgustedly and unable to think of anything else to say, pulled a lump of dough from the bun he was holding and threw it at Robin.

After exclaiming "Well, that's nice I must say," Robin did likewise. Just then their father returned to the kitchen inadvertently attracting some of the missiles intended for Richard.

"All right, all right, just pack it in," he said, cuffing Richard and Robin none too gently round the head. He looked down at them in disgust then turned to Richard. "You should know better."

"He started it," said Richard pointing at Robin.

"No I didn't," shouted Robin over-loudly, his voice full of righteous indignation, belied by the wide grin on his face.

"Never mind who started it, just pack it up." He surveyed them grimly for a moment, then resumed, "You wouldn't be so cheeky if you mother was standing here right now." Unconsciously Richard and Robin shook their heads. "Right so don't go on because you think I'm soft or I'll give you both a proper belting. Now you," he pointed at Robin, "finish eating your breakfast then clean this mess up, and you," he turned to look at Richard, "hurry up and go and get the coke, we've been burning coke dust and cats' doings for the last two days."

Everyone laughed at this joke but Robin chipped in, "I wondered what that smell was coming from the fire." Then dodged a half-hearted clout from his father who walked off mumbling to himself. "Shouldn't let that bleedin' cat into the porch."

Richard spoke to his father's retreating back. "They'll be shut today. I'll go tomorrow." His father turned around. "Alright but don't forget to get there early." Richard nodded assent then with his brother and sister, resumed eating his breakfast. Peace and quiet returned to the kitchen, if only for a short while.

* * *

The heat in the kitchen and smell from the frying pan was overwhelming as Richard sat in his place at the kitchen table. As he had to go out early tonight to church he was to be the first to have his tea. It was not one of his favourite meals. His mother placed a plate of food in front of him with the admonishment.

"Eat up and grow up to be a big boy."

This was accompanied by her patting him hard on the head as she walked off to watch television with the rest of the family. Richard looked at his plate on which were spread a greasy fried egg and two even greasier pork strips. Each was at least a quarter of an inch thick, two inches wide and seven to eight inches long. Each strip was made up of alternate rows of glistening fat and pork meat, and at the top, the pork rind, with short bristles sticking out. Just looking at it made him feel nauseous. The thought of having to actually put it into his mouth, chew and then swallow, was something he would rather not even think about.

Resignedly he picked up his knife and fork. It would not have been so bad if he could cut away the fat and just eat the meat. Unfortunately he knew that his mother expected him to eat all of it – including the bristles. Slowly he cut into a pork strip with his knife, having difficulty in cutting through the rind, which had blobs of grease hanging on the bristles, but he finally succeeded in doing so as Robin strolled into the kitchen and paused by his chair.

Robin leaned over the plate, ignoring Richard's woeful expression, and sniffed appreciatively. "Lovely grub, eat it all up, there's a good boy," he said, and then hurriedly dodged away from Richard's thrown fist.

Richard had, unfortunately, forgotten he was holding a fork in that hand on which was tenuously held the piece of pork he had just cut. As he aimed his fist at Robin it flew off the end of the fork, narrowly missed Robin, and hit the wall with a splat! It hung there for a moment, finally sliding down the wall a few inches before dropping onto a pile of crockery.

His face full of startled amazement at the thought of almost being savaged by a piece of pork strip, Robin burst into giggles, which he hastily muffled by jamming both his hands over his mouth. Richard too began to laugh but his features froze as his mother's voice rang through the air.

"What's going on out there? Robin come away and let Richard eat his food in peace. Or else."

Robin stopped laughing immediately. "Yes, Mater," he replied. "I'm just going upstairs." Then sticking his tongue out at Richard he dashed out into the hall with a big grin on his face.

Richard stared morosely after him for a moment before, without making a sound, getting up out of his chair and tiptoeing over to the draining board to retrieve the piece of pork. It was lying on a plate, and apart from acquiring some dirt off the wall it did not look too bad. Richard dropped it onto his plate and eased himself quietly back onto his chair. He looked at the piece of pork he had already cut and realising he would have to leave a clean plate; decided he might as well eat that piece now as later. Picking up his knife and fork he scraped the piece of pork clean and, having carefully scrutinised it for any missed dirt, put it into his mouth. Giving it one or two hasty chews he swallowed it: having to force it down since it was still, more or less, one large lump. When he felt it start to come up again he rushed to the sink, filled a cup with water and poured it down his throat, hoping his mother had not heard him. He knew she did not like them drinking anything with their meals since she said it ruined their appetites.

Taking what remained of the water in the cup back to the table, he gripped his knife and fork more tightly than before and began to attack the two pork strips. Cutting them into small pieces he put them in his mouth and after a few quick chews swallowed the large pieces. As he usually did when he ate this particular meal, he pretended he was a pirate in the eighteenth century, or a sailor in Nelson's fleet, as he had read in books, having to eat salt pork on a long voyage. Richard had seen HMS Victory on a school trip and knew what such a ship looked like. With a vivid imagination it did not take much for Richard to picture living with others next to a cannon on the lower gun deck. Eating salt pork off pewter plates and, as his father said with relish, rolling his eyes when recounting his navy days, having to knock the weevils out of the biscuits before you could eat them. Or if you fancied a bit of fresh 'meat' you left them in.

That had been one of the more happy days he had spent on a school outing and afterwards he had excitedly told his father all about the trip around the dockyard to see destroyers and a minesweeper before actually being shown around HMS Victory. As he had hoped, his father, infected by Richard's enthusiasm in what had been a major part of his life, had begun to tell a few of his own experiences. Slowly at first then with greater speed as with subtle pumping from Richard he began to remember people, places and things he had thought he had buried so deep that they would never be recalled.

Richard smiled at the recollection of that day. His mother's absence from the house seemingly allowing his father to speak out unrestrained; especially after he had once had to tell Richard that he knew nothing about the war, as he relived events from his past. Occasionally bursting out into great guffaws of laughter as he explained an incident which, although in itself quite funny, did not bring out for him the pleasure his father obviously got when he recounted it. Perhaps he was holding something back, thought Richard, something he was unwilling or unable to share – even with his son.

At other times he would remember something sad or so horrible that he did not want to discuss either it or anything else about the navy. When this happened it didn't matter how much Richard used all of his wiles and skills to cajole him into continuing, his father suddenly just didn't want to remember. Richard knew that whenever it happened his father would be unlikely to speak to him or Robin again like this for quite a time, if only because their mother was so rarely out of the house.

His mother had no real friends to speak of. Her neighbours she despised because she thought they were common, stupid and ignorant; without any education, culture, or any hope of acquiring any. For the same reason neither Richard nor his brother were allowed to mix with the children who lived nearby. This made it especially hard on Robin, who did not, as he did, have the escape of meeting people who were regarded as acceptable at church. Whilst the people, with whom she would have liked to have been friends, and with whom she had only the most tenuous of links, such as the people at church, did not really want to know her.

With his mind centred on such thoughts and assisted by the now cold fried egg he managed to gulp down the last of the pork. Thankfully he wiped the sheen of sweat off his forehead and away from his eyes before taking the plate and cup to the sink so that he could wash them. All he had to do now was keep the pork down for an hour or so, otherwise he might sick it up again. He did not relish having to eat that particular meal twice; it was bad enough having to watch Robin eat regurgitated porridge. The idea of having to eat partly digested pork strips and a fried egg made him feel ill. He hurriedly dismissed it from his mind and concentrated on washing up. Having done so, he looked around for something sweet to eat to take the taste of pork out of his mouth.

"Can I have a piece of sugar, please," he paused only for a second before adding "mater?" After all these months he still had not got used to the word and was glad that his friends did not know. He would rather die first.

"All right." Came the peremptory reply.

Eagerly Richard spread some margarine onto a slice of bread, then sprinkled sugar on it until it was mostly covered, then poured the sugar that had not stuck to the margarine back into the bowl. Holding the bread horizontally he carried it over to the sink before biting into it, at ease knowing that any grains of sugar would fall into the sink and not onto either the table or floor to be trodden noisily into the lino. His mother hated that and heaven help anyone who did such a thing. He bit into the bread, his teeth jarring then crunching hard on the grains of sugar, which at first bravely resisted his attempt to crush them, then giving way with a suddenness that made his teeth jolt. Licking the sugar which had collected around his mouth he bit again into his 'piece', the slightly savoury taste of the margarine complemented by the intense sweetness of the sugar.

Looking at the clock he hurriedly finished eating. Licking his lips and fingers he washed the knife then left it on the draining board to dry. Rushing upstairs he washed and changed, looking hastily out of the window at the sound of raindrops spattering against the glass. Finishing, he hurried downstairs, put on his raincoat and tied the sou'wester around his head. Dodging passed Robin in the kitchen, who muttered at him.

"I'm glad I'm not going out tonight."

Richard only smiled, and then quickly assumed a serious expression as he stood by the door to the back room. "I'm off to church now, mater."

He waited until, as usual, his mother raised her head from the magazine she was reading and looked him up and down. Seemingly satisfied with his appearance she spoke. "OK, off you go but don't be late back."

Richard nodded his agreement, which seemed to suffice as, without any further comment, she resumed reading. Turning the door handle Richard opened the door from the kitchen to the porch and stepped outside. He was unable to prevent the thought from entering his head – he was free again.

Seizing his bike with one hand, he opened the door with the other, only just managing to hold onto it as the wind threw it back against the porch wall. Rain spattered onto his oilskin sou'wester as he wrestled his bicycle through the door and then, with some effort, closed it behind him. Immediately he jumped onto his saddle, to stop it getting wet, and cycled off down the path. A blast of wind caught him as he left the shelter of the side of the house and cycled off down Northdown Hill.

It was just the same as Good Friday last year, he thought, slitting his eyes against the force of the wind and rain. Himself and Barry leading the choir into the church, looking odd just in their cassocks, as if they were only partly dressed. The Meloids in their tin, in his cassock pocket, had rattled as he walked and he made a mental note to leave them in his place in the pew before the service started this year. As they appeared from the vestry corridor the congregation had stood up, their coats, evidence of the cold wet night, had twinkled where they were still spattered with drops of rain. A strong draught was blowing through the south door making the heavy velvet curtains swing to and fro.

Richard sighed as he relived the memory a sudden blast of rain bringing him back from daydreaming about the past to the present. Good Friday, not hot cross bun day, he thought was one of his favourite services of the year. Only partly because of the music, which ebbed and flowed as a background to his thoughts, nor because of the solemnity of the occasion:

although these contributed. It was most of all the quiet and tranquillity of the darkened church at this time that he liked, which was in contrast to what he imagined it must have actually been when Jesus was crucified. With these thoughts going around in his head Richard leaned into the stormy rain and, cycling harder, disappeared into the gloom cast by a broken street lamp.

Chapter 17: **Fossils and fighting**

Freewheeling down Harbour Street, Richard looked up as he passed under York Gate. Like the buildings and houses, which lined the street it was made out of split flints. Music from the juke box in the York Gate cafe came and went as he passed by. Behind the Espresso coffee machine the 'Teddy Boy' assistant could barely be discerned from the rising steam. Richard applied the brakes on his bicycle cautiously as he turned the corner at the bottom of the hill. There was a lot of sand on the road today, which could easily cause him to skid and come off his bicycle if he were not careful. Passing the low windows of the Tarter Frigate public house, whose doors he had yet to darken and whose very presence so near the beach he knew displeased his mother, he slowed with just enough momentum to get him beyond the low concrete slipway that led down to the beach and allow him to rest on the stout wooden railings which ran along the whole length of the edge of the jetty.

Getting off his bicycle Richard looked quickly around for sight of Emma. He knew he was early, purposely so, he said to himself as he leaned his bicycle against the solid wood railing, and then walked across to the other side of the jetty. Going passed the boathouse, some of the doors of which were open, their contents spilling out over the ground in front. Half-mended lobster pots, oars and nets, whilst inside the whites of the eyes of a fisherman, moving as he stitched a net, gave it an air of mystery and menace. This miscellany of items jogged Richard's memory so he backtracked to look at the notice board next to the Harbour Master's Office. In spite of already having checked the time in the local newspaper he was still relieved to see it confirmed. The tide was on its way out so they had plenty of time to walk along the beach to Stone Gap, or even further if Emma wished.

Richard resumed his walk along the jetty and leaned on the rotting wooden fence on the seaward side. A stiff, continuous, breeze was blowing here taking the tops off the edges of the khaki-coloured waves, which creamed as they broke over the seaweed covered chalk rocks. Richard looked up to the end of the jetty and then back again down to the honey coloured sand in Stone Gap. There were only one or two people about. Up on the headland Bleak House stood; a dirt brown guardian atop the white chalk cliff surrounded by greenery from the garden. Richard pushed himself away from the fence and returned back the way he had come. Rounding the corner of the boathouse he paused as he saw Emma standing by his bicycle. He smiled and ran to meet her, glad of the opportunity to see her other than for a few minutes after church. Although her boarding school had closed for the Easter holidays, as at Christmas, a few of the girls – including Emma – whose parents were abroad had remained at school. To make their stay less tiresome they were allowed a lot more latitude than they were in school time. Richard shuddered to a halt and kissed Emma lightly on the lips, then took her hand in his. He gazed into her eyes for a moment then impulsively gave her another kiss before asking.

"Shall we walk along the beach?"

He surreptitiously looked down to see what shoes she was wearing but Emma noticed and laughed. He was relieved to see that she had sandals on.

Emma nodded, "Yes, let's." They walked along the jetty and down the steep slipway that led onto the sands to Stone Gap. Though exhilarated to be in Emma's company again he still remembered to ask how she was and her friends, not forgetting Marmaduke in his eagerness.

Whilst Richard expected it, the wind took him aback as they left the shelter of the jetty and ran down the slope to the sand into Stone Gap; he hesitated for a moment, wondering if Emma might find it too much, but he needed have worried. Emma laughed as the wind caught her hair: her white teeth bright against her lips. Channelled by the cliff on their left and the concrete breakwater on their right the wind was so strong that to breathe it seemed you need only to open your mouth for the air to be forced into your lungs. Richard stepped forward tugging Emma along, who ran to catch up, spontaneously Richard too picked up speed and laughing, hand in hand, they ran across the sand the wind roaring in their ears.

After a while they slowed to a walk across the now firm sand, still damp from the retreating sea. Sometimes having to step over chalk boulders; at others, each taking one side their arms, joined by their hands, forming a temporary bridge between their bodies. Richard paused for a moment to look at the remains of a dead green crab lying twisted and broken on the sand, but quickly moved on when noticing Emma's unease. They walked away from the wet sand to above the high tide mark where the sand was dry and sat down.

The wind was less fierce here. Richard sat and gazed out to sea. The April sun had barely warmed the surface of the sand, whilst the wind was pleasantly cool, heralding the end of the really cold winter weather with a hint of the summer to come. With Emma, still holding her hand, Richard watched the green sea, the water in the waves twisting and tumbling over itself in the rush to the shore before breaking with a perceptible sigh as it hissed across the sand. Each wave left behind partially formed spume and bubbles that hesitated for a moment before finally being absorbed by the sand before it too was covered by the next incoming wave.

After a while Emma sighed. "Isn't it beautiful here?"

Richard nodded; he thought so as well, but not just because of the sea. He was going to say nothing and merely squeezed Emma's hand slightly but then found himself confessing, "I know."

He paused, wondering what it was that compelled him to share his thoughts like this, then continued, "I often come here. It's a very beautiful bay, especially this time of year when there are no holiday-makers about."

They both looked around the wide expanse of the bay and the deep sandy beach, protected at the back and sides by tall white chalk cliffs. Since at high tide it was cut off from Viking Bay for a few hours by the tide and the only other way down to it was by means of a narrow footpath, obscured by shrubs, leading to the beach from Stone Road, it was usually only frequented by local people; except in July and August when holidaymakers spilled over from Viking Bay in their search for a few square yards of sand.

Emma's voice broke through his thoughts again as, with a squeeze, she let go of his hand and hugged her knees, rocking slightly back and forth. Looking sideways at Richard, she bit her lip, and then spoke. "I shall miss this."

Richard turned his head and stared, taking Emma's hand back into his. Her words had somehow had a note of finality about them. Very quietly he said, "What do you mean?"

Smiling wanly Emma said, "It's not definite yet." Then in a rush, "But it might be." Emma looked down at the sand then releasing her hand again moved round to face Richard. "You know my father's in the Foreign Office?" Richard nodded dumbly, his heart, unbidden, beginning to beat a little faster. "Well," continued Emma, "he's being moved to Washington, in America, this summer. "It's not absolutely definite just yet," she said again, "but if he is moved then I'll probably leave Landen Hall and go to school in America."

"Oh," replied Richard, not being able to think of anything else to say. He couldn't quite conceive of America as a place other than that represented on television, which only provided a confused amalgam of gangsters, cowboys and Indians. "When will you know for sure, do you think?"

Emma gave a slight shrug and a half smile. "I don't know," she paused, "but don't let's worry about it. It might not happen," she said, trying to inject a cheerful note into her voice.

Emma reached out and picked up Richard's hand, which he was trailing aimlessly back and forth in the sand; making small ridges and then smoothing them over before starting again. Richard sat holding Emma's hand as he alternated between gazing into her eyes and out to sea. After a short while he pulled Emma down to the sand and moved back a little so that they were now lying on the sand facing each other. "I love you," said Richard, "I don't think I've ever loved anyone else. Emma moved forward slightly and kissed him.

"I love you, too. Don't worry if I have to go to America, I'll write every week."

Richard smiled and kissed Emma again. He didn't want to say so but knew even then that if Emma did go away they would probably never see each other again. He suddenly thought back to the time before his family had moved down to Broadstairs from London a few years ago, that he thought he had loved the girl next door whose name he could not now even remember.

Even though she was here with him he could sense that Emma was, somehow, already slipping away and there was nothing he could do about it. It really didn't bear thinking about. Even if he did it wouldn't make any difference. Richard had acquired early, a certain fatalism about life, usually reserved for when you were older. He, like his brother and sister, had had to bear so many disappointments and anguish that he had learned not to expect too much in life. Even the present wasn't really guaranteed. His attitude to life was something that had been caused by an accumulation of hurts and disappointments mostly at the behest of their mother. Although in themselves they had been small and should have meant little, they had become significant by their sheer number. But this now was different. His love for Emma equalled or even excelled the only other important things in his life, that of his love for his brother and sister and his singing in the choir. Whether he would be able, as he had in the past, to overcome yet another major disappointment was something he would rather not dwell on, especially since it might, just might, never happen.

"Come on," said Richard at last. "If you're meant to be out collecting fossils for your geology class, we had better go and find some." He stood up and put his hand down. Emma took hold and Richard pulled her to her feet.

"All right," she said grinning. Both of them brushed the sand off their clothes then hand in hand they walked up the beach, their progress marked by the squeaking noise of their shoes on the sand.

Arriving at the cliff-face, Richard looked up at the cracked and faded sign warning the public to be aware of falling chalk. Richard then scrutinised the chalk face with an expert eye, looking for the tell-tale signs of the calcified fossil sometimes yellower than the white of the chalk proper, which indicated that there was a fossil below the surface. Emma moved off slightly whilst Richard hurriedly continued to scan the cliff face. He was keen to find a fossil as quickly as possible, both to impress Emma and ensure that her school would be satisfied that Emma had been collecting fossils so paving the way for further meetings, especially if this might be one of the very last times he would see her.

Unable to locate anything he moved along the cliff face studying the chalk intently as he went, with Emma following on behind. After about fifty yards Richard became slightly worried. He never usually had this much difficulty in finding fossils. He was famed among his friends as the fossil finder. Richard stopped suddenly and eyed the cliff where he was standing. Whilst he was unable to spot the signs of any fossils he had noticed a split in the cliff face, which he might be able to prise open. Taking his father's jack knife out of his pocket he pulled out the spike and poked it into the crack at various places to find the deepest point. Having found it he pushed the spike in hard then cast around for a flint.

"I'm looking for a suitable flint to use as a hammer," he said to Emma, whose face cleared since she had been puzzled by his eyes roving around the ground. She too looked around for a suitable flint. After discarding a number of flints Richard found a large one, which was narrowed at one end so that he could grip it tightly whilst using the larger end as a hammer head.

Returning to the embedded knife he used both implements as a hammer and chisel to work up and down the crack in the cliff to loosen if from the main body of the cliff. After doing this for a short while, which involved a great deal of wresting of the knife from the suction of the chalk, Richard felt that he had probably reached the point when the cliff would soon fall. "You'd better stand back a bit," he cried, holding back the cliff with one hand and the knife with the other. Emma nodded, then stepped back a few paces. "Is this far enough?" she asked. Richard looked. It seemed okay but you never knew, "Just a bit more to be on the safe side." Emma nodded again and stepped nimbly around some rounded chalk boulders, the residue of some previous rock falls. Richard nodded his agreement, the first making sure of his footing he removed his hand from the chalk face. He had resolved to run quickly once he pulled the knife out in case even more chalk fell down than he had bargained for.

"Ready?" he called.

Emma nodded then said, "Ready."

Richard pulled the embedded knife away from the cliff so forcing the chalk away from the main body. He ran away as he did so to stand by Emma, not looking back despite hearing the noise of the fall behind him. He looked at Emma, her eyes wide with amazement as he reached her, causing him to look round quickly. The noise, louder than usual, should perhaps have warned him. The slab of chalk he had intended had fallen down but had brought down with it an even larger area above it.

"Amazing," said Richard, awed by what he had done. Whilst he thought the cliff were white, they now looked grey in comparison with the colour of the newly exposed chalk.

He was about to step forward to look for fossils in the newly fallen chalk when he stopped by a sudden premonition. He was still holding the flint in his hand. Without knowing why he threw it hard at the cliff. It sailed through the air in an arc, to land with a dull thud just above the wide white scar. The chalk appeared to tremble for a moment before another section, as large as the first, suddenly fell down onto the pile of newly fallen chalk.

"Is it safe?" asked Emma as odd pieces of chalk still dropped off onto the now settled mound.

"I don't know," replied Richard. "I'll just throw some more flints at it to make sure." Scouting around, he picked up some fist-sized lumps of flint and threw them at the chalk he had laid bare, and the surrounding area. Apart from one or two lumps of chalk there was no other movement.

"It should be alright." Said Richard as he moved forward cautiously, stepping carefully over the broken chalk on the ground, eyeing it thoroughly as he went. He saw an Echinoid peeping out of the chalk. "Here's one," he cried triumphantly, pointing with his jack-knife at a fossil, which appeared to be emerging from the chalk.

"Let me see," said Emma excitedly, crouching down beside Richard.

"Would you like to dig it out?" asked Richard, proffering his jack-knife.

"Emma shook her head. "No, you had better do it."

Richard nodded and very carefully dug and cut the surrounding chalk away from the fossil. The chalk was damp and sticky and clung to the knife blade, making it difficult for him to work. Now and then the blade broke free and skidded across the chalk, making Emma draw in her breath. Finally, reversing the knife he dug the spike into the chalk and eased the Echinoid fossil clear, to a cheer from Emma that made him feel good.

Now that it was free he sat down in the sand in a more comfortable position and began to scrape away the excess chalk. It did not take too long to see that the fossil was not whole and the part embedded in the chalk had, somehow, been crushed and broken, as a lot of fossils were. Richard expressed his disgust.

"Is it not any good then?" asked Emma, taking it from Richard's out-stretched hand and examining it.

Richard shook his head. "Not really," he said, pointing with his knife. "Half of it is crushed and when you have cleaned away the chalk the broken pieces will probably just fall off." He stood and looked up at the cliff, talking to himself. "You really need a whole one." He moved to the cliff and began a concentrated study of the rock face. After a few minutes he found a beige convex shape, highlighted by the surrounding very white chalk. "I've found another one," he cried out, causing Emma to put down the fossil she had been examining to come and stand next to Richard.

"Where?"

"Here," replied Richard pointing to the fossil, what was about as big as a pocket watch. Estimating its size by the exposed piece and allowing a little bit extra to be on the safe side, Richard dug carefully around the fossil, removing fairly large lumps of chalk and scraping them laboriously off his penknife.

"What if it is broken once you manage to get it out?" asked Emma.

Richard paused for a moment. The thought had occurred to him as he was digging. There was really no point in spending a lot of time digging this fossil out of the cliff face if it was broken like the other one. "I'll dig round the fossil like I am now, then here, here and here." He pointed with his penknife at three points around the fossil equidistant from each other. "And I'll scrape away the chalk carefully to see if it is whole before working on it properly."

Emma nodded approval to this plan as Richard resumed his work, digging quickly to remove the bulk of the chalk. Having finished the rough digging he very painstakingly began to fine away the chalk at one point of the fossil following the curve of the shell until it reached the bottom. "That side's alright," he said, eventually, turning to smile at Emma.

"Isn't it exciting," she said, craning forward to get a better look, as Richard stood back to make room for her.

After touching the fossil lightly with her fingers, Emma moved back and Richard resumed his work. After what seemed ages, but was really only a few minutes, he said triumphantly, "That side is alright as well." Now that he knew the full size of the fossil Richard worked quickly, removing the remainder of the chalk around the sides prior to levering the fossil out of the chalk with the spike of his knife. He had almost done this when he heard a voice say.

"What have you got there?"

Startled, Richard turned around. He was surprised to see Graham Poole who he had succeeded as Head Chorister at St Peter's. Richard had never really liked him. He used to bully the smaller boys and especially took great pleasure in forcing you to play a game of 'knuckles' with him, often prolonging the game after you had conceded he had won, only so he could inflict more pain.

"Nothing," replied Richard, knowing that it wouldn't matter what he said. Graham was well known for sticking his nose into other people's business just for the sake of it. Graham stepped forward threateningly, pushing Emma to one side, making her stumble backwards, which made him smile.

"It's just a fossil," said Richard hurriedly, hoping that his curiosity satisfied, Graham would go on his way.

"Good, that's just what I'm looking for," replied Graham, making Richard's heart sink as he determined what to do. "Go on, get out of the way so I can have it," said Graham.

Richard was very reluctant to do so. One reason was that he wanted Emma to have this fossil. It was a perfect specimen, one of the best he had ever seen. Not only that, but Richard could see that Emma was frightened of the bigger boy and that made him angry. He did not like the way Emma had been pushed or the look of confusion and fear on her face.

Leaving the knife embedded in the chalk, which surrounded the fossil Richard turned to face Graham. He was reluctant to fight him, not only because Graham was bigger and had a reputation for bullying but also because of how it might affect Emma. On the other hand he did not want to see Emma get hurt, nor was he prepared to give up this fossil. Richard was faced with a dilemma he seemed unable to resolve. He decided to wait and see what would happen. Now that he had stepped out of the shadow he was conscious, of the sun on his back, making him progressively warmer. Behind Graham he noticed the wind blowing stray wisps of Emma's hair from side to side. Whilst in front of him Graham, with beads of sweat on his freckled face stood in a more menacing pose.

"Are you going to let me have that fossil or not?" he finally demanded, and pushed Richard, forcing him to step backwards.

Having made up his mind Richard decided to declare his intentions. "No, I'm not," he said and readied himself for a fight, feeling annoyed and slightly ridiculous both with himself and this bully for getting him into this situation: especially in front of Emma.

Richard had almost decided to change his mind and resign himself to giving up the fossil when Graham stepping forward, grabbed hold of two handfuls of

Richard's jersey and attempted to lift him up. As he clearly did not have the strength to do so and since the wool of Richard's jersey was very old and worn, he only succeeded in stretching it further. Graham had barely begun saying the words, "If you don't let me have...." and was going to say 'that fossil' when Richard acted.

When Richard thought about it afterwards, up to that point he had no clear idea of what he was going to do. Only two things compelled him to do what he did and he would not have been able to say which was the more important.

First there was fear. Not from the position he was in, or of what Graham would do to him, but of his mother. He knew that if he returned home again with a badly distorted jersey, what his mother would do to him did not bear thinking about. He just had to be able to give a good account of what he had done to prevent it. A veteran of many beatings, he knew how tenuous was the balance between his mother's very occasional good humour and her rages, which he, his brother, sister and father, found incomprehensible. It would take very little for him to be badly beaten because of his jersey being stretched again.

Second was his love of Emma. He had found it so easy to love her. If he had to decide at this moment what was more important, more precious; his love for Emma or that for church music, he did not know how he would decide. Their relationship had from the very beginning been special to him but over the months he had slowly begun to realise how important it was. Now that it was again being threatened he was prepared to go to any lengths to protect it.

Richard stepped quickly backwards, half a step and then forward, at the same time moving his arm backward and then forward and with all his strength he hit the other boy hard in the solar plexus. He didn't realise this was the name of that particular part of the body but he remembered that his Dad, who had boxed for the navy, had told him time after time that if you want to take the '*wind out of somebody's sails*' that was the point to aim for.

Graham went 'Oof' and clutched his stomach, bending double as he did so that his face was almost level with Richard's waist. He looked up at Richard and started to say something but he was so badly winded and was trying desperately to suck in air that the words died in his throat.

What Richard did next he remembered later with regret, but something was driving him uncontrollably. Because of his fear he wanted really to humiliate and injure this boy since he had caused Emma and himself so much distress; but most of all to save himself from a later beating from his mother when she saw the sorry state of his jersey. Swinging his arm back again he brought his fist forward with all his weight and smashed it into the boy's nose. It cracked ominously and immediately began to pour blood. Richard noticed the look of fear, which suddenly appeared in the other boy's eyes as he fell backwards to land heavily in the sand. He also saw Emma's original look of concern for his safety was being replaced by confusion at what had suddenly happened to Graham Poole. Involuntarily she stepped back, her face white and her limbs shaking.

Richard was angry with himself and with Graham Poole. He knew, as did a very few others that if pushed to the limit he and his brother Robin had a temper – probably inherited from their mother – which occasionally, as now, rose to the surface when in a 'kill or be killed' situations. Richard cursed himself and his luck. Had Emma not been there he would have probably kicked Graham as he lay on the sand in front of him. Only the look of alarm in Emma's eyes, when he drew back his foot as he considered the matter, held him back. He returned to the cliff face and retrieved his knife from the chalk. Hesitating whether to remove the fossil he had half decided against it. From being something precious it would only remind him and Emma of this day. Against this was the need for Emma to show the school proof of her search. With a vicious twist of his hand the spike on the knife ejected the fossil into his hand. Closing his Dad's jack knife with a loud snap he put it in his trouser pocket and returned to Emma's side.

Graham drew back as he passed him and, to his dismay, so did Emma as he approached. His hands still shaking from the adrenalin pumping through his veins he took Emma's hand in his. She too was shaking, but not for the same reason. "Come on," he said gently, "let's go." Emma did not respond but allowed herself to be led away from the spot but not before a last look at Graham, whose face was now covered with blood.

They had gone only a few yards when Richard, his mind still in a turmoil from what had suddenly happened to his tranquil day out with Emma, stopped and looked back at Graham prone on the sand, dabbing his nose with a handkerchief. Richard was still undecided whether to go back and hit him again. Somehow he had felt cheated. Graham had not to his mind been hurt enough for what he had done – especially to the damage to his relationship with Emma. He had started to make a half step towards Graham when he felt the restraining tug of Emma's hand in his. He looked at her.

"Come on Richard," she said, and then stepping forward suddenly kissed him. All thought of further revenge dissipated with that kiss. Letting go of her hand Richard hugged Emma with his left arm. Then taking up her hand again they walked back along the beach the way they had come.

* * *

The knock on the front door, when it sounded, was so loud that Richard thought for a moment it had gone off in his head. He had jerked up at the noise bur oddly his brother; sister and mother remained dozing in front of the fire. Only his father who was reading the paper in the kitchen raised his head and then drew himself upright then, staggering from stiffness, moved slowly towards the door leading from the kitchen to the hall. "All right, all right," he grumbled as the knock on the door sounded again, this time more insistent than the first.

Richard smiled at his father's tone. He was about to continue reading when, his curiosity aroused, Richard eased himself off the floor. Stepping carefully around his brother's feet he followed his father through the kitchen to the hall, closing the door to the kitchen behind him just as his father reached the front door. His father turned and eyed him sourly then gestured for him to get out of sight. Richard smiled then sat on the bottom step of the stairs behind the door, and watched as his father pulled the door open.

"Mr Luckhurst?" enquired a man's voice. Richard craned his neck to look through the crack between the door and frame and saw a man he vaguely recognised. Then he realised who it was as, standing beside him was Graham Poole.

Richard's father nodded and said, "Yes!" not quite sure what was expected of him. The man pulled the boy in front of him as Richard squinted through the crack, wondering what was going to happen next and if he should make a run for it. After he had returned Emma to her school he had completely forgotten about the fight. His initial fears that it would somehow turn Emma against him had vanished as they had walked back from the beach. That having been his only worry concerning the fight he had promptly forgotten about it. He was now intrigued as to what Graham and his father were doing here.

"My name's Mr Poole and this afternoon you son beat mine up. Well, I want him punished for it."

Richard's father straightened up. He hadn't liked the look of this man or his gangling spotty son. Any reluctance and drowsiness flew away like dust in a storm. He eyed Mr Poole and then his son.

"Well!" demanded Mr Poole when nothing appeared to be forthcoming.

"Well what?" said Richard's father, seeming to ready himself as if for a physical assault. He imagined he could feel his blood flowing a little faster and his breathing quickened imperceptibly. He knew the signs from his navy boxing days and narrowed his eyes slightly knowing that it gave him a menacing appearance. It had often worked in intimidating his opponents and he smiled inwardly as he saw Mr Poole hesitate slightly. Mr Poole cleared his throat nervously.

"I want to see your son punished for hitting my lad." Richard's father eyed Mr Poole balefully.

"He's not here," he replied. "And anyway how do I know that your son didn't start it?"

Richard's face split into a wide grin. He hadn't known how his Dad would react to this news but hadn't expected this.

"Of course he didn't start it, just look at his face." Richard's father looked. Mr Poole's son's nose was a swollen mass of bruising with traces of blood around the nostrils.

"That doesn't prove anything other than my boy is faster with his fists than yours. Anyway, your son's bigger than mine. Why should he want to go and fight someone bigger than himself, eh?"

Mr Poole looked at his son's face and then back to Richard's Dad. "So you're not going to do anything about it?" Richard's father merely shrugged his shoulders in a helpless, dismissive gesture. "In that case," continued Mr Poole, "I'll inform the police, I'm sure they won't take it so lightly."

Richard's father sighed as he stiffened slightly. "Now there's no need to get aereated over this. Boys will be boys. It's only natural they get into scrapes now and again – what can we do about it?" He paused, watching the words sink in. "I'll tell you what I'll do. I'll have a word with my lad when he gets home and find out exactly what happened. In fact I'll bring him along to your house so the four of us can have it out together to find out the truth." He was pleased to see that the Poole boy had drawn back at this remark, which had not gone unnoticed by his father. Richard's Dad seized on this and continued magnanimously, "But then we don't want to make a mountain out of a molehill, do we? I'll speak to my lad and if he did start this fight then I'll tan his hide. I can't say fairer than that, can I?"

Mr Poole looked down at his son. "I suppose not."

Richard's Dad smiled then continued. "But on the other hand if I find out that your son started it then I'll be the one who goes to the police, all right? We can't have bullying of smaller boys going on, can we?" He saw with satisfaction Graham Poole's face pale with fright and that Mr Poole began to look uncertain.

Mr Poole gazed about him at the peeling yellow paint on the walls of the house, a cracked window in the door that badly needed painting and then back at Richard's father. He suddenly felt anxious to get back to his own house over the hardware shop at the roundabout. He had only come here in the first place because his wife had insisted. He knew his son had been in trouble before for bullying smaller boys from the reports from his school's headmaster. Taking a deep breath, he replied, "Yes, all right, I'll leave it up to you." He pulled his son's arm. "Come along, Graham. Sorry to have troubled you, Mr Luckhurst." Raising a finger to his hat he dragged his son quickly down the path.

Richard's Dad watched them go then smiled to himself and closed the door quietly. He looked down at Richard still sitting on the stairs. Richard stopped grinning and returned his father's gaze. He had been amazed at how his father had handled Mr Poole and was glad it had been him who had answered the door and not his mother. He felt his father was waiting for an explanation. So he spoke.

"It wasn't my fault Dad, he started it." He stopped for a moment; he didn't want to tell his Dad about his meeting with Emma. Still, a half truth was better than a lie. "It was down the beach. I wouldn't let him have a fossil I was digging out of the cliff so he pulled my jersey. Well I only hit him twice!" He smiled as that seemed sufficient justification to explain his behaviour.

"That's all right, Ricky. Only if there is a next time hit him an extra hard time for telling tales, all right?" Richard nodded as his father, stepping past him to climb the stairs, tousled his hair. Richard stood up. "Thanks Dad, I will." Then he walked back the way he had come to join his brother and sister in the back room.

Chapter 18: 'Happy' Birthday

The helicopter floated effortlessly through the sky, its yellow rotor blades cutting through the air as it rose higher and higher. It seemed as if nothing could stop it when gradually its blades slowed, speeded up again, faltered and suddenly stopped. Reluctantly but relentlessly it was forced by gravity downwards barely scraping over the wall to crash in the thick, overlong grass.

Richard smiled happily. Having survived the Easter weekend it was now Tuesday and his birthday. But most of all, tomorrow he would be meeting Emma again. Completing his happiness it was a warm sunny day and once he had finished playing with his toy helicopter he had some other presents inside waiting for him. Holding in his hand the mechanism for making the helicopter fly he walked to the wall, which was about four feet high. He leaned over and saw the helicopter lying at an angle where it had crashed. Jumping up on top of the wall Richard looked to see where he would put his feet when he jumped down, making sure that it would not be on the helicopter. Having chosen a place he jumped. As he did so, the place where he was about to put his foot moved slightly. Almost immediately he saw the outline of a hedgehog, so camouflaged by the grass and weeds that he hadn't seen it when he first looked. He couldn't land on the hedgehog or he would crush it. Moving his foot slightly out of the way he landed heavily twisting his ankle on a clump of earth.

The relief at having saved the life of the hedgehog, which now scuttled off through the nearby privet hedge, gave way to the pain from the jolt his ankle gave him from the wrench it had taken, then anguish as, in trying to steady himself, he thrust out his hand and felt the plastic blades of his helicopter crack under the force of his unintended blow. Richard lay there stunned. A few minutes ago everything was perfect and now he had a twisted ankle and a broken toy. Gingerly he moved his hand away, noticing the indentation in his palm from the broken blades.

Slowly he picked up the helicopter and tried to push the broken blades together, but to no avail. Richard felt crushed. The few minutes he had played with the helicopter had been marvellous; he had gained a feeling of release as if it was himself flying through the air. Now it was over, the realities of the capricious nature of life rushing back to being him down to earth. How could he possibly explain to his mother that what had happened was an accident. How would she react? Richard looked glumly at the broken toy then turned it in his hands as he wished again and again the he could undo what had happened so quickly. He knew only too well how his mother would behave when she saw the broken toy. From the pit of his stomach a wave of nausea sprang up and swept unbidden over him. He looked again at the broken blades, willing them to stick together but nothing happened. A tear emerged from his eye and he brushed it away angrily. Finally shrugging his shoulders, he climbed awkwardly back over the wall holding the broken toy in his hands and careful not to put too much weight on his twisted ankle. His only consolation being that he had saved the hedgehog from being maimed or killed, he limped into the porch, opened the kitchen door and stepped inside leaving his shoes on the mat in the porch.

His father looked up from reading the newspaper as Richard entered. Smiling at his son, he was about to ask how the helicopter had flown when he saw the broken toy in Richard's hands. Richard's father's shoulders slumped in resignation, to which Richard shrugged his in reply and mouthed, "Where's Mater?" His father silently pointed to the back room. Taking a deep breath Richard, thinking it was better to get it over with on his birthday when his punishment might be less severe, walked into the room where his mother reclined in an armchair, her feet on the pouffe, reading a magazine. As usual she was picking her teeth with her long painted fingernails, all the time making little sucking noises. At the sight of his mother Richard's courage failed him and he started to back away. As if noticing this movement, his mother looked around swiftly, eyed him up and down before noticing the broken toy in his grass streaked hand. Her eyes, as they stared into his, demanded an explanation, which Richard haltingly began.

"I'm sorry but it's broken..." Richard stopped as his mother dropped the magazine and, with surprising agility for someone who a few moments ago was lounging on a chair, was up on her feet, head bent like a vulture over a piece of carrion, eyes glittering feral-like. Richard unnerved by his mother's quiet, began his explanation again, speaking quickly in an effort to get his explanation out before he was hit – as he knew he undoubtedly would be – since it might somehow lessen his punishment.

"It went over the wall and when I jumped over, there was a hedgehog in the way so I accidently fell on the present: but the hedgehog is all right," he finished, holding the helicopter up for her to see, adding, "It was an accident."

His mother looked at him as if he were mad, making Richard wonder if he had spoken too fast so that she had not understood him. He started to repeat what he had said when from the corner of his eye he saw, too late to avoid it, his mother's right hand swinging round to hit him hard on the side of his head, making his ears sing and causing him to stagger backwards, awkwardly, on his twisted ankle. He gasped as a jolt of pain shot through his foot and up his leg. Lurching about for a few seconds, whilst retrieving his balance he had dropped the broken toy helicopter, causing its last remaining blade, which had been hanging by a fragment of plastic, to snap off. Richard paled still further as he saw this and then bent over to pick it up.

"Leave it!" commanded his mother. Richard paused, frozen in a crouching position before slowly straightening up. His mother stared at him, her mouth twitching uncontrollably, a finger pointed accusingly at Richard.

"You ungrateful little wretch," she began, but seemed unable to continue. Turning away she rushed to the sideboard, knelt down to open the door and took out Richard's other birthday presents; two exercise books for his writing, a red and blue biro and two pencils. Looking round and up at Richard she said, "So you like breaking things we get you, do you? Well I'll save you the trouble." Taking hold of the exercise books she carefully tore them in half and then half again, dropping the pieces in the fire. Grinning maliciously at Richard she then snapped the pencils in half and then bent and broke the biro pens, dropping them to the floor. Standing up she walked over to the helicopter now lying on the floor. Pushing Richard out of the way she then commenced stamping on it hard so that it shattered to pieces.

Richard's heart sank. Whilst he thought it might have been possible to repair the broken blades with some plastic glue, this was now impossible. Having finished trampling on the toy helicopter his mother grabbed hold of his right ear, twisting it so that his head looked up at her face at an angle. "Now clear up that mess up and put it in the dustbin, then get up to your room and stay there," punctuating this statement with further slaps to his face and head. Satisfied for a moment, she resumed her reclining posture on the armchair.

Richard, his head ringing from the blows, limped into the kitchen, passed his father who without saying a word put his hand on Richard's shoulder and gave it a squeeze. Richard turned his head and smiled and going into the hall retrieved the dust pan and brush from the cupboard under the stairs. His head was beginning to ache from the blows it had received, whilst the pain in his ankle was now throbbing with a pernicious regularity.

Limping into the back room he quickly swept up the debris of his helicopter and then the remains of the pens and pencils, wondering if anything could be salvaged. He looked around at his mother who fixed him with her eyes. She must have known what he was thinking.

"I said put everything in the dustbin or God help you!"

Richard sighed inwardly, knowing that it would be foolish and dangerous to defy such an order. Quickly he scooped up the remnants and put them into the dustpan. Standing slowly, favouring his leg with the twisted ankle, he limped out of the back room, his mother's voice following relentlessly after him.

"And there'll be no party tonight, either."

Pausing slightly at his mother's words Richard then resumed walking to the outside. Limping to the back of the porch he lifted the dustbin lid and with a final look at the contents of the dustpan, emptied it. His broken presents fell into the rubbish, mingling symbolically with the ashes and cinders of yesterday's fire.

He had replaced the lid and was about to return to the kitchen when Robin came clattering along the path on his bicycle, returning from the shops. He seemed to be in hurry and the expression on his face combined urgency with fear.

"You're in big trouble," said Robin quietly, looking quickly from side to side and over his shoulder just in case there mother was lurking about, as she was apt to do. Richard raised his eyebrows. He couldn't tell from his brother's voice how badly he was in trouble. Neither could he think of anything he had done recently that should concern his mother, other than the broken toys, but Robin couldn't know about that yet. The incident over his fight down the beach had been sorted out by his Dad. Not that it mattered too much since the cause of the fight was the other boy pulling his jersey. His mother could hardly blame him for what happened and might even be on his side. He ran quickly over the events of the last few days but there was nothing there, which would seem to warrant his being in trouble. The only thing was his being with Emma but his mother couldn't possibly know anything about that.

"What about?" he asked, not too concernedly.

Robin looked around again before continuing.

"I met Barry down the roundabout. You know that boy Graham you beat up?"

Richard nodded; he hadn't actually beaten him up although he wished he had after what he had done to himself and Emma.

"Well, you know he came up here with his dad to complain and Dad sent him off with a flea in his ear?" Richard nodded again. It looked as if it was going to be a long story, he smiled to himself at this thought, but so far it didn't sound ominous.

"Well, that boy's mum bumped into Mater yesterday," he stopped here and curled his lip with a look of distaste as having to use that word, making Richard laugh, but he stopped quickly when Robin didn't join in.

"Well, that boy's mother told Mater that the fight you had with her son was because of a girl."

Richard's heart lurched suddenly. He felt ill.

"Oh no, she'll murder me," then groaned involuntarily as Robin nodded his agreement.

"Uh huh, were you with Emma?" Richard nodded then briefly told his brother what happened that day, at the end of which Robin merely shrugged.

"Anyway, Barry who heard this from his mum, told me to warn you, so you could get a story ready." Richard laughed and, after initial puzzlement, Robin joined in.

"Got any ideas?" he asked at last, knowing that it was pointless trying to think of anything to lessen his trouble. He was going to get it whatever he said.

"I could say it wasn't Emma but someone else?" he suddenly thought out loud. Robin thought about that for a while.

"Maybe," he said hesitantly, "but that might make it worse if she thinks you go out with lots of girls."

Richard nodded his head. "But that's better than saying it was Emma when I've been told never to see her isn't it?"

Robin paused for a moment before saying. "I suppose so. I don't understand why she regards girls as if they were the spawn of Satan. It ain't natural."

Richard was about to comment on this when a piercing whistle cut through the air: their mother's summons that demanded instant obedience. Robin and Richard stood up automatically. Robin moved off.

"Coming," he shouted. Richard pulled a face then joined his brother, limping behind him. He was as ready to face his mother as he would ever be.

* * *

Richard stood naked in the cold bathroom shivering from the draught blowing through the cracked pane of glass in the window and his bare feet on the lino. The bath was now beginning to fill up with water from the cold tap, which he had turned on at his mother's command. He watched the cold green-white water tumble into the bath and as he did so he ran over the day's events in his mind.

It had started off quite well. As it had been his birthday he had been regarded as special for the day. No cleaning or washing to be done. No washing up. Just eat and play. Coming down to breakfast and the excitement of receiving some presents was just like a mini Christmas. Then, whilst Robin had done the shopping, he had gone out to play with his toy helicopter. Here, despite his best intentions, things had gone out of his control, ending in disaster with the destruction of his presents. If that wasn't enough Robin had brought him further bad news with which, when he had gone into the house, his mother had confronted him.

To start with she had been almost casual in her approach as if only being able to half remember what she had been told. Knowing what was behind it had made her manner all the more unnerving, so much so that when finally she came to the point about his meeting with Emma he had been almost relieved. The fact that he had been out with a girl, normally the worst 'crime' he could ever commit, paled to insignificance compared to the fact that he had disobeyed his mother's order, given to him at Christmas, that he should not see Emma, or any other girl. What puzzled him was the fact that she had waited until today to tell him off when, according to Robin and Barry, she had found out yesterday. It did not make sense. He interrupted his thoughts to flick briefly through yesterday. But at no time had his mother given any indication of knowing where and who he had been with when he said he had gone down the beach.

Returning to his main line of thought, Richard didn't dwell on the further beating he had got following the questioning and his admission when he returned indoors. He was still too numb from the earlier one, from breaking his toy helicopter, for it to have any real effect on him. He had also noticed that his mother had been playing with him. She had not put her full weight behind the blows, which were normally hard enough to pitch him to the floor. Although not immediately apparent it was clear that it had been only a preliminary beating prior to the main punishment, which was why he was standing here now. His heart had chilled when he had been told to come up here and prepare the bath. It had been over a year, at least he thought, since his mother had done this to him and he had hoped that it was a punishment he had either grown out of or his mother had tired of it. She had certainly not used it on any of his brothers.

He turned his head at the sound of the kitchen door opening and shutting. There was then a short silence, quickly followed by the sound of his mother clumping up the stairs until she reached the landing. Marching into the bathroom she looked down at Richard for a moment, watching him shiver, then leaned over the side of the bath putting her hand in the water to see that it was really cold. Satisfied that it was she dried her hand on the towel and turned to Richard, saying peremptorily, "Get in!"

Richard hesitated for a moment and then moved to the side of the bath. Lifting his foot over the edge he put his toe into the icy water and would have withdrawn it had his mother not shouted at him.

"Get in now!"

Reluctantly Richard put his foot down in the bath and then lifted his other foot over until he was standing in the bath, the cold water reaching almost up to his knees. Goose pimples sprang out all over his body as the cold water took effect. His mother stood watching him for a moment then turned off the cold tap and folded her arms. "Right sit down." Richard looked at the clear translucent green water and could see his feet starting to turn red with the cold. The look his mother gave him put an end to his hesitation and he started to sit down but the water was so cold he just had to stop. He looked up, his eyes pleading.

"It's cold."

His mother just stared, nodded, and seeing that he still hesitated pushed him down so that he fell backwards into the cold water. Richard's mother held him down in a sitting position for a moment then asked quietly.

"You know what this is for don't you?"

Richard now beginning to shiver uncontrollably, nodded, even though he felt he did not.

"Good, I don't like people not doing as they're told."

With that she got hold of him and pushed him under the water, holding his head down. Richard, knowing what was coming from previous times, had taken a deep breath as he went under and closed his eyes. He now counted in his head to see how long he would be held down. Reaching twenty he started to get worried. Opening his eyes he looked up at his mother holding him under. Even through the distortion caused by the green-white water he could see that she was smiling. He knew he couldn't hold his breath for much longer and started to struggle in an attempt to sit up. Still his mother held him down as he succeeded only in getting an arm or a leg about the surface, as he flailed from side to side in his efforts to get up. In the end he gave up resisting and lay quietly on the bottom of the bath watching the air bubbles emerging from his lips and rush to the surface. At first one or two bubbles following each other, then several more and finally, when he could hold his breath no longer, a flurry of bubbles swooshed to the surface. Richard was about to inhale the water when he was jerked viciously out of the water.

"Well!" his mother demanded, "have you learned you lesson now?"

Richard was too concerned with trying to breathe, to reply, taking in great gulps of air before, as he knew would happen, he was pushed under again. Even so he had better not delay too long before replying. Turning his head towards his mother he nodded slightly, hoping that would suffice.

A resounding slap across the side of his head quickly followed.

"When I ask a question," his mother said in a dangerously quiet voice, "I expect a reply." Not getting an immediate response she started to raise her hand again but lowered it as Richard nodded urgently saying.

"Yes."

His mother seized on this. "Yes what?"

Richard swallowed for a moment. "Yes I have learned my lesson." Then feeling very cold, his teeth now chattering uncontrollably and his feet starting to go numb with the cold, he added, "Can I come out now, please?" He pleaded.

His mother looked at him for a moment then asked,

"Are you sure you have learned not to tell lies and not do things you shouldn't?"

Richard nodded, adding quickly, not wishing to be slapped again, "Yes, I have."

"Hm," replied his mother. "I don't think you have." Getting hold of his forehead she pushed him under the surface once again, before Richard had time to take a proper breath of air. Again Richard opened his eyes and looked at his mother holding him under the water. One tiny part of him accepted that he had lied and not done as he had been told and for that he should be punished. But another rebelled at the form this should take. He hated being immersed in a cold bath until he thought he might drown; but his mother seemed to revel in this particular form of punishment, which he couldn't explain.

Richard had had enough. Again he struggled to force his head off the bottom of the bath to reach the surface and as before his mother succeeded in holding him under. Sensing that further attempts were useless, Richard released some air from his mouth, lessening the pressure somewhat on his aching lungs. Still his mother held him under and Richard started to feel himself beginning to blackout; bright spots of light appearing before his eyes. His mind too, beginning to wander, drifting away, wishing to be anywhere but here, held under water in a cold bath. Unbidden came a sound, elusively at first, and then stronger and louder until he recognised it as the twenty-third Psalm sung to the tune of 'Brother James' Air'. He had sung a solo part in this anthem a few weeks ago and then the descant. Trying to escape the present horror that engulfed him he thought back to that day and began to sing in his mind. In doing so he unwittingly released some of his precious air then drew in water as he attempted to breathe.

His mother, noticing the air bubbles, ignored it, thinking it was just another ruse to avoid being held under. Richard's whole body began to convulse uncontrollably with spasms, as its defence mechanisms took over. Still his mother held him down. It was only when Richard stopped that she reluctantly released her grip and removed her hands.

At that point Richard's father, hearing the commotion downstairs, burst into the bathroom and seeing Richard lying still on the bottom of the bath, surged forward and pulled him out, water cascading onto the floor. He turned angrily on his wife.

"For heaven's sake, are you trying to kill the boy?"

Laying Richard on the floor he viciously forced air into his lung by pummelling his chest and moving his arms back and forth as he had been taught in the Navy. After a few seconds Richard drew in a large breath of air, almost immediately convulsing into a spasm of coughing interspersing with retching as his lungs finally emptied themselves of some water. After a short while Richard was able to control his breathing and smiled weakly at his father. His mother seeing he would survive, had left the bathroom and returned downstairs.

As his father dried him Richard began to shiver with cold and the reaction from what had happened. His father helped him into the bedroom and sat him on the side of the bed whilst he went to the airing cupboard. Richard began to be properly aware of his surroundings. The music in his head, which had not left him during his ordeal, began to fade as slowly and softly as it had begun until it was only a memory. He suddenly felt very tired and did not protest as his father having pulled a clean shirt over his head put him into his bed. The punishment was over for the time being. Richard's last thought as he drifted off to sleep were that he had survived again. That was all that mattered.

Unseen at the door, Robin looked at his big brother and slowly shook his head from side to side. This was so wrong, he thought. It really can't go on like this.

PART SIX: WHITSUN

Chapter 19: **Understanding time and Pilchard fishcakes**

Walking slowly up the back garden path, away from the house, Richard stopped every now and then to take a longer look at the nursery rhyme characters that his father had drawn into the cement before it had set. Crouching down he traced his finger around a curve of Humpty Dumpty, one of his favourite characters, and looked at its smiling features somehow, especially on this beautiful day, at odds with what was going on around him.

Through the partially opened window he could hear his mother's high pitched voice as she asked Robin what time it was. There came a hesitant mumbled reply followed almost immediately by the inevitable slap as Robin got it wrong, followed by his mother's voice giving the right answer. The whole cycle then repeated itself.

Although it was a few years ago, it only seemed like yesterday when Richard had been taught to tell the time by the same method. He had sat on a kitchen chair, his mother on a chair beside him with the kitchen clock in her hand. Turning the knob at the back of the clock she changed the position of the hand, and then asked him what the time was. Invariably he gave the wrong answer.

Although at that time he could count beyond twelve and had a vague idea of the concept of time, in relation to days, hours and minutes, faced with having to decipher the differing angles of the hands on a clock, without any preliminary instruction on the concept of 'o'clock', left his mind a complete blank. As a consequence on being ordered to say something he had a guess at one of several thousand possibilities floating around in head. Usually this was wrong and was quickly followed by a hard slap on his uncovered thigh. Though the slap was not in itself initially very painful, after a while the repetitiveness of the punishment made his thigh at first slightly sore and then painfully so. The inflamed skin became so sensitive by repeated slapping that the mere hint of a further slap, heralded by a raised hand, made him gabble out answers in the hope, usually forlorn, that he would chance on the right one eventually and so ward off further punishment. The slap that followed usually sent a shudder down his leg. The only thing he could liken it to was being slapped on freshly sunburned skin. Just thinking about it made his palms and face feel sweaty. A further slap from inside the house did not help as he heard Robin crying and his sob-wreaked, "I don't know." Richard wished he could go out but he had been confined to the house for falling off his bicycle and slightly damaging it in the process.

He moved down to the end of the garden but this did not help much in reducing the amount of noise. The slaps and Robin's crying seemed to echo down to the end of the garden. The noise confined, and amplified, by the shrubs and trees that grew there. Sitting down on the grass Richard pulled out a grass stalk and stuck it between his teeth. He lay back and watched the clouds drifting by, hoping that he could doze off but each time he thought he would another slap, sounding like a Christmas cracker insisted he stay awake.

A cat mewed behind him and he turned to see 'Flopdown' balanced precariously on a concrete fence post. This was not the cat's real name, although he had now forgotten what it was, but it had acquired it by its habit of flopping to the ground suddenly and rolling about. 'Flopdown' had done this the first time Richard had seen it, when it had come up to him to be stroked. At first he had thought that there was something wrong with its legs, or that it was trying to avoid being stroked, but it was neither of these. "Flopdown, Flopdown," he called.

Meowing the cat looked at him then down at the ground where it was going to land. Tensing itself it jumped, paused, sniffing the grass then strolled over to where Richard was sitting before collapsing suddenly to the ground. Richard smiled and, stretching out his hand, stroked the cat. As usual its glossy black coat was covered in dust, pieces of grass and other debris, which it had picked up in the garden. Richard brushed some of it away in an effort to clean him up a little whilst Flopdown, as he usually did, thinking it a game, took hold of Richard's hand tightly with his front paws and raked his arms with his two rear paws. The first time Flopdown had done this Richard had pulled his arm away, which had startled the cat, then he realised that Flopdown had kept his claws in. Whether automatically or from knowing the harm he could do with his claws Richard knew he would never know. Richard distracted himself by playing with the cat until he heard his mother's shouted voice.

"Go on, get out, you're stupid, just like your brother"

Lifting his head, with his back on the grass so that almost immediately his neck began to ache, Richard watched the house. After a few seconds Robin emerged from the porch but instead of immediately joining Richard he stood there, pulled a face and stuck his tongue out; then put his thumb to his nose and twiddled his fingers. Having completed his insults he walked slowly towards Richard and dropped down beside him. As expected his face was dirty from the tears, which had run down his cheeks. He had looked like that too frequently lately, thought Richard, about to say something to comfort his brother, but Robin pre-empted him.

"What's so bleedin' important about being able to tell the time?"

Robin carefully pulled up his shorts and pointed to his thighs, which were bright red from repeated slapping.

"Look at my legs, they're so sore that if you blow on them it hurts!" He demonstrated this by doing just that, wincing as he did so.

Richard killed a smile, which had begun to form on his lips. It wasn't funny really.

"We've all got to learn how to tell the time sometime," he finally said.

Robin looked at him scornfully, "What for? We'll never be able to afford a watch. And even if we do, why does she," he turned to look at the house before continuing, lowering his voice as he did so, "have to hit us all the time? "It's not fair." He stopped as his eyes filled with water.

In the last few weeks Robin had taken more than his fair share of punishment from their mother, thought

Richard as he looked at his brother. "She's a sadist that's what she is," said Robin after a few moments' silence. Richard looked oddly at his brother.

"You don't even know what it means," he said finally.

"Oh yes I do, I looked it up" said Robin with a superior note in his voice. "She enjoys causing us pain. And she won't let us do anything. You're lucky; you can meet your friends at church. But I hardly ever get out of the house apart from school. And she's always sneaking around our room hoping to find something incriminating. She even opens your letters."

Richard nodded at this last remark since he found it very irksome especially as it always led to third degree about whatever was going on. "And" continued Robin, "She's definitely a sadist since she likes hitting us all the time, even when we haven't done anything wrong. It never stops. It's not right." Having spoken he leaned back again and nodded his head.

Richard was very surprised at this coming from his young brother. He had never thought of his mother's behaviour towards them in this manner and just thought her to be, as his father often said, "Nervy and unpredictable" or, if he thought about it longer, perhaps she was a bit mad or barmy, so not really responsible for her actions. It had never occurred to him that she might actually enjoy inflicting pain on him and his brother. The thought that this might be true was, he found, a little frightening. It added a new dimension to the punishment she handed out, especially the immersion in the bath of cold water, making him even less secure than he had been: and that wasn't much. It was not something he really wished to think about, but now the thought was in his head he had to pursue it.

"Do you really think so?" he asked Robin, who nodded in return.

"Yes, and one day, when I'm bigger I'm going to get a lot of pleasure from giving her two slaps for every one she gave me. I'll give her a really good belting."

Richard laughed at this outrageous statement. "You'll never do it," he said. "You'll die of old age before you're even half way through."

Robin frowned, and then acknowledged, with a rueful smile, the possible truth of his brother's remark. He was about to say that he didn't care how long it took when their mother's strident whistle rang through the air: an immediate summons. "Now what?" said Robin, but like Richard he didn't hang around to discuss the call but with rapid strides caught up with Richard so that they entered the house together.

Shutting the back door quietly behind them, Richard and Robin stood with their backs against the door near the open door that led to the back room where their mother sat reading the 'Daily Mirror'. Marilyn was also there, having come downstairs from her room once Robin's lesson on how to tell the time was over. Richard noticed that Robin had stood so that he was partially obscured by himself so ensuring that he was out of the direct line of fire from whatever might come from their mother, be it physical or verbal abuse.

They waited for their mother to stir. There was nothing unusual in this, although its effect, unknown to their mother, was wasted on them. They were so used to this scenario that having to wait those extra few minutes did not heighten the tension or increase the level of their fear. If they were in trouble there was no doubt that they would be punished, it was more a question of when, rather than if, or what form the punishment would take.

Abruptly their mother put down the paper and stared straight at Robin who moved even further behind his older brother. "You – get upstairs and tidy your room. Anyone who can't tell the time doesn't have the right to go out and play, so get!" she finished, pointing her finger in the direction of the stairs. Needing no further urging Robin left his brother's side and walked quickly around the kitchen table to the door to the hall, opened it and went through. Closing it quietly behind him he rushed upstairs.

Richard heard him go, glad that Robin had not received any further punishment, which his mother was likely to dish out just because she was in a bad mood. Bending over Richard rubbed his knee, which was still red and sore from his fall off his bike that morning. This did not go unnoticed by his mother. "What's the matter with your knee?" she asked him suddenly, making him jerk up then relax again. He wasn't in any trouble, at least anything of which he was aware, and for the moment was unafraid.

"Nothing much. It happened when I fell off my bike this morning, that's all," he replied, daring to look his mother straight in the eye.

"Hm," said his mother, surveying the grazed knee. "Put some gentian violet on it." Richard nodded his acquiescence and was about to go when his mother's command stopped him.

"Wait!"

He paused, awaiting the next order. "As you've got nothing better to do except talk to your stupid brother you can cook dinner." Richard nodded. This was nothing new; he often cooked dinner and now merely needed to find out what it was he had to cook.

"What's for dinner, Mater?" he asked as his mother returned to her newspaper.

She lifted her head. "Pilchard fishcakes," she replied going back to her paper. That would have been the end of the conversation had not Richard said automatically, revealing for once his true feelings.

"Oh no, not again."

As the last word came out of his mouth Richard wished he could somehow retract them. Whilst knowing that he had said the wrong thing, he did not like the sudden ferocious look on his mother's face as she got out of her seat. Marilyn just looked at him and shook her head from side to side, sadly.

Richard began to quake. 'You stupid berk', he told himself. The trouble was he had been too confident recently. It had been some time since he had been in real trouble, which had made him unwittingly relax his usual guard. Normally, like his brother and sister, he never spoke spontaneously but carefully weighed his words just in case there was anything in them that his mother was likely to take the wrong way. Like now, for example, it wasn't that he didn't like Pilchard fish cakes. He did. But lately they seemed to eat them every other day, so now he – and he knew the others – were sick to death of them. It was always the same, whenever their mother happened on something that was easy to cook and they said they liked, or only partially liked, they were fed it to the exclusion of everything else. All such thoughts now fled as, with her face only inches from his own, his mother asked quietly.

"What did you say?"

Richard was sensitive to his mother's moods and knew he was in big trouble. The quieter she spoke initially the worse trouble you were in.

"I, I quite like fishcakes, I mean, I do like fishcakes, it's just, just...." He didn't finish, knowing that if he had said that they had eaten a lot of them lately, he would only be compounding his error. His mother was ahead of him though.

"You get fishcakes because you like them, don't you?" she prodded him in the face with her forefinger, the long nail making a mark in his cheek. "Well?" she demanded, thinking him dilatory in replying.

Richard nodded, following up quickly with "Yes, but..." As usual he got no further as he was interrupted by his mother.

"Do you think it is easy thinking up different things to eat all the time with hardly any money in the house?" Richard shook his head and watched his mother warily. She was now beginning to pace up and down the small kitchen, her voice rising in pitch. It was only a matter of time now before she hit him on one of her passes. She was gradually working herself up into a frenzy and when she reached a certain point Richard knew that the violence would start. The only thing he was unable to gauge at present was the extent of it.

"I work my fingers to the bone for you and the others. Do I get any thanks?" Richard nodded, not daring to speak but found that in doing so he was inadvertently contradicting his mother who was shaking her head from side to side. He stopped in mid-nod, a gesture his mother seized on. "I do, do I, well tell me how?"

Richard stood there nonplussed, unable to think of anything to say that would appease his mother. After the silence had dragged on for a few seconds Richard was becoming desperate. The tension was building up until it was a palpable presence in the air between them. Finally it came. The first slap across his cheek; breaking both the tension and any desire in Richard to even attempt to justify what he had said, or what had been behind it. Admittedly it was his own fault in not properly taking account of his mother's mood, so soon after Robin's lesson on being taught how to tell the time. Together with having been free of any recent punishment, and from the wrong side of his mother's tongue, had made him think, though heaven knows why, he reflected, that perhaps he was immune to her capriciousness for a while.

Richard switched off. His mother was not yet into her stride and it only needed the minimum of his attention to keep her going. The occasional 'yes' or 'no'; a partial shrug of his shoulders, sufficed to indicate to her satisfaction at least, that he was paying attention to what she was saying. She walked towards him now, poking her finger at his face to accentuate the particular point she was making.

"Well, do you understand?" she said at last, staring at him unblinkingly, waiting for his reply.

Needing to swallow Richard did so, and then spoke. "Yes."

His mother looked at him a mixture of pity and scorn on her face. "No, I don't think you do." Then slapped him hard, making his head bang against the wall. "Stand up straight when I'm talking to you!" Richard stood at attention, watched closely by his mother, until satisfied by his stance, she walked away resuming her tirade.

Richard stood there and, although he was very careful not to show it on his face, fumed. He hated it when after a, usually, long harangue, his mother asked him the question 'do you understand' and if he did – which admittedly was not as often as he liked, mainly because his mother went round in circles, endlessly repeating herself usually with enthusiasm because she thought the point she was expounding on was a newly formed aspect of her hypothesis, seemingly unaware that she had said the very same thing only a few minutes before – and he said 'yes', she always added in that martyred pitying voice, 'No, I don't think you do.' Sometimes Richard felt like screaming out 'I do understand, I do.' At others he felt that if there was some information missing vital to the point she was trying to make, which he didn't know, given his age, why didn't she tell him so that he could understand; and if she was not prepared to do so, why bother to ask the question in the first place.

These thoughts all stopped and Richard paid attention once more as his mother came towards him her raised voice warning him that another slap was on its way, giving him time to prepare. This time a backhander on his right cheek so that another part of his head rebounded off the kitchen wall.

In the back room Marilyn rustled the newspaper noisily in an effort to attract her young brother's attention. She had been willing him to stand away from the wall ever since Richard had backed up against it in order to avoid his mother's blows. Now of course he was getting a double punishment, firstly from the slap and secondly as his head hit the wall. Every time this happened Marilyn winced. No wonder he gets headaches all the time she thought. Unable to stand it any longer, she put the newspaper down, got out of her seat and unseen by her mother, tried to attract Richard's attention. It was difficult in case her mother saw her and would automatically assume she was either fooling about or mimicking her. Waving her hands frantically she finally caught Richard's attention.

With his mother turning away for a few seconds, as she usually did being unable to stay in one place when she was in full spate, he flicked his eyes over to his sister long enough for her to mouth, "Stand away from the wall," gesturing with her hands as she did so. Without any acknowledgement and looking quickly back at his mother, Richard hurriedly shuffled his feet half a pace forward. Marilyn sighed with relief and on tiptoe hurried back to her seat and resumed reading the newspaper. Whilst there had been nothing she could do about Richard getting punished, as least he wouldn't now get two whacks around the head for one. Not that it was over yet. She could, like everyone else in the family had learned to do long ago, switch off her mother's voice and concentrate on what she was doing. Today was Richard's turn to bear the brunt of his mother's wrath, as he did more than any of them. Tomorrow it might be Robin's again or even hers.

Having already expended a great deal of energy on Robin, Richard's mother did not keep him much longer. After a few more slaps he was told to get upstairs and help Robin to clean out the bedroom. He would also forgo his dinner since he hated fishcakes so much. With his head still ringing Richard climbed slowly up the stairs, not making any noise. Entering the room he caught Robin in mid-leap as he hurriedly tried to get off the bed and making a pretence of tidying up the room.

"Relax, it's only me," said Richard closing the door behind him and going to sit down on his bunk. Robin dropped the clothes and toys he had picked up and went and sat on his brother's bed. He pointed to the floor with his finger.

"What was all that about?" Richard grimaced and briefly outlined what had happened: the drama of not wanting Pilchard fishcakes again finishing with a shrug of his shoulders at his mother's parting shot that he would get no fishcakes for dinner.

Robin smiled. "Well, that's no hardship, it's a pity we can't all have the same punishment." Richard looked obliquely at his brother as he continued, "Well, you've only got yourself to blame. I don't know what got into you. You're either getting very brave or very stupid, you berk!"

Shrugging Richard lay down on his bunk bed. Probably very stupid, he thought to himself and looked at his brother who seemed very deep in thought. Robin feeling his brother's eyes on him looked around.

"You know – that's it," he said, his eyes gleaming as if he had happened on a great truth. "What we ought to do is stand up to her. If all three of us did it she can't hit all of us at once!" Richard gazed out of the window at the sky and then looked back again at Robin.

"Why not, what's to stop her? She's bigger than us and what about Dad, whose side do you think he'd be on?"

Robin stopped to think about this for a while. It still seemed a good idea despite his brother's misgivings. He just needed to think about it for a bit and all the answers would come to him. Of one thing at least he was certain: he was not prepared to put up with being hit by his mother all the time. Why should he have to flinch every time his mother walked past? It had gotten so bad that he now flinched everywhere if someone got close to him. It wasn't right. Getting punished for doing something wrong was acceptable, but in this family almost anything you did was wrong in his mother's eyes. It didn't matter what you did; if she objected to it then you were usually beaten to within an inch of your life just to make sure that you didn't do it again. Robin knew this didn't happen in his friend's houses. They didn't walk around expecting to get hit all the time.

"Robin, get down here at once!"

Robin jerked upright, forgetting in his panic that he was sitting on a bunk bed, and cracked his head hard on the iron frame of the upper bunk. It was so sudden and painful he immediately dropped to his knees whilst a red mist studded with bright lights danced in front of his closed eyes.

"Are you alright?" said Richard dropping down beside him.

"Robin!" screamed his mother, "get down here this instant or do I have to come up there and get you?"

Robin started to crawl to the door whilst Richard attempted to lift his brother to his feet as Robin cried out, "I'm coming – I'm in the bathroom." This seemed to mollify their mother since they heard the hall door to the kitchen slam shut. Richard half carried and half dragged his brother out to the landing and leaned him against the banister.

"Are you alright?" he asked, his voice full of concern.

Robin started to nod his head but stopped when he felt the beginnings of a flush of nausea run through his body. He felt that he was going to be sick but he knew that he could not afford to wait much longer or his mother would think that he was being deliberately slow. "See," he said to Richard, "she gives me a pain just by speaking."

Richard started to smile but stopped when he saw that Robin was not joking. Robin made as if to go downstairs but Richard held onto his arm. "Wait!" he commanded, then rushed into the bathroom and pulled the chain then turned on the cold tap in the sink, counted to ten quickly then turned it off again.

"Go on" he said to Robin who smiled at his brother's quick thinking.

"Thanks Ricky," said Robin then he staggered downstairs.

Richard waited on the landing until he heard Robin open and close the door to the kitchen and his mother's voice. "What were you doing in the bathroom – I told you to tidy up your room." Not waiting to hear his brother's mumbled reply, Richard returned to the bedroom and began to tidy up, knowing that it would not be just Robin who would get into trouble if their mother did not like the state of their room. He was also a bit worried about Robin. Increasingly lately he had been thinking about revenge on their mother for the way she continued to treat them. Perhaps it was all getting too much for him. Richard resolved to ask him to come down the beach with him tomorrow. He doubted if he would come though, since he preferred his own friends. Thinking of ways and means of both helping his brother and of drawing some of his mother's ire away from Robin, even if it meant more for himself, Richard got on with tidying up their bedroom.

Chapter 20: The day of the Conger

Gripping a tighter hold on his end of the oar, Richard listened with the others to Barry's instructions.

"Right, when I say 'heave', you lift. Right?"

He waited until Richard, David and Jim had all nodded their heads before taking a deep breath and saying loudly, "Heave!" At the signal all four lifted the small but heavy wooden boat. The rope at the back, which had been inexpertly tied through the iron ring bolted to the stern, stretched before taking the strain, making Richard and Barry lift their arms higher than should have been necessary. Having got the boat off the sand, Barry shouted, "Let's go!"

All four staggered forward, watched bemusedly by Herbert who followed after, carrying the emergency paddles for the boat.

"You look like a load of ducks waddling along," he called but the others were too busy straining with the load to reply.

Gradually the sea got closer and with a mad rush borne of desperation and imminent exhaustion, they completed the few remaining yards to the water's edge. David and Jim at the front of the boat dropped the oar they were holding, which had been pushed through the iron ring at the bow and jumped back to avoid getting their shoes wet. At the back Richard and Barry continued to push, with the momentum the boat had gained, so that the front of it slid into the sea. Richard and Barry dropped their oar and sat down on the sand and rested with Jim and David.

"Phew," said Jim, "why is this boat so heavy? It's only small."

Barry, whose boat it was, just looked at him sourly before saying

"Because it's made of solid wood, not like this fibreglass stuff you get nowadays." He thumped the side of the boat hard with his fist a few times to emphasise his words, then looked up as Herbert arrived and sat down with them. "Are you coming with us Bert?"

Herbert looked at the boat; it seemed hardly big enough to carry four let alone five. He shook his head from side to side.

"I don't know. I get seasick easily."

Richard nodded, sympathising; he knew how easy it was to get sick especially if there was a heavy swell. He looked at the sea. It was sheltered here in the harbour but out in the bay it was a bit choppy.

"You don't think it might get too rough?" He asked Barry as Jim and David got up and walked back to get the fishing rods and hand-lines.

Barry stood up and looked around and then up at the sky, which was dotted with clouds but they were not moving too fast.

"No, should be alright." He bent down to untie the rope from the iron ring in the stern and so release the oar.

Removing his shoes and socks, Richard stowed them in the small locker in the bow. Walking into the water he paused for a moment as the sudden cold made him clench his teeth. Then stepping forward, his toes digging into the wet sand, he took hold of the oar and drew it out of the front iron ring whilst Herbert put the paddles under the seats. Barry kept these paddles for use in an emergency should they lose an oar. Taking the rowlocks from the locker Richard put them in the holes provided on each side of the boat.

Barry finally finished untying the oar from the ring in the stern, which he did with many "bleedin's" watched by Herbert who thought it best to keep out of the way. David and Jim returned with the fishing tackle then took off their shoes and socks, put them in the locker and waited for Barry to do likewise. Barry sat on the sand, tucking his socks into his shoes whilst surveying what he regarded as his crew.

"Right, Herbert, you go up front." Herbert grimaced; he was still not sure about it but at least the sea didn't look too rough. He climbed in.

"Ricky, you and David can start the rowing and Jim and me will be in the stern."

Richard and David stepped into the boat and placed the oars in the rowlocks. Barry and Jim waited until they had signified that they were ready then took hold of the boat and pushed it into the water. Slowly at first, the boat eased itself off the sandy bottom, then suddenly released it lurched forward making Barry and Jim grab hold to restrain it with outstretched hands.

"Stop rowing, for Gawd's sake," gasped Jim as he stumbled over a submerged mooring chain and nearly fell into the sea, scraping his shin on the side of the boat in the process. Richard and David reversed their rowing action to stop the boat.

"In you get, Jim," said Barry. Jim started to climb in the side of the boat, causing it to rock wildly from side to side.

"No, you idiot, over the stern," said Barry, trying to hold onto the boat.

"Don't call me an idiot," replied Jim, but moved round to climb over the stern, followed quickly by Barry.

Herbert glanced over the side. With five people in it the boat looked awfully low in the water. He shut his eyes and swallowed as Barry, with one final look around, called out, "Right, pull away. Off we go."

Jim rubbed his skinned shinbone and muttered sourly, "Anyone for the Skylark? I don't think." The others stifled their grins and put their backs into rowing.

* * *

As it left the shelter of the jetty the boat lifted and dropped under the long swell of the sea. The pea-green water at once translucent as the oars dipped into it accentuating its limpidity; but opaque if any of them tried to stare into its depths. Above them a hopeful seagull glided near them a few times then, with a plaintive cry and an impatient flap of its wings, it flew off to seek titbits elsewhere. Flying first out to sea then wheeling back to head for the shore crying out once more as it flew over them.

Herbert watched it go, wishing that he could be heading back to shore. Whilst it had been fun all of them jammed in the small boat when they had been in the calm of the harbour, out here, at sea, the boat suddenly seemed very small, overloaded and unsafe.

He looked down as the crest of another wave passed them by, only a couple of inches from the top of the side of the boat. He was not a good swimmer and wondered how much farther they were going to go out. He decided to voice his fears.

"How far are we going out?" he asked.

Lifting his hand from the sea, from where he had caught a piece of seaweed, Barry looked up. "Not far," he said, inspecting the seaweed. Herbert's sense of relief suddenly drained out of him as Barry continued, "Only as far as the yellow Sailing Club buoy." Unconcerned he threw the seaweed back into the water and began to help Jim bait the hooks with pieces of cut-up dogfish heads and guts they had collected from the fishermen.

Herbert looked away, torn between nausea from the baiting activity and the fear as he looked at the yellow buoy. It seemed miles away. Although David and Richard were rowing hard they didn't seem to be getting any closer. He hoped Richard and David thought it was too far as well as himself.

As if he had spoken aloud Richard stopped rowing, as did David, and keeping his oar out of the water twisted round to see how far they had to go. Turning back he raised his eyebrows at David who returned the gesture.

"It's a bit far out, isn't it?"

Barry looked up as Richard continued.

"It'll take ages to get out there and when we want to come back the tide will be against us, making it twice as hard."

"And it might get rough," chipped in Herbert, not afraid to voice his fears now that someone else had spoken out. Barry was prepared to be swayed by the majority. Even though it was his boat he was not keen on hard rowing.

"What do you think Jim?"

Jim looked about. He was impatient to get on with the fishing. Now that they were about a hundred yards passed the end of the slipway, which jutted out from the east end of the jetty, farther out than he was usually able to fish with very clear water, he just wanted to get on with it.

"This'll do."

David nodded his agreement. Barry, bowing to their greater fishing expertise, nodded as well. "Drop the anchor Bert," he cried. Herbert looked around; he couldn't see any anchor. Richard shipped his oar and lifting his feet over the side and twisting on his seat now face Herbert.

"It's in the locker. Get your feet out of the way and I'll get it out.

Reluctantly Herbert moved back on the covered top of the locker and lifted his feet out of the boat-well. A sudden unexpected swell made him slip to one side and he grasped hold of either side of the boat, which now felt as smooth as glass as he feverishly tried to find something on which his fingers could find some purchase.

"Hurry up Ricky," he whispered, his voice appearing to have disappeared with his last reserves of courage.

"Here Bert," said Richard handing him the end of the anchor rope. "Tie this through the ring at the front, using a round turn and two half hitches."

Herbert dutifully took hold of the rope's end and after staring at it for a second stuck it through the iron ring. Hesitating, he looked round at Richard who was holding the small anchor in preparation for throwing it over the side. Feeling Herbert's eyes on him he looked up.

"What's a round turn and two half hitches?" asked Herbert. Richard started to explain but seeing Herbert getting more and more confused with each passing word gave up. Swapping places with Herbert, who did so gratefully, only too pleased to be actually in the well of the boat, rather than being perched on top of the locker, Richard hurriedly tied the anchor rope and then dropped the anchor over the side. The sound of the splash drew the attention of the others and they all waited until all the rope had been paid out to see if it would catch on the rocks first time. The boat drifted for a few yards then the rope went taut.

"Hooray!" they cried spontaneously, pleased that they did not have to waste time drawing it up and throwing it in again at a different place, time after time as sometimes happened, trying to get it to catch hold.

"Let's hope we can get the bleedin' thing up again," said Barry only half jokingly. He had already lost one anchor, which his father had grudgingly replaced, and he did not relish having to ask him for another one.

The five boys set about fishing. As they were the only ones who had fishing rods it was agreed that Barry and Jim would fish from the stern whilst the others, who had hand-lines would drop their lines over the side, or as far as they could swing them out at the front. All having cast their rods and lines, each sat and waited to see who would be the first to catch anything.

Perched on top of the locker Richard alternatively gazed down at his line and then at those of the others. The heavy doughnut-shaped weight had carried his line and limpet baited hook right down to the bottom. All he could do now was to wait. He daydreamed. This was the best thing about fishing. You could sit pretending to do something when really you were doing nothing at all. True, sometimes you caught fish, or at least Jim had. Richard had never caught a fish and wasn't particularly keen to do so anyway. The taste of freshly caught fish had never appealed to him. It was too salty for a start. Watching them being scraped and cleaned out and the bloodied guts dropped into the sea didn't do much either to enhance the flavour or increase his appetite. If he had to eat fish then give me a nice clean white fish on a marble slab in the fishmonger he thought; anything else – forget it. He looked down again at his line and wondered whether it was time to haul it in but decided to leave it for a bit longer, as Jim cried out excitedly.

"I've got a bite." He waited for a second or two to make sure that whatever it was having taken the bait was well and truly hooked, then swiftly and expertly reeled in. As more and more line came in, bringing with it pieces of weed, some pale yellow like rotted cheese, others dark and robust, the tension heightened to dissipate with a chorus of "Oh's" as the line suddenly went slack and two empty hooks broke the surface. His puzzled features betraying his hidden feelings of frustration, Jim swung the line in and caught it with his other hand. After inspecting the hooks carefully he showed them to Barry, commenting unnecessarily, "The bait's gone."

Barry looked at one of the hooks that appeared to have been partially straightened. "That's odd," he said, then let go of the hook to take a firmer grip of his rod, which had just dipped slightly. "I've got a bite." Again the air was full of tension as he reeled in, only to find, like Jim, two empty hooks.

David laughed, "Those fish are cleverer than you think." Jim gave him a sour look as he cut free the damaged hook and replaced it with a much larger one.

"Let's see them bend that," he said as he pushed it carefully through another piece of dogfish offal and expertly cast his line into the sea.

Unable to bear the waiting any longer Richard pulled in his line. It felt heavier than before and though, from past experience, he knew it was more likely to be due to a piece of seaweed rather than a fish, he was unable to stop himself becoming increasingly excited the more line he pulled in. The last few yards emerged from where the opacity of the sea gave way to translucence. There was something on the hook, he could not quite see what, but it was green. His heart sank a little as with a final pull it emerged from the water. "A crab!" he exclaimed. The others laughed as, with a great deal of difficulty since it did not want to leave the source of food, he pulled the green crab off the bait and showed it to Herbert who drew back. Richard looked at it for a moment; it was only a green crab – you couldn't even eat it. He waved it in the air. "Anyone want it for bait?"

Barry and Jim shook their heads, content to stay with dogfish pieces. "No, I'll stick with worms," said David whilst Herbert pulled a face: the thought of someone disembowelling a live crab in the confines of the boat made him feel ill. With a last look Richard, taking a firmer hold of the crab, threw it far away to land with a solid splash into the top of a passing wave.

Things settled down again in the boat. The long smooth swells of the sea having a soporific effect on the occupants as the boat moved slowly up and down with each passing roller. "Ricky?" Came the voice, but he ignored it: content to gaze out to sea at the horizon. "Ricky!" This time the voice was more insistent so he turned his head. Now that he had got Richards attention Herbert continued. "Are their octopuses in the sea?" Richard nodded sleepily but Herbert shook his head. "I mean are there any in the sea here?"

Richard thought for a moment. He had always regarded the octopus as an exotic sea creature to be found in warmer seas, like the Mediterranean but not around here. He yawned then stretched, and gave his line an experimental tug before replying. "I don't think so, Bert: at least I've never seen one." It was not something on which he had any strong views and he was happy to concede the point.

"Well in that case," said Herbert pursuing the matter, "what's that down there?!"

Richard turned around so that he could see better and followed the direction of Herbert's pointed finger. There, about fifteen feet from the boat, floated a squid-like object with two long tentacles and several short ones. Richard looked at it as it bobbed up and down, seeming to be drifting aimlessly. With the exception of Jim, who was concentrating on his rod with a puzzled expression on his face, the others leaned over the side of the boat wondering to each other what it was.

"I don't think it is an octopus," ventured Richard at last. "Its body is too long and the tentacles are too short."

"Perhaps it's a squid," said David, reaching for an oar. "Let's try to get it in. Holding on to the oar, which was about seven feet long, he stretched out as far as he could go, tipping the boat so much that some water came over the gunnels.

"Watch out!" cried Herbert, alarmed, "we'll sink!" David stopped and having given Herbert an exasperated look, sat and fumed. Tempted to try again even though he knew it was just too far to reach.

Barry cast around looking for something to throw at it and, unable to find anything better, picked a dogfish head out of the bucket and threw it at the object. With his unerring aim it landed on the body of the thing causing it to sink momentarily, and then bob back up. The boys cheered spontaneously as Barry beamed. They watched the dogfish head spiral down, twisting over and over as it sank to the bottom.

Richard turned to Jim and asked him what he thought it was but he was still concentrating on holding his rod tightly, occasionally looking over the side of the boat with a mystified expression on his face. Finally, Richard's calls being to no avail, Barry dug him hard in the ribs.

"Oi, Jim, what's that over there?" Jim jumped and turned around suddenly, realising that everyone's eyes were on him. He followed the line of the oar held out by David, looked at it for a second and said, "It's a cuttlefish. Dead." Without another word he returned to his rod.

"Oh," said Herbert, "a cuttlefish. I suppose that's a sort of octopus or a squid?" The others nodded their heads in solemn agreement as they watched it drift out of sight. They turned as Jim exclaimed suddenly.

"I've got a bite." Then quickly began to reel in. All watched expectantly as the line came in and then slumped as once again the bare hooks broke the surface of the water. "I don't understand it!" said Jim swinging the line in and resting the rod against his shoulder whilst he inspected the hooks. Not a shred of the bait remained. He showed them to Barry who shrugged saying. "There's a fish down there that thinks this is a bleeding cafe."

The others laughed but Jim glowered. He took his fishing seriously and was not going to be made a fool of by a fish. Fuming he lifted out a tobacco tin from his bag. Opening it he took out a slightly smaller hook and wired it on next to the big one. Baiting it with a large lump of dogfish he flicked the line out to where he had been fishing. Clenching his teeth, he settled down to wait as did the others. Although they had lines in the water they all thought it would be more entertaining to watch Jim in what, for him, had become a personal vendetta.

They watched Jim as he pulled the rod towards him and then letting it drop back again. A few minutes passed then he tensed but after reeling the line in a few turns he relaxed and let it out again. The others watched expectantly and were soon rewarded by a sudden cry and frantic reeling by Jim. They all leaned over Jim's side of the boat to see better causing the water to slip over the side into the boat again so reluctantly they drew back. In seconds the hooks on the line emerged from the water still with the bait on them.

Barry expressed his disgust. "You must have imagined it. There's nothing there!" Jim ignored him and carefully inspected the bait on the hook before showing it around for everyone to see.

"Look, part of the bait's missing. I must have reeled in too soon before the fish could get caught on the hook."

Richard inspected it closely before agreeing. About a third of the bait was missing. Not only that, it appeared to have been chewed off. He looked at Barry.

"Reel your line in and see if you have caught anything." Barry shrugged; he had forgotten that he had a line in the water and soon reeled it in. The bait had gone. "Are you sure you put the bait on properly?" asked Richard.

"Of course I bleedin' did," replied Barry in exasperation. "I'm not stupid. I know how to bait a hook."

Herbert looked at the hook as well. "It must be a very clever fish to take the bait without touching the hook."

Jim nodded his head, sage-like. "I agree." He looked to where he had placed his line before. "And I'm going to catch it."

Without another word he cast his line to almost the same place as before. This time after the weight had hit the bottom he wound the line back until it was fairly taut then held it lightly with his fingertips. He turned to grin at the others. "I'll get him this time," before staring at the place where the line entered the sea.

Once again they all settled down to wait. Richard stared at each passing wave as it reached the line, hanging there for a second before moving on. A cloud obscured the sun, making it suddenly chill and dark: the boat somehow seeming smaller and more vulnerable that it had before. Richard watched the shadow edge come towards them, and then swiftly passing to bathe them in light and heat again from the sun. The minutes passed. Slowly Richard sat up on the locker top, stretching his legs to ease his cramped muscles. Herbert lost interest and dabbled his hands in the water now and then picking up a filament of passing seaweed, inspecting it before returning it to the sea. Richard loved the peace and tranquillity that flowed through him at such times. Each passing wave adding to the sense of serenity he felt: an antidote to the awfulness and pain linked to his life at home.

"I think I can feel something on the line," said Jim, so quietly that only Barry and David heard him properly. Whilst not hearing the words the tenseness in his voice caused Richard to lean forward as he watched Jim take a firm hold of the line in his hand. Holding and pausing for a second or two, without warning he suddenly yanked the line as far as his outstretched arm would go. Then letting go of the line he turned the handle of the reel as fast as he could; so fast that the ratchet made an angry buzzing noise.

"I've got it, I've got it," he yelled jubilantly, his eyes aglow. His reeling in became slower and slower until he finally had to stop. All the boys looked at him expectantly.

"Come on, Jim," said Richard, "Reel it in." Jim grasping the handle hard shook his head and not daring to look up, said, "I can't – it's pulling too much and the line might break.

Barry put his arms around Jim and grasping the rod with his left hand and getting hold of the handle with his right hand helped Jim to turn the reel. It moved slowly under the pressure of the two of them. Barry, his voice quavering with the strain, spoke, "It must be a bleedin' monster," he puffed, "never known anything like it."

Surreptitiously Herbert moved away to the side of the boat at the mention of the word 'monster', and wished he hadn't been so keen to relinquish his position in the front of the boat on top of the locker.

He wondered how he could get it back without making it seem too obvious that he was afraid.

"It's coming up to the surface," cried David leaning over the side of the boat. "It looks like a giant eel!"

Barry and Jim's faces were distorted by the effort of reeling in as they watched the line now moving violently from side to side with the rod almost horizontal with the water as the catch neared the surface. "I can't reel for much longer," gasped Jim, "my fingers are getting numb."

Richard looked at the rod and line and then at his friends. "You've reeled in enough," he shouted. "Just lift the rod and it will come up out of the water."

As if they were one, Barry and Jim stopped reeling in and pulled at the rod trying to lift it into the vertical position. At first nothing happened, then it began to lift a little at a time. Richard, suppressing a laugh, glanced at his friends who looked so comical, especially Barry, whose face was getting red and bloated from the strain. Without warning the catch suddenly shot out of the sea causing Barry and Jim fall backwards into the well of the boat but still holding the rod upright.

"It's a bleedin' great conger!" exclaimed Barry as the conger eel, about six feet long, swung in from the sea above their heads as the boat heaved about in the sea and water came in over the gunnels.

Herbert sat, transfixed, as the conger eel hurtled towards him, twisting and bucking in its efforts to escape from the line, which held it prisoner. The eel had almost reached him when, in a desperate attempt to get out of the way, and forgetting he was in a boat Herbert threw himself backwards and disappeared over the side, managing to cry out briefly before he vanished beneath a passing wave.

Richard watched, amazed, as the conger eel flew back again to the other side narrowly missing David as Jim and Barry sat there apparently paralysed.

"Drop it back in the sea!" he cried as he leaned over the gunnel to grab hold of Herbert who had surfaced spluttering and helped him to get a hold of the side of the boat.

"In you get Bert," he said, getting hold of Herbert's arm in order to pull him in. But Herbert drew back. Not wishing to lose the catch Jim had dropped the eel into the boat so it was now thrashing about snapping at anything it could whilst the others jumped out of its way. Watching the drama Herbert felt safer in the water, even though it was cold. He shook his head.

"No thanks." He moved away to the front of the boat and held onto the anchor rope keeping one eye on the Conger eel and another on the water just in case there were other giant eels lurking nearby.

Richard watched as the eel flailed about on the bottom of the boat, whilst Barry and Jim, their feet up on the seat, looked on. "Well, don't just sit there," cried Richard, "do something."

David, moving to join Richard behind the front seat, added, unhelpfully, "Yeah, you're supposed to kill it by hitting it on the head." He laughed because he was out of harm's way and by the fixed look of terror and amazement on his friend's faces as they saw what they had brought up out of the deep.

Swallowing deeply, Jim let go of the rod, thrusting it more firmly into Barry's grasp. He was determined not to lose his biggest catch ever; even though he was scared of it. Opening his hands in order to get hold of the eel he followed the eel's spasmodic movements, still hanging from the line, prior to grabbing hold of it where he thought its neck was. Being an eel this was difficult to gauge but he thought it was behind its head where there were two horizontal fins. Jim had just decided to make a grab when the eel finally managed to tear itself loose from the hook, which had held it prisoner. Before Jim had the opportunity to either get hold of the eel, or move his hands out of the way, the eel seized one of his hands with its sharp teeth.

"Argh!" cried Jim, "get it off, get it off!"

Barry dropped the rod and, without thinking, took hold of the eel and pulled, making Jim cry out even louder.

"Stop, stop, it's pulling my fingers off, STOP!"

As the eel's skin was slimy it slipped through Barry's fingers anyway. With Jim shaking his hand in an effort to get rid of the eel and pulling the jaw open with his other hand; and Richard and Barry wondering what to do, David couldn't stop himself from laughing. Whilst sympathising with his friend and wishing to help him, he hadn't seen anything so funny in years. Jim looked so comical that tears ran uncontrollably down his cheeks.

In the water Herbert's teeth were starting to chatter but the sight of the, in his eyes, giant eel attempting to eat his friend made him feel ill. He wished it was all just a bad dream and that he was really at home in bed.

Jim was now getting desperate. He wanted to get rid of the eel at any cost. The eel's teeth had dug into his hand so hard that the wound was beginning to bleed profusely, which only seemed to incense the eel more. Jim felt that the teeth must now be down to the bones, the very thought of which made him think he was going to faint. Whilst his friends stood by wondering what on earth to do, whilst avoiding the whip-like tail, Jim, using his other hand continued to attempt to prise the eel's jaws apart but couldn't do so. He gave up trying especially as the others seemed reluctant to help him do this.

"Get it off!" cried Jim. He was rapidly reaching the stage where he would just throw his head back and scream in an effort to release the pent-up tension that was building up within him.

Barry had a sudden thought. "Quick, Ricky. In the locker: an axe."

Richard moved almost before Barry had finished speaking. Fumbling about amongst the paraphernalia in the locker his hand rested on a wooden handle. Closing his fingers around it he pulled out the axe. In one motion he leaned over the front seat and grabbing hold of Jim's hand pulled it down to the wooden seat.

"Get hold of the body," he said to Barry as, without waiting he raised the axe and brought it hard down on the eel, partly severing its head. Barry put his foot on the body of the eel, whilst a second and finally third blow from Richard with the axe completely separated the eel's head from the body. Dropping the axe to the floor Richard took hold of the upper and lower jaws of the eel and with great effort managed to pull it apart enough to release Jim's hand. Very gingerly Jim cradled his hand with the other one, resting it on his chest. He looked very pale and Richard wondered if he was going to be sick. He was about to ask Jim how he felt but was distracted by Herbert's voice.

"Is it safe to come in yet?"

Having moved around from the front of the boat, his wet face was now peering over the side. Richard reached out his hand and took hold of one of Herbert's arms, whilst David took the other.

"In you come Bert," he said, as they pulled and dragged him bodily over the side so that all three were jammed into the front half of the boat; whilst Jim and the still wriggling carcass were in the back half. Now that he was out of the water and exposed to the wind, Herbert's teeth began to chatter more loudly.

"I'm cold," he said.

Richard looked at Herbert's dripping clothes and nodded. "Yes, we had better go back in now. Jim needs to get his hand seen to, what do you think Barry?"

He looked down at his friend who was staring fascinated at the wriggling remains of the eel, every now and then prodding it with the axe when it showed signs of slowing down, whilst the large eyes in its separated head looked at him balefully.

Barry looked up. "Eh?" Oh, all right," he turned to Jim, "What do you want done with the eel Jim – it's your catch?" Jim was too busy inspecting his hand to reply.

"Can you eat it?" asked David.

Richard shrugged whilst Herbert, his voice full of loathing, replied, "I can't think of anyone in his right mind wanting to eat that." Then he flinched as the head moved suddenly, caused by a passing wave rocking the boat.

Chuck it over the side," said Jim suddenly. His hand was beginning to throb with pain and what had seemed like a triumph, the biggest thing he had ever caught, had turned into a disaster. He looked at the eel and wished he had never caught it in the first place. "Go on, chuck it!" he said emphatically.

Barry shrugged he was not bothered. It was not really his catch although he had helped to bring it in. "Give us a hand, Ricky, David." Together they all picked up the eel and, with difficulty because it was heavy as well as very slippery, heaved it over the side. All of them, save Jim, watched as twisting in the waves it sank into the sea, finally disappearing into the depths. Hesitantly Barry picked up the head then threw it quickly over the side. Having rinsed his hands in the sea he shook them before drying them on his shorts.

"It's gone," he said to Jim, who had been looking the other way.

Jim turned around as Richard and David sat down and took hold of the oars. "Good, let's get back. My hand's giving me gyp."

"Bring in the anchor, Bert," said Richard as he and David began rowing to loosen it from its hold on the seabed. Herbert strained with all his weight on the rope until he felt it come free then quickly pulled it in. Finally lifting the seaweed-covered anchor and dropping it into the boat having accomplished this he sat down and exhaled noisily.

Richard and David began to get into a rhythm with their rowing whilst Barry sat tidying up the fishing tackle, every now and then casting any eye at Jim who sat gazing at the shore. Barry shook his head wonderingly. "Biggest bleedin' eel I've ever seen." He paused in what he was doing before continuing, "Pity we couldn't have kept it – could've had it stuffed.

Although smiling at this remark, Richard was a bit worried about Jim who had gone very quiet. "How's the hand Jim?" he managed to get out in-between rowing.

Jim uncovered his hand and held it out. Herbert, looking over Richard's shoulder, winced with a sudden intake of breath and then sat back on the anchor rope and resumed teeth chattering. Jim's hand had been badly mauled by the eel, the bite having been worsened by Barry trying to pull the eel off whilst its teeth were still embedded in the flesh. Where the skin was not ragged and concealed by partly congealed blood, Richard could clearly see the teeth marks.

"Does it hurt?" asked David without thinking.

Jim, having resumed cradling his lacerated hand, in his other hand, merely nodded. The shore looked as far away as ever and he doubted if he would make it to the beach without fainting. He took another covert look at his hand, being repelled and fascinated by it at the same time. A sudden stab of pain increased his nausea, making him speak out. "Can't you row any faster?" he said querulously, and then looked down at his hand again.

David, who knew they were rowing as fast as they could, in fact faster than he had ever rowed before, looked at Richard in astonishment. He was about to say something but both Richard and Barry shook their heads. Frustrated, he took his anger out on Herbert, his words punctuated by the rowing strokes. "For heaven's sake, Bert, stop that bleedin' noise from your teeth."

Unabashed, Herbert turned around from staring at the slowly approaching shore. "I'm cold. You would be if you had to sit in this tub soaked to the skin like me."

His indignation caused them all, save Jim, to laugh, dispelling if only for a short while the miasma of gloom, which hung over the boat. After the laughter had died down, each of them reverted to their own thoughts with only Barry saying belatedly, "Bleedin' cheek calling my boat a tub."

With Jim nursing his torn hand they felt restrained, unable to talk about what had happened until they were all safely ashore and Jim had had his hand attended to. Roll on tomorrow, thought Richard, his arms now aching from the unaccustomed strain of fast sustained rowing. He would be seeing Emma again. Even though her school did not, like his, have half-term holidays, now that the winter was over the girls were allowed a little more free time to do as they wished. He hoped it didn't rain and as the thought flew through his mind Richard looked up at the sky as if he could somehow divine the next day's weather.

With thoughts of tomorrow spurring him on he slowly began to increase his rowing rate. David, after looking at him oddly for a moment, followed suit making the stubby little boat go faster than either he or Barry, whose boat it was, ever thought possible. With Herbert sitting in the bow his teeth chattering; Richard and David vying with each other over who could row the fastest; Jim rocking slowly back and forth as he held his bloodied hand; and Barry trailing his fingers in the sea watching the wake, the small boat finally disappeared around the edge of the jetty on the last leg of its journey back into the harbour.

Chapter 21: **A box of chocolates**

The golden parcel glittered in the ray from the sun as Richard's mother rotated it in her hands. Her eyes gleamed with anticipation as she turned to look at Richard and Robin, who waited with some slight apprehension.

It was their mother's birthday. For the past three or four weeks they had debated what they should buy her. Unfortunately they did not have much money between them – especially as their mother didn't allow them to have either a paper round or any other part-time work. Both of them received pocket money based on a penny for each year of their age. Richard now got a shilling and Robin ten pennies. After buying sweets and a comic it did not leave much to buy a present. Richard's additional money from singing in the choir had long since been spent and there was a dearth of weddings as this time of the year so no extra money was coming from that source. However, combining what little money they had was sufficient to buy either some nylons or a box of chocolates. They had discussed this with their Dad who said that he had already bought some nylons and would also get some flowers for the big day.

Not being able to get any more ideas from their Dad, Richard and Robin had haunted Woolworths in the High Street for several Saturdays. Perfume was another alternative suggested by Robin as they had stared bemusedly at the counter one afternoon, but they did not really have enough money – and what if she didn't like the smell they had chosen. Wistfully Richard had contemplated the perfumes, remembering the present he had bought Emma for Christmas.

Finally they had made up their minds. It was Robin, who suggested, as they traipsed around the sweet counter yet again watched balefully by the shop assistant, that as their mother had liked the box of Black Magic chocolates they had bought her for Christmas so much, they should buy her another one. Richard agreed readily. Any present was better than none and the worry of choosing something suitable was beginning to wear him down. Thankfully they purchased the box of chocolates and with the remaining few pence some wrapping paper, sellotape and a card. Hurrying home they had shown their Dad their purchases and his approval of their choice had been greeted with sighs of relief. Taking great care in wrapping the present they had hidden it away until their mother's birthday. They had got out of bed extra early this morning to ensure that they did so before their mother was up and had put the card and present at her place on the kitchen table.

Now the moment had arrived. Richard shivered suddenly in anticipation. Although he rarely admitted it to himself there were very few days that his mother was happy; when his brother, sister, himself and also his Dad could say and do almost anything without worrying about incurring the instant wrath of their mother. Usually the sound of her walking about upstairs in their room, making the ceiling creak, was enough to fill them with dread, which increased in intensity as she stomped downstairs, and reached a climax when she burst through the kitchen door, more often than not with some bitter question on her tongue. This morning, sighed Richard thankfully to himself, it was going to be different as he watched his mother slowly unwrap the present, not wishing to tear the expensive looking wrapping paper, then in her urgency to get at the present, not caring; ripping the paper until the present was revealed.

Richard watched, noticing his mother's features change from eager expectation to first puzzlement, indignation, and then anger as she looked at the box of chocolates, now somehow naked and defenceless without the gaudy covering of wrapping paper.

"Chocolates!" she cried, "*Black Magic* chocolates!" Her voice rising with her growing rage.

Richard looked at Robin who returned his gaze, noticing the look of bewilderment on his young brother's features, which was mirrored in his own; before a further outburst from their mother made Robin's face drain of blood so quickly that you would have thought someone had turned on a tap.

Their mother turned to look at them both. Her face full of fury. "I had *Black Magic* chocolates from you at Christmas and now you buy them again for me on my birthday." She looked accusingly at Richard. "Are you so stupid? Have you no imagination?" she continued, looking now at Robin and then back again at Richard. "Are you so stupid? Have you no imagination?" she continued, looking now at Robin and then back again at Richard. The knuckles of her hands turned white as she attempted to tear the box apart. After straining at the reluctant box it came to pieces with a suddenness, which surprised even her, scattering chocolates around the room like confetti at a wedding. Some hit Richard and Robin standing nearby, others fell to the floor near her feet. "That's what I think of your present, you stupid boys!" she spat, whilst stamping viciously on the chocolates that lay on the floor, grinding them into the lino.

Richard and Robin watched appalled, not believing what they were witnessing. Their mother had liked these chocolates at Christmas, which was months ago. She had not received any since and now this had happened. What a waste of money. Any further thoughts he might have had like this fled like birds before a storm as his mother turned on him.

"Whose idea was it? Was it yours?" she said rushing up to Richard and poking him with a long fingernail hard in the cheek. Before he could reply she rounded on Robin. "Or was it you?" pushing him backwards with the palm of her hand.

Robin knew it was his suggestion even though his brother had agreed with him. His eyes turned to Richard in mute appeal, which did not go unnoticed, though misinterpreted, by their mother who now swung back to Richard.

"So it was you, you stupid little boy. I half suspected as much." Holding up her little finger she said, "I've got more brains in my little finger than you have in your whole head." She stopped momentarily at a loss for words, which she overcame by slapping Richard hard around the head. "Get out of my sight, I'm sick at looking at you, go on, get out and don't bother coming back."

Richard turned. His silence had condemned him. Even if he was not guilty of suggesting the present he was equally culpable in that he agreed with Robin's idea. Not wishing to see his young brother get hit instead of him he walked towards the door that led to the porch and stepped outside.

Their mother now turned her attention to Robin. "You, you're just as useless, go on, and get out of my sight." Robin hurried out just as Marilyn came into the room with her present. He shot her a warning glance then carried on as his mother spoke. "Ah my darling and what have you got your Mater for her birthday?"

Robin closed the door quietly, glad of the distraction to his mother, which had enabled him to get out of the room without any punishment. He turned left out of the porch to the back garden and sat down on the bench there, next to Richard, who looked at him.

"Many happy returns of the day," said Richard ironically. Robin laughed and punched his brother lightly on the arm. For the moment his relief at getting out of the house in one piece overwhelmed his other emotions. They both sat there for a while letting the slight breeze blow away their disappointment. Finally Robin broke the silence.

"It's not fair, you know."

"I know," said Richard.

"What a waste of money and effort."

Richard shrugged, he was resigned to his mother's irrational moods and bouts of anger and tried to live with them, whereas Robin was not.

"I don't know why we bother," continued Robin "we must be..." he groped for the right word, aware of its existence even though not knowing what it was.

"Masochists," said Richard.

"Yeah," said Robin, "that's it, masochists. She treats us like dirt and what do we do? Take our hard saved money and go and buy her a present only to make her angry." It's not fair. I don't know why we stand for it." He stood up suddenly, his voice now tinged with anger. "No, it isn't right. I'm going to go in there and tell her exactly what I think."

He made as if to walk into the house but Richard reached up with his hand and stopped him, surprised at the amount of resistance from Robin. He had really meant it. Robin looked down at this brother's restraining hand and then at Richard who pulled him back to his seat.

"Don't," said Richard. "It's not worth it."

Robin desisted, he was still very angry: in fact angrier now than he had been when he had stood up. He had expected Richard, of all people, to understand how he felt. "Why not? It's about time someone stood up to her. It's not right the way she treats us. None of our friends get this sort of treatment from their mothers. There should be a law against it. Look," he pointed to his thighs still bruised and swollen from the slaps his mother had given him when she had been teaching him to tell the time.

Richard nodded. "Because," he said "for one thing she's bigger than you are and can hit a lot harder." He paused for a moment to let this sink in. When Richard saw that it had he continued, "And remember that time Marilyn had been hit hard and Mum then threw a fork at her which stuck in her stomach and Marilyn said she would get back at her and tell the doctor who did it."

Robin nodded, a queasy feeling beginning to inhabit his stomach. He remembered standing in the kitchen next to Richard, shaking uncontrollably out of fear, having seen the fork fly through the air and bury itself in Marilyn's stomach. It had hung there for a few seconds then slowly slid out and fallen to the floor, accompanied by drops of blood. It had been too much for Robin and he had run out of the room but the noise of the fork landing on the floor had brought Marilyn out of her shock and she had threatened to go to the police. But their Dad, so he heard later, had told her not to, but he could not remember why. He nodded again, not wanting to ask the rest, which he had forgotten, but knowing Richard needed prompting if he was going to find out. He had to in case it was important. "I remember her being hit by the fork," he trailed off, letting Richard pick up the unasked question that hung between them.

"Well," said Richard, speaking slowly making sure he did not leave anything out since it had haunted him ever since. "After Marilyn had threatened to tell Dr Castle and the police, Mum had stood up, walked over to her and said in a very quiet voice. 'If you don't like it here you can go and live in a children's Home away from your brothers or be sent to Australia with other badly behaved kids. You tell anyone I did that and I'll say you're uncontrollable and they'll take you away. They'll believe me before they believe you, so you go ahead and tell the police and say goodbye to your brothers whilst you're at it.' That's what she said," finished Richard.

Like his sister before him Robin had, if only for the moment, had all the resistance driven out of him by his brother's recollection. The way he had spoken, his voice mimicking that of his mother, had sent a chill all through his body and made him break out in goose pimples. He did not want to live in a home like some of the boys at his school. Then as he weighed it up in his mind his anger resurfaced. Yes, it would be worth it if they could only get rid of their mother. If only for a little while so they didn't have to live as they did now, in constant fear of their mother. Living each moment of their lives in dread of her breaking out into one of her rages and no matter who was right or wrong it always ended up with one of them getting hurt, sometimes badly. Well not any more, thought Robin.

He looked at his older brother and could not really believe in his mother's threat. Whatever happened he would see him again. But what to do, how or when to do it, to rectify what was an impossible situation seemed beyond him. Robin stared at his feet, wondering what to do. He resolved that the next time he was beaten he would go to the police. He paused in his thoughts. That was probably no good. Lots of children got hit by their parents. True. But he did not know of any of his friends who got hit as hard – cricket bat was the current implement being used – or as often as he and Richard did. What was worse than the punishment was living in constant fear of being hit. His sister and Dad were not immune once their mother got going. Even his dad used to take it when, if he really wanted to, Robin did not doubt that he could beat her up. That's it, thought Robin, smacking his right fist into his left hand making Richard turn his head to stare at him before resuming his morose scrutiny of the grass, the next time she hits me I'll just hit her back and see if she likes it. He shivered in anticipation, each passing second confirming his belief that it remained the only possible solution to their trouble. She may murder me, he thought, but I don't care, I'm sick to death of being treated like some worthless slave.

Now that he had started ruminating about the solution to dealing with their mother Robin found that he couldn't stop. It wasn't just being hit all the time that got on his nerves, although that was in itself quite bad, but it was something he and the others had learned to live with. It was the fact that even when she wasn't hitting anyone she was constantly griping, whining, criticising and nagging. Nothing was ever right. Nothing they did was worthwhile and she was always telling them how worthless they were. With quick stabs of her sharp tongue she could flay you alive. Although not always understanding exactly what was going on Robin used to cringe with embarrassment as, like his brother and sister, he had been forced to watch his Dad being humiliated. Merely, it seemed, from the pleasure she derived from exercising the power she held over another person. At such times Robin had felt like standing up and shouting out loud, go on Dad, hit her, hit her and shut her up for heaven's sake. But he never had. Like his Dad, her very dominating presence seemed to deny others free will.

The more he thought about it the angrier Robin became: most especially his indignation at the most recent event being foremost in his mind. The sight of those chocolates being scattered around the floor and trampled underfoot made his blood boil.

"We must be mad. None of us like her so why on earth do we waste our money and buy her presents?"

He shouted out loud, not realising that he had done so.

Richard turned and looked at his brother and smiled. He had almost, he imagined, been able to hear his brother's mind churning over in the last few minutes as he had been looking for answers to probably unfathomable questions.

"Simple," he replied, making Robin look up, "because if we didn't our life would be even more unbearable that it is now: if that is possible." He laughed at Robin's face whose mouth was gaping open in astonishment, then became even more fish-like as he groped for the right words, finally finding them.

"But, but that's not fair!" was all he could immediately think of. "Whatever we do," he finally added, "if we buy her presents or we don't buy her presents we still get told off and hit." He stopped as another idea hit him suddenly. "Suppose she knows that we only buy her presents to stop from being hit. That's it!" he shouted standing up as the full import of the idea hit him. "She knows we don't like her, because she treats us so bad, so even though we buy her presents it doesn't make any difference to the way we are treated because she knows it is all false, so we don't get treated any better." He stopped again, astounded by the ideas running around in his head. "She's just playing with us, laughing at us all the time."

Robin sat down again, his flash of insight over. It was not only the thought that they were wasting their time and money but what he thought was the fact that their mother knew of, accepted and used their hypocrisy through fear of her as an amusement. It was one further reason why he wanted revenge for all she had done to them. He paused, waiting for Richard's confirmation. When it was not immediately forthcoming he prompted him. "Well, what do you think?"

Richard shrugged, and then shook his head before speaking. "You may be right, only I don't think it is worth the risk of trying to find out. Dad thinks that the only reason we're still breathing is because of mother's day, Christmas and her birthday.

Robin went "Humph" and lapsed into silence, his mind going round and round at what he could do to get back at his mother for all the fear, pain and heartache she had caused him and his brother and sister.

"I think I agree with Dad, you know," said Richard. "A quiet life."

Not getting any response from his brother he too lapsed into silence. Sitting back against the porch wall he gazed up at the clouds pacing each other through the sky. At least it was warm he thought. Having to stay out of the house in May was easy compared to January. Sheltered from the cool breeze blowing over the fields at the front of the house by the porch, he whiled away the hours until lunchtime, as he had learned to do early in his life, by daydreaming. Although relaxed his body, as he knew it would, like Robin's, respond instantly to any whistles from his mother, or calls from his Dad to come into the house. It was such an automatic reflex that he had frequently rushed into the house after hearing a whistled summons without being fully aware of what he was doing, or why. He just knew that when whistled they had to get in the house at once otherwise there would be trouble. Arriving in such a state of panic he was often unable to take in fully what was being said to him so that he usually exacerbated his position making any punishment due him much worse. Perhaps, he thought, he ought to try and slow his reflexes down. Being late but more aware might be preferable in future. Having decided that, his body relaxed further into a somnolent attitude. Doing nothing was the best thing to do at times like this.

Chapter 22: **Breaking point**

Pedalling faster and faster Richard raced down Broadstairs High Street. He was going so fast now that it was impossible for him to peddle any more. Keeping himself alert to any traffic, which might suddenly emerge from a side street Richard gripped the handlebars of his bicycle tightly, his lips drawn back in a fierce grin. He was free. He had escaped. He felt like shouting; he was so happy to get out of the house with its overwhelming atmosphere of fear and misery. More than that, hopefully, he would shortly be meeting Emma and this morning, after the fiasco over his mother's birthday present, none of it had seemed likely or possible.

Dinnertime had come and gone until finally their dad had come out and said for them to come in and get something to eat. Having carefully eased themselves off the bench and stretched the cramp and fatigue out of their bodies, they had gone inside to eat a cheese sandwich each and drink a mug of milk. It had been strangely quiet. On asking where Marilyn and their mother were, their dad had told them that as a special treat, for her nice present, Marilyn had been taken to Dreamland amusement park by their mother. Richard, although disappointed at not being included in the outing, was both relieved at not having to come face to face with his mother again and pleased that he would now be able to go out that afternoon and, as arranged, meet Emma.

Robin had been less sanguine. He had at first thought that his Dad was playing a joke on them. He couldn't believe that he would not be included in such an outing since it was such a rarity. When all his doubts had finally been dispelled he had sat hunched over his sandwich, saying nothing, with tears running down his face. He couldn't understand why he and Richard were being punished in this way for doing something good.

Having obtained reluctant permission from his father to go down to the harbour that afternoon, provided he was back before five o'clock when his mother was expected to return from Dreamland with Marilyn, Richard felt a bit guilty about leaving Robin behind and had suggested that he might want to come with him; even though in his heart, he really would rather have gone alone. Robin had merely shaken his head and pulled a chunk out of his sandwich with his teeth, which he hardly bothered to chew before swallowing it convulsively. Richard had looked at his Dad who merely mouthed 'leave him be' and left the room. Just before he left Richard had made a final attempt to persuade his brother to go out but Robin had just shook his head.

"Come on Rob," Richard had persisted, making Robin raise his head, his face dirty from tears and his eyes red and swollen.

"It's not fair, Ricky. Why can't we go to Dreamland as well? All we did was buy her a present and look what happened." Pausing for a moment to rub his eyes he had continued, "What's she trying to do to us, eh?" His voice hardened suddenly. "You know, I really hate her. I'm going to get her back for all the things she's done to us." Getting up abruptly he had left the room saying with finality, "You see if I don't." He then ran heavily up the stairs and, going into the bathroom, slammed the door behind him.

Richard had made to follow after his brother but the kitchen clock caught his eye. He would be late if he didn't hurry and anyway Robin easily got into funny moods and came out of them just as easily. Consoled by this thought Richard had said a hurried goodbye to his Dad, who had grunted in response, got on his bicycle and hurried down to Viking Bay.

Applying his brakes as he reached the junction with Albion Street, Richard cruised along the narrow road of Sea Approach and stopped by the railings lining the promenade. Richard gazed out to sea and along the shore picking out familiar landmarks as if he were greeting old friends anew. High up on the promontory to his left, Bleak House where Charles Dickens once lived. It didn't look very cheerless up there; its facade of brown bricks seemed to ooze friendliness. Looking down, his eyes flickered quickly over the old boat house, with the figurehead from a ship, the Scottish Soldier, and finally the arch of two whale bones. His eyes roamed to the end of the jetty. He paused to look over the Viking ship, shaped in wire on the roof of the jetty shelter, which was lit up at night in the summer with light bulbs; then on across the bay to the other side where the bandstand stood, a monument to Victorian splendour surrounded by the flowers that served as a decoration to that part of the promenade.

His eyes, stopping there for only a few seconds, only to look at the clock on top of the bandstand, swept back across the bay to scrutinise the jetty. He had agreed to meet Emma by the red painted mine, which stood next to the Harbour Master's office. Empty of explosives, it was now adorned with a weathered brass plate seeing donations for a seamen's charity. Richard shook his head. He could not see Emma standing there even though this was the agreed time. Mind you, he thought, he had only just made it himself. As cycling was not permitted on the promenade Richard got off his bicycle and with one foot on a pedal, scooted along the cliff top. With deft twists of the handlebars he easily avoided the early holiday makers, mostly OAPs at this time of the year, heralding the beginning of another holiday season.

Arriving at the jetty Richard leaned his bicycle against the stout wooden railings and looked down at the sailing dinghies on the sand in their enclosure: Mainly 'Merlins', 'Rockets' and 'Snipes'. Whilst out in the harbour the sturdier and much heavier 'Forelands' strained against their mooring chains. Up against the wall of the jetty leaned the smaller rowing boats, including Barry's.

Richard smiled as he remembered the recent fishing expedition. As soon as they had landed Jim rushed off across the sand not caring about his fishing tackle, jumped on his bicycle and cycled off up Harbour Street, a thing he or any of them rarely did as it was so steep and sand-strewn. Without much being said, and accompanied by the chattering of Herbert's teeth, they had laboriously hauled the boat out of the water, carried it to the harbour wall and with much grunting and straining, heaved it up into its present position, where it was secured in place with the rope. This task having been accomplished; they had thankfully collected their belongings, Barry taking Jim's fishing tackle with him, and made their separate ways home.

Richard wondered for a moment how Jim was getting on as his eyes wandered back and forth along the sands and the jetty before looking towards Harbour Street expecting any moment that first glimpse of Emma. An endless stream of people came and went around the corner of Harbour Street, causing Richard every now and then to leap up, as he thought he had caught sight of Emma, only to have to fall into repose as the girl concerned got closer and he saw that it was not her.

Like the cumulus clouds moving sedately overhead the minutes passed by. As the sky darkened with the gathering clouds, the idea gradually began to crystallise in Richard's mind that perhaps Emma would not be coming after all. He thought back to their last meeting when they had agreed to meet here. Richard admitted to himself that Emma had not been certain whether she would be able to get out of school. Richard also remembered agreeing cheerfully that it wouldn't matter if she could not. He would still try to see here after church on Sunday. Now, faced with the actuality, Richard was not so happy. He had really been hoping to see Emma today: more so after morning's debacle with his mother's birthday present. He was going to ask Emma if she knew the reason for his mother behaving like she had.

A gust of wind, coupled with an extremely dark cloud momentarily covering the sun, made Richard shiver suddenly and caused him to rub his arms to drive away the chill. He looked up at the sky. There were many more clouds about, some white and grey but mostly black, with here and there, disappearing even as he looked, a few patches of pale blue sky. Turning, Richard looked at the clock on the wall next to the Harbour Master's office; it was half an hour past their arranged meeting time. Richard began to wonder how long he should wait before going home. Around him people were leaving the beach and pier, not waiting for the first few drops of rain which would undoubtedly fall before too long. A particularly large black cloud drifted overhead pattering down a few drops of rain, which fell heavily into the sand near Richard's feet. Moving back from the railings Richard sought shelter by the wall of the Harbour Master's office but the expected downpour did not materialise. The black cloud moved off seeking a better place, thought Richard, to shed its watery burden. People in transparent plastic raincoats strolled by, smug in their preparedness, but looking unreal, thought Richard, their bodies and arms covered in the clear plastic seemed like the silver bubble of air that enfolds a water spider.

Emma's not coming, Richard finally admitted to himself, looking up at the sky. Individual clouds had given way to a mass of greyness, which seemed to impress on Richard a sombre mood. He knew somehow that there was no point in waiting any longer and he had better get home before it really rained hard. In any case if it was also going to rain in Margate his mother and Marilyn would soon be on their way home. He had better; as his Dad had warned him, get home before them. It would be bad enough having to explain his absence; he didn't want to worsen any imagined wrong-doing his mother might accuse him of if he came back wet as well. Apart from being out in the first place, his mother would want to know where he had been and why he had not come back sooner, and what it was that had detained him.

This thought acting as a spur to his going, Richard cycled up Harbour Street. Although one part of his mind had accepted that Emma would not turn up, another part urged him to go home by the route Emma would have taken rather than take the quick way home, just in case he caught a glimpse of her. Reaching the top of Harbour Street, his mind made up, Richard turned into Albion Street on the first leg of his journey to St Peter's pursued by the rain.

* * *

Despite cycling fast Richard did not quite manage to stay ahead of the rain on his journey home. His hair, face, jersey and shorts, save the part that rested on the saddle, were quite wet as he careened down the path at the side of the house and put his bicycle into the porch. After wiping his wet face with the palms of his hands, the only other part of him that was fairly dry, he bent down and untied his wet shoes, leaving them in the porch to dry. Opening the door to the kitchen he stepped quickly inside. The kitchen was empty and for a brief moment he felt a sense of relief as he thought he had got home before his mother had returned from Dreamland with Marilyn. He stepped into the back room to greet his brother and Dad, hoping that Robin had got over his morbid mood. After one step he got no further, and stood by the door, unable to move by what he saw.

His brother Robin lay on the floor. His face and legs were a mass of red bruising. Blood oozed from the cuts in his lips and over his eyes, whilst his left arm lay twisted at an impossible angle. Above all was the tortured way his chest heaved up and down as he took a breath. His mother stood nearby, like an animal at bay, breathing heavily, leaning against the wall, the bloodied poker in her hand waving to and fro before finally dropping, with a dull thud, to the lino. Richard rushed forward calling to his brother, willing him to get off the floor.

"Rob, Rob, are you all right?"

He never reached Robin, as his father suddenly rushed into the room and roughly pushed him out of the way. He knelt down beside Robin looking at his injuries, then as gently as he could, straightening Robin's arm, making him writhe with the pain it caused. His Dad looked back at Richard, his weathered face unnaturally white with shock.

"Richard, quickly, run up to the telephone box, dial 999 and call an ambulance."

Richard stood there, unable to move, just looking at his younger brother, not fully able to take it all in, least of all what was being said to him. His Dad realising this, left Robin and taking Richard firmly by the arm, propelled him out of the back room, through the kitchen and into the porch. He shook Richard roughly.

"Listen to me, Ricky, you're a fast runner, faster than any of us and Robin needs help, so run up to the telephone box and call an ambulance." Richard's Dad, seeing the light of growing awareness appearing in his son's eyes, lifted him up and taking him out to the porch dropped him into his shoes, opened the door to the porch and pushed him outside, then returned to the back room.

Richard first walked then trotted to the front gate. He had a task to perform that solely filled his mind. He must get help for his brother Robin. He must run. As if he was running the hundred yards in school, at which he excelled, he sprinted up the hill. Although it was about four hundred yards to the telephone box he ran as if it was only a hundred. It was still raining. His feet made hardly any sound as he flew up the hill trying to go faster and faster.

Halfway up the hill he shot past a German shepherd dog that had been sitting by the front gate of its owner's house. It automatically drew back as Richard, unheeding, ran passed, then, either annoyed by the disturbance or thinking it a game, the dog ran after Richard, barking noisily. Richard heard the dog but ignored it even when it caught up with him and snapped at his heels, growling and barking. Finally the harassment became too much and he kicked at it sideways with his left foot, then continued running. The dog shied off then came at him again, this time with greater determination than before. Richard kicked once more with greater force and as he did so his shoe flew off. This distracted the dog sufficiently to allow him to concentrate on reaching the telephone kiosk, which he could see at the top of the hill. Running awkwardly, but uncaring, with only one shoe on, his stockinged foot getting wetter and wetter from the puddled pavement he continued on his way unhindered by the dog. The German shepherd sat contentedly chewing the shoe, and then with a last glance at Richard's disappearing form, it picked up the shoe with its teeth and carried it back as a trophy back to where it had been sitting.

Meanwhile Richard had at last negotiated the few remaining yards across Whitfield Avenue, where his other shoe came off. He ignored it and rushed into the telephone kiosk which thankfully was empty. Richard was breathing heavily from his running but nevertheless picked up the telephone and dialled '999', taking deep breaths while at the same time trying to slow down his breathing so that he could talk when required to do so. The telephone rang in his ear then a woman's voice answered.

"Emergency, which service do you require?"

Taking a deep breath Richard expelled it with the one word, "Ambulance." Although he thought he had said it clearly the woman asked him to repeat it. He made a conscious effort to breathe slowly and then said it again, "Ambulance." After a few seconds a man's voice told him that he was speaking to the ambulance service. Richard blurted out his story, twice. The man he was speaking to was not entirely convinced that this was not a hoax played by an irresponsible boy. Finally accepting the soundness of the request he advised Richard that an ambulance was on its way.

With two hands Richard put the telephone very carefully on its rest and slumped against the iron and glass side of the kiosk. He had done it. A gust of wind spattered some rain against the glass, urging him out. Feebly Richard pushed against the door with one hand but it refused to budge. Forcing him to concentrate, since reaction was beginning to set in, he stood up and pushed against the door with his whole weight and stumbled outside.

As if to make up for his earlier exertion he walked very slowly across Whitfield Avenue, picking up his shoe as he went but not bothering to put it on, then on down Northdown Hill. Rain was falling more heavily as he walked but this did little to further wet his already soaked clothes. With the slope of the hill to speed him on he increased his pace down the hill until he reached the gate opening where sat the dog with one paw over his most recently acquired possession. Richard eyed the dog and the dog in turn eyed him back. Richard was in no mood to argue.

"Give me back my shoe, you stupid dog!"

The dog aware that a challenge had been made stood up still keeping a paw on the shoe. Richard went to take the shoe but the dog growled and snapped at his hand.

Knowing that he was going to need both hands to retrieve his shoe Richard put on the one he had on his foot and tied it up. The dog, taking this as a signal to leave, picked up the shoe it had with its mouth and turned away as if to go back into its house. Richard suddenly stretched out and grabbed hold of the shoe whilst the dog tightened its grip, growling menacingly as it did so. Richard pulled, as did the dog. After a few minutes of this, it was apparent that they were at a stalemate, whilst the dog had probably now realised its mistake in that picking up the shoe it could not use its teeth as a weapon.

"Let go, or else," said Richard. He didn't know exactly what the 'or else' would be but he did not wish to be delayed any longer. From the corner of his eye he had seen the ambulance arrive outside his house and wished to hurry home, but he also knew that if he didn't get his shoe back now he might never see it again.

Keeping hold of the shoe tightly with his left hand he drew back his right arm, balled his fingers into a fist and punched the dog hard on the nose. The dog released the shoe with a startled yelp and stumbled backwards as did Richard who, after examining the shoe briefly, put it on and ran off down the hill. The dog, recovering from its initial shock, ran after him barking but after a few yards a twinge of pain running through its nose made it stop. Contenting itself with a few more barks and a growl at the retreating figure it went back to its house and barked and whimpered to be let in out of the rain.

Chapter 23: Some times will last forever

Cycling automatically, not having to think of the journey, Richard made his way to church, the events of yesterday crowding his mind. For the first time since he had joined the choir Richard had said that he wanted to stay at home for news of Robin rather than go to church, but his Dad had said 'no'. He had more than enough to do to visit the hospital and their mother at the police station whilst Marilyn could look after herself. Besides, his Dad had said, wasn't he singing an important solo this Sunday? He had mentioned it often enough all week. Richard had started to protest, surprising even himself when he said that it wasn't important, but aware of the strained look on his Dad's face, he desisted.

As he cycled Richard thought about the previous afternoon, trying to understand what had happened. The police had arrived at the house shortly after the ambulance, their presence unexplained. When the ambulance had finally rushed Robin off to hospital the police had gone into the front room with his Dad and mother, whilst Richard and Marilyn had been told to stay in the back room. Although he and Marilyn had strained to hear what was going on, even putting tumblers up against the wall, they could barely make out the muted questions of the policemen and the monosyllabic replies of their mother with, every now and then, the deeper voice of their Dad. After about ten minutes the door to the front room had opened suddenly, causing Richard and Marilyn to scramble around and hide the glasses, managing to sit down just as their Dad entered the room. Without any preliminaries he addressed them both; for once speaking quickly, not wasting any words.

"Your Mum and I are going out for a bit. Tidy this room up then have your supper and get to bed right?"

The tone of his voice was sufficiently sombre to brook no argument. Marilyn had just said, 'Yes, Dad,' whilst Richard could only nod once, briefly.

Their Dad looked at them both for a moment then nodded his head. "Right." he said emphatically as he left the room closing the door firmly behind him.

They had remained where they were listening intently to the sounds from the hall as their parents made ready to go out with the policemen. Not daring to speak in case they missed anything that might be said. But nothing was. Finally the front door closed with a slam. As if it were a signal, Richard and Marilyn looked at each other and then rushed out of their seats. Reaching the door first Richard opened it and hurried through the hall into the front room, stopping by the edge of the curtain to avoid being seen from the outside. With his sister crowding behind him, Richard leaned his head forward just enough so he could see what was going on. A procession of four was walking towards the front gate: first a policeman, followed by his mother and Dad, with the other policeman bringing up the rear.

The leading policeman on reaching the car opened the rear door, allowing Richard's mother to get in, followed quickly by their Dad. Meanwhile the other policeman had walked around the front of the car, got in the driving seat and started the engine. When his partner had got in, the car rolled slowly down the hill. Richard moved out from behind the curtain to look out of the window and watched the car until it disappeared out of sight.

Richard stood there for a while until Marilyn had told him to help her tidy up the back room. Unable to stand the thought of washing up Robin's blood from the lino he had left most of the work to Marilyn and was pleased when she suggested that he make the supper. After a hurried cheese on toast Richard had washed up, locked and bolted the back door and then gone to bed.

Richard felt drained as he tried to fall asleep but merely lay in his bed, hands behind his head staring at the supporting wire and mattress of Robin's bunk above him, his mind running over and over the day's events especially his return home. After a while he heard the front door open and close quietly. Richard ears pricked up as he listened to the sounds of movement downstairs, lights being switched on then off again, doors opening and closing. After a few minutes the light on the landing went on, framing the bedroom door in light. Only one set of footsteps sounded on the stairs, which he recognised as belonging to his Dad. His only thought pertaining to his mother's absence was merely that nothing else untoward would happen that night. Turning over onto his side Richard had tried to go to sleep again. Whether he had or not he really didn't know.

* * *

It dawned on Richard that in daydreaming about yesterday he had arrived at the church and so stopped cycling. Looking up at the clock Richard saw that it was only ten fifteen. It was much too early to go into the vestry and get ready for the eleven o'clock service and he did not, in any case, wish to talk to anyone. He heard a shout and turned to see Barry coming along Church Street, near the entrance to the Smithy, cycling towards him. Quickly Richard pushed his bicycle into the courtyard outside the vestry and leaned it against the wall. With a twinge of remorse he paused for a second, wondering whether he should stop and talk to his best friend but finally decided against it: he really didn't want to speak to anyone at the moment. Hurrying across the trodden path which ran through the small graveyard bordering the east end of the church, he trotted past the war memorial and up the driveway along the south side of the church to the graveyard.

Richard stopped suddenly, looked around quickly to check that he had not been followed or watched and then forced a way through the barrier of shrubs, weeds and small trees that lined the footpath at that place. Ignoring the thorns snatching at his jersey and the stinging nettles brushing his knees, Richard continued through the scrub until he reached a clearing. He walked on past a large holly tree and some young shrubs until he reached the point he had aimed for.

The grave was very small and, although the inscription was weathered and unreadable, must, from its size, have belonged to a child. It was adorned with a small marble statue of a kneeling, weeping angel which had its arms clasped around a cross. Richard always sought this spot when seeking solace. The statue seemed to imbue the grave and the clearing with an air of tragic poignancy; a quality of stillness that would eventually overcome any troubles. He sat on the side of the grave and watched idly whilst two butterflies danced with each other around the clearing. A slight breeze ruffled his hair and gradually the clearing and the sun's heat had the desired soporific effect he desired on his body. Richard started to relax and leaned back against the weeping angel. He began to think again about what had happened yesterday, both with Emma and to Robin: most especially how it would affect himself and his brother and sister.

Richard was rudely woken from this reverie by the sound of someone crashing through the undergrowth. As the person got closer the sounds were accompanied by muttered curses. Richard recognised the voice as belonging to Barry. The noises stopped suddenly as Barry marched triumphantly into the clearing.

"Hullo Ricky," he called.

Richard looked up; the comfort he had sought from the peace and tranquillity of this place, and had started to achieve had been forcibly interrupted. Not only that, he had always regarded the weeping angel and the clearing as his own secret place, which he was unwilling to share with anybody, even his best friend. He looked at Barry, his face, he hoped, severe and forbidding.

"How did you know where to find me?"

Barry surveyed the clearing. "That was easy," he countered, squatting down next to Richard. "You always come here."

Richard, amazed at the sureness in his friend's voice, and that someone else knew so much about him, looked away and plucked a piece of grass from the ground and put it in his mouth. He was reluctant to tell Barry to go away but neither did he want to start a conversation. Barry aware of his mood and knowing part of the reason for it was prepared to wait. He had been surprised when Richard had not stopped when he had called him. He had gone into the vestry expecting to find him there but instead had obtained sketchy details of what had happened to Richard's brother, Robin, the previous day from Jim. That he had been beaten half to death by his mother before being taken to hospital. He knew, almost immediately, where his friend would be and decided to seek him out. Lying down in the grass next to Richard, Barry put his hands behind his head, content to gaze at the clouds drifting by in the azure sky.

Richard relaxed slightly then watched as a bumble bee alighted on a piece of clover. Idly he stretched out a finger and very gently stroked its back. He loved the velvety vibrant touch of a bumble bee and although he had stroked at least a hundred bees he had never been stung. Richard felt a great affinity with the bee and watched with regret as it flew off seeking another flower.

Barry looked on slightly envious of Richard's ability to be as one with nature. He rolled over onto his stomach and stretched out his hand to a nearby clump of Bluebells, which had sprung up out of the long tangled grass, their sweet gentle fragrance filling the clearing. With the tips of his fingers he brushed the Bluebell nearest to him for a few times before he managed to catch hold of it. Pulling firmly but gently in order not to break the stalk, he eased the Bluebell free. Carefully scrutinising the bottom white end of the stalk, that contrasted oddly with the green, to make sure there was no dirt or insects on it, he put it in his mouth and with his front teeth crushed the end. He loved the subtle taste of Bluebells almost as much as he liked their shape and smell. The delicate bell shaped flower was in reality six separate pieces with curly edges, some very dark blue and others so faint in colour that they were almost white at the tips with only a hint of blue, all with delicate yellow filaments inside.

Taking the chewed end out of his mouth Barry put the flower close to his nose and breathed in deeply. The sweet smell swamped his nostrils. Somehow it always made him think of the church, perhaps because there were so many Bluebells in the churchyard near the vestry that in May the smell permeated the vestry and the church. Whatever it was, it brought with it a flood of happy memories of the times he had sung in the choir. Taking a final sniff he put the chewed end back in his mouth again and rolled over onto his back. After watching the clouds for a while the heat from the sun in this sheltered place made him sleepy so he closed his eyes. Relishing the gentle breezes that caressed his cheek and caused the long grass to swish about; enveloping them both in the perfume of the other flowers, but mainly the Bluebells, as the wind moved the air in the clearing, first this way then back again, bathing them in fragrance.

Richard watched as another large bumble bee hurtled into the clearing and buzzed around their heads before finally alighting onto a Buttercup. As the bee was so heavy the Buttercup stalk bent over so that it became a hoop with the bee hanging upside down, its wings brushing the grass. Richard smiled at the sight, and then sighed as the bee flew off. "Alright, what do you want?"

Barry looked away, pretending to spot something which required his total attention, pleased that Richard had at last broken from his introspective mood and was beginning to get back to normal – hopefully. Although they had been friends all through junior school Richard had often had moments like this when, frequently for no discernible reason, he would suddenly go off by himself leaving his friends feeling puzzled and dejected.

"Nothing," he replied. Richard sighed, impatiently this time. "At least, nothing special," said Barry hastily, not wishing his oft-time moody friend to lose himself again. "I just want to help," said Barry after the silence had stretched on for just a little too long. That is all he had really come to say. He didn't like to see his best friend the way he was now. In fact he had never seen him so low before and was really at a loss what to do. "Just help," he said again quietly, but it was enough to prompt Richard into speaking.

"It's not fair, it's not right!" he finally blurted out.

Into Barry's mind came unbidden the nonsensical response his mother gave whenever he said the same thing, 'and it's not raining' but he didn't as Richard continued, explaining what had happened the previous day. Richard talking so fast that Barry had difficulty in following all that his friend said. Finally, the story told, Richard ran down and stopped.

"Robin's out of danger and going to be kept in hospital so we won't be able to see him for a bit. It's not fair!" Richard repeated. Barry wondered if he should say something to console his friend but before he could think of anything suitable, Richard continued.

"You know, the last six months have been the best in my life. Being made Head Chorister and meeting Emma, it's, it's all been wonderful. And things at home have been no worse really than usual. Well normal as far as our house goes." He looked at Barry who nodded understandingly.

Barry knew only too well what Richard meant. It may have been normal to Richard to be beaten as frequently as he and his brother were but all his friends dreaded even visiting Richard's house, because of his maniacal mother. Before Barry and his friends had got to know Richard they had thought that the cuts and bruises which littered his face were because he liked getting into fights. As a result, when he had joined the school some years ago on moving into the area, they had tended to avoid him. It was only when Barry had fortuitously seen Richard getting a good belting once from his mother in the front garden that the truth had emerged. Barry still had a vivid memory of that day. Too vivid, he thought, shuddering.

"It was really perfect," said Richard wistfully. "Emma is lovely, don't you think so?" Barry nodded; he did, certainly nicer than some of the girls who wouldn't leave him alone.

Richard smiled wanly to himself; he was still worried about why Emma had not turned up yesterday. Although, as sometimes in the past, they had made only tentative arrangements to meet, she had never failed to turn up before. Still, he would, hopefully, see her after church this morning. It was this that had been keeping him going when all he really felt like doing was sitting down somewhere and crying.

"Come on," said Barry finally, trying to inject a light-hearted note into his voice, "we had better get going. You're singing a solo, don't forget." He stood up and brushed pieces of grass off his shorts looking down at Richard still sitting on the side of the grave.

Looking up, his eyes squinting against the bright sunlight, Richard said. "I don't feel like it. I can't be bothered."

Barry stood there, shocked. Music was his friend's life. Richard seemed to spend more time at the church than any of them and he had the best voice. He squatted down again, saying quietly, "Come on Ricky, you know you don't mean it and do you really want to let the others down?" He waited for a few seconds to let the words sink in, knowing, above anything else, that this would appeal to his sense of honour. After a few more seconds had elapsed, without anything else being said, Richard got to his feet and followed Barry out of the clearing.

Walking side by side along the path leading out of the churchyard Richard's spirits began to rise a little. Just being at church, which always meant so much to him because of the peace and security it gave him compared to his home, seemed to ease away his troubles. Talking to Barry had also helped. It was because he was starting to feel a little lightheaded that his heart gave quite a leap when, rounding the corner of the church, Richard saw some girls from Emma's school whom he thought he recognised. He waved at them causing them to stop. Richard hurried forward, almost breaking into a run.

As he got closer he saw that they were friends of Emma; in fact the ones who had given him the letter all those months ago. "Hullo," said Richard breathlessly as he ran up to them and was pleased to hear them respond. Then oddly two of the girls looked meaningfully at the third, whose name he remembered was Gabrielle, then with a quick smile at Richard walked into the church.

"See you inside," said Barry also going by. Richard followed them all with his eyes for a moment then turned to the remaining girl.

"Hullo Gabby."

"Hullo Richard," she said, then smiled and just waited, making Richard hesitate wondering how best to approach the subject. Not knowing he suddenly found himself blurting out, "Where's Emma? She was supposed to meet me yesterday and didn't turn up. Do you know where she is? She's not ill is she?" Richard stopped, as much to take a breath of air as well as temporarily running out of things to say and wanting, anyway, answers to some of his questions.

Gabrielle had begun to smile at Richard's outpouring but checked herself. Now she didn't know what to say. Well, that was not exactly true, she thought to herself, fumbling in the back of her mind for the right words in the hope that they would somehow lessen the impact of what she had to tell Richard. The silence lengthened and realising that Richard was about to speak again, Gabrielle spoke out.

"I'm sorry, Richard, but Emma has left school." She paused, seeing the look of distress on his face, wondering whether or not to say the rest but decided she had to press on. Medicine in small doses was usually worse than having it all at once. "She won't be coming back. She's gone to America to join her parents.

Richard's senses reeled from this news. He couldn't believe it was happening. The worst he could think of, when she hadn't turned up was that she was ill. Not that she had left school and St Peter's forever. His mind flashed back to that time they were at the beach, just over six weeks ago, when Emma had mentioned that she might have to go to school in America because of her Dad's job in the Foreign Office. Because of what had happened later, the fight with Graham Poole, it had slipped to the back of his mind. Emma had never spoken about it again.

"Before she left, Emma wrote you a letter."

Richard, who had been looking down at the ground, whilst his mind had been racing, looked up sharply at this: a glimmer of hope beginning to emerge amongst the dark thoughts of despair lurking in his mind. But it died before it had time to properly form when he saw the look on Gabrielle's face as she continued.

"I left it in my locker. I was going to give it to you today. It was in my bedside locker but a mistress found it and took it." Gabrielle hurried through the rest, wanting to get it over quickly. "The mistress, Miss Hardbottle," she mouth distastefully, "said she had read it and tore it up and wanted to know if I knew who you were but I said I didn't know. None of us did. But of course she didn't believe us." Unable to bear the look of total despair on Richard's face she said a hurried goodbye and ran into the church.

Richard stood there unable to move. His mind running over the conversation he had just had, vainly looking for some consolation in a word or phrase that would give him some shred of hope. There was nothing, except for the letter she had written him, a letter that was now lost. His mind spun fantasies around its possible contents. Had it contained some element of good news, with a promise, no matter how slight, for a future meeting, or had it been a final farewell, too painful for Emma to bear personally so she had written the letter instead of meeting as previously agreed? Unheeding of the people entering the church, some of whom, knowing who he was, were surprised at his presence and wondering why, when the service was shortly to begin, Richard stood there rather than being dressed for the service and in the vestry. The two alternatives Richard had thought of were going round and round in his mind, raising his hopes and then dashing them again. He would probably have stayed there all morning and missed the service had not Barry, now dressed in his cassock and ruff, come outside to collect him.

Barry, concerned at Richard's odd mood, and having heard about Emma from Gabrielle, had thought Richard had wandered off somewhere. He was relieved to see him where he had left him. Smiling at the passers by Barry went up to his friend. "Ricky!" he hissed, "Come on, you've got to get changed." He was a bit disconcerted by the blankness in Richard's eyes and was pleased to see them finally focus on him.

"Oh. Oh – OK," said Richard beginning to concentrate on what was going on around him, walked into the church behind Barry.

Nodding to the church warden just inside the door, he remembered to bow to the altar as they reached the nave. But, no matter how hard he tried, part of his mind kept saying to him 'you're never going to see Emma again,' whilst the image of his young brother prone on the floor, with his mother leaning over him, with a bloodied poker in her hand, also intruded unbidden in his thoughts. Alternating now between despair and anger, at the two thoughts uppermost in his mind, he shook his head violently to clear his mind as he followed Barry into the corridor that led into the vestry.

* * *

Richard listened, seemingly isolated from those surrounding him by the events of the last two days, as the organ played the introduction to the anthem, 'A Prayer of St Richard of Chichester'. In the three bars before he began his solo he swallowed twice then, taking a couple of deep breaths to sustain him, began the first part of his most favourite anthem. His pure clear voice echoed around the chancel before reverberating into the darkest depths of the church, each note appearing to hang in the air for a moment before seemingly, reluctantly giving way to the next when it sprang forth.

As Richard sang the events of the last six months ran through his mind. His voice catching slightly as he relived what happened yesterday, then this morning's bad news about Emma. Despite the way his mother had treated them he could not understand what had taken place to cause her to hurt Robin so badly. He also could not accept the idea that he might never see Emma again Richard felt his eyes well with tears making him struggle to finish the solo. As a tear ran unheeded down his cheek, quickly followed by another, he was, more than anything else, filled with surprise. He had supposed that his tears had all been beaten out of him by his mother who had, when hitting him, forbidden him to cry otherwise she would give him the same punishment all over again and 'really give him something to cry about.' They now ran unchecked down his cheeks as his solo came to the last few bars. Around him the other choristers were preparing to take over the main theme whilst he would continue his solo with the descant. Because of his reverie Richard was beginning to lose his concentration on what he was singing. Although he had made no conscious decision not to continue with the anthem he was now becoming so totally wrapped up in his own thoughts, over the events of yesterday and today, to care over much about anything else.

Richard's voice faltered again, slightly, as he ended the solo but across the aisle Barry breathed a huge sigh of relief. For a short while, during which he and the other choristers began to sing the main melody before Richard took up the descant, he thought all would be well. Then he noticed that Richard was standing very still and although he appeared to be looking at the music his eyes were not following the notes as they were being sung. Barry looked across at Jim, indicating with his eyes and a shake of his head that he thought something was wrong with Richard. Jim in the same row as Richard, but at the other end, leaned forward slightly but could only see that Richard was standing stock still. He looked back at Barry and shrugged his shoulders. Barry grimaced then looked at Richard standing in his place as tears rolled down his cheeks. A warning jangled in his ear: the descant! He quickly made up his mind, with Richard staring into space it was unlikely that he would remember that he had to sing the descant. Barry had practiced it a few times with Richard so he would just have to do it. He would not let his friend down.

As the cue for the descant came up he took a deep breath and launched himself into it. He accepted as he sang that his voice was not, and probably could never be, as good as Richard's but he would do his best. Although he knew this he had never really admitted it before, even to himself. But the purity of his friend's voice when he had sung the solo, coupled with the feeling that Richard had somehow been able to put his whole being into the words he had been singing had left him very moved. Thinking these thoughts Barry sang determinedly on, watched by wide-eyed fascination by the other boys who did not know he was capable of it.

Richard, though still lost in the labyrinth of his thoughts was beginning to find his way out. Gradually the words and music filtered unconsciously into his mind. With the sudden perspicuity of insight, which hits some people once or twice in a lifetime; and others not at all, he saw the way ahead. He had never really appreciated before, or tried to quantify, the things in his life that were important to him: the things which were fundamental to his very existence and happiness. There was his family, which really meant his brother and sister. He could not envisage a life without them. Though they often quarrelled and fought among themselves this did not detract from how they really felt about one another, particularly in times of stress when they would close ranks against adversity – especially their mother – and share their burdens. He just knew at that moment Robin would get better again soon and be back home with them before long. Most of all, now that people knew what she was really like their mother might be kept away.

Then there were his friends who Richard regarded as an extension to his family. He hoped that they felt about him in the same way. Finally there was his singing in the choir. He came to church not only to obtain relief from his mother, although that was an added bonus; nor because he believed in God, which he didn't really understand but provided him with the stability and strength that he didn't get from his home life; but because he loved the music and the peace and joy it gave him. It had unknowingly and gradually become a very important part of his life. Richard loved singing for its own sake and especially because it carried him to normally unobtainable heights. He knew that whatever else happened in his lifetime the effect of the years he had spent singing in the choir would always be with him.

As if he had been deaf, and now could suddenly hear, he found himself surrounded by the voices of his friends. He looked across at Barry who was now beginning to struggle to maintain the descant, his throat beginning to ache with the effort. He pleaded with his eyes for Richard to join in. Richard smiled, gave a slight nod and locating his place, softly at first and then with greater power as he found his voice, took over the descant. Barry now relaxed a little and would have reverted back to singing the main melody had not Richard indicated with his eyes and an upward motion of the anthem sheet held in his hands that he should continue with the descant. Getting his second wind and with Richard's encouragement, Barry continued singing with his friend.

Richard smiled as he sang. His and Barry's voices now singing below and then above that of the other boys who sang louder to ensure that they would not be overwhelmed by this descant duet. The anthem drew rapidly to a close. As one, with a final sustained note, Richard and Barry ended this most beautiful of anthems. Richard just knew, when they had finished singing and the note echoed to silence around the church, that whatever happened in future, the good and especially the bad, it would for him sound forever.

This story is set in the village of St Peter's in Thanet, now part of Broadstairs.

If you would like to know more about the history of St Peter's church, there is a comprehensive history available – including information on hidden pre-Reformation painted panels – by G M Hogben.

Copies of the book – 'The History of St. Peter-the-Apostle Church in Thanet' (281 pp) may be purchased from:-

The Parish Office
St Peter's Church Hall
Hopeville Avenue
Broadstairs
Kent CT10 2TR

Telephone: 01843 866061

Or by contacting mumzio@hotmail.com

It is priced at £10, plus p&p and is full of interesting information about the building and the people who have worshipped there over the last 800 years.

All money raised from the sale of this book goes to support St. Peter's church.

www.ingramcontent.com/pod-product-compliance
Lightning Source LLC
Chambersburg PA
CBHW021210090426
42740CB00006B/175